LITTLE WING

"We travel together, passengers on a little spaceship, dependent on its vulnerable supplies of air and soil . . . preserved from annihilation by the care, the work, and I will say the love we give our fragile craft"

From the last speech of Adlai Stevenson

LITTLE WING

EASTABOUT THE SOUTHERN OCEANS | RAUD O'BRIEN

WATERLINE

Copyright © 1997 Raud O'Brien
Text, photographs and illustrations are by the Author

First published in the UK in 1997
by Waterline Books, an imprint of Airlife Publishing Ltd

British Library Cataloguing in Publication Data
  A catalogue record for this book
  is available from the British Library.

ISBN 1 85310 770 0

Typeset by Hewer Text Composition Services, Edinburgh
Printed in Great Britain by St Edmundsbury Press Ltd, Bury St Edmunds, Suffolk.

Waterline Books
an imprint of Airlife Publishing Ltd
101 Longden Road, Shrewsbury SY3 9EB, England

Contents

Dedication

To my father, 1919–1995, whose lines written for the launching of the "WRAITH OF ODIN" in 1951:

"MAY THAT VIKING GOD STAND TO THE HELM
WHEN AURORA'S TRESSES STREAM OUT ACROSS
THE SKY AND THE WILD WHITE HORSEMEN OF
THE SOUTHERN SEAS = THUNDER ASTERN"

have moved me deeply for years; and to my mother,
his companion in adventures on land and sea for over 50 years.

Acknowledgements

I would firstly like to acknowledge the assistance of Kim and Julie Blyth in translating the initial draft from pencil on paper to storage on disk, thus drawing me inexorably into the PC age to complete the task.

Also to Kay and Sylvia, Goddesses of the world of Instant Print, for their advice and assistance along the way towards the mock-up copy (as close to the finished article in appearance as my funds would allow) . . . and not forgetting, of course, the crew at Facelab for film development and slides, prints and bromides without which no mock-up would have been possible – thanks George and Mary, Dave and Ian. The excerpt from Beryl Markham's *West with the Night* reproduced with kind permission and excerpts of the lyrics of *Follow that Dream* composed by F. Wise and B. Weisman reproduced with kind permission of Williamson Music Co. Chappell and Co. Inc, New York. Special thanks to Luce Fleitout for *Irlande, La France et Angleterre*.

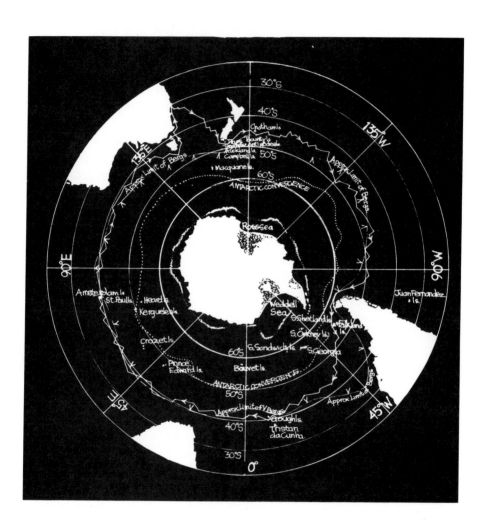

Chapter One
Life's Ending, Re-starting

R apidly my eyes scan the surrounding rock for suitable crystals. Fingernails hooked over them would be my hand-holds. Some rugosities lent 'faith in friction' to support my feet. Only featureless granite lay ahead. Nearly 100 feet above my last runner, this was slab climbing at its delicious best; committed, thoughtful, the soul singing with the pure joy of an endless string of delicate moves taking me ever further into that realm of no latitude for error.

Cruising the second pitch of Bird of Prey, at Booroomba Rocks, Australian Capital Territory. An autumn morning, sky predominantly blue, with occasional cumulus floating over the headwalls of the Prow, above and to my right . . .

The year was 1988, and already my inclination toward leading climbs with long run-outs and little or no protection was recognised among my climbing friends. Few realised, though, the place these held in the mental preparation for my voyage.

Many autumns had lengthened their shadows across the slabs and had the climbers scurrying for their evening meals back at the campsite since this story really began. Many a winter had deposited its covering of snow upon the tops and many a summer had then parched them with its heat. And at this stage I still did not know that climbers placed protection or even used ropes! I merely thought they never made mistakes, as I had climbed, since childhood, until . . .

Light spreads slowly around me, and consciousness, seemingly a totally new sensation, struggles to hold a more than temporary place in my mind. People, strangers as far as I can tell, are standing around and I am in a strange bed, a strange room. Not the familiar black walls and ceiling, varnished wood and paintings of home. Some harshly overlit domain. The walls hard and shiny, tiled I think, and lots of stainless steel . . . Finally I recognise two faces in the crowd, my parents, and ask,

'Where am I?'

'Mona Vale.'

'Is that very far from here?'

Quite a reasonable question, I thought, still disoriented, and after all, I had travelled far since last I remembered. To at least a couple of the strangers surrounding me, though, it seemed to confirm their fears: that after over eight days unconscious if I resurfaced at all it would be as a zombie, a mental vegetable. Wasn't that the proof? Not the sort of 'intelligent' question one would expect from a recent university graduate! And look at that eye, it's pupil jammed into the corner, unmoving. And all the other signs emerging as consciousness fought to gain control . . .

Very slowly, comprehension seeped in, and I understood what they were trying to say. I had made the mistake I had assumed climbers never made. I had fallen, unroped, approximately 80 feet to the rocks below, having spotted an interesting-looking line to ascend the cliff, working through and around the overhangs above. It had proven too difficult, I came unstuck and fell. It had been 3 a.m., mid-winter, 1972, on Barrenjoey's south-eastern cliffline. A stupid time to be climbing without ropes, and particularly for me, as I was due to head off to bushwalk and climb in south-west Tasmania the following week.

A friend who had come around to the beach with me, and who had had the sense not to climb at such a ridiculous hour, dodged my falling body as it bounced off the track. I became wedged in a huge split boulder below. Having ascertained that I was still alive, at least marginally (I had an erratic, almost non-existent, pulse due to head injuries, and blood pouring out the back of my head from a cut which later had twenty-three stitches put in it at hospital), he ran back across the sandhills and beach to get help.

Three or four ambulances later – several got bogged in the sand before they resorted to carrying me the full distance by stretcher apparently, I arrived – 'Is that very far from here?' – at Mona Vale Hospital Intensive Care Ward, where approximately eight and a half days later I regained consciousness of sorts as described.

Well, Intensive Care wasn't so intensive that year, and wanting to get up and try moving around after such a long rest, I resented being put in a caged bed and resolved to get out. I hadn't noticed yet the deficiency in my vision from having the left eye jammed unmoving in its socket, nor had I noticed my virtually total paralysis down the left side. I worked my way to a corner at the foot of the bed where seemingly an escape route lay, and with puzzling difficulty attempted what should have been the easy task of climbing over the rails . . .

The pattern of a white-tiled corner, glistening and hard, rushes up to meet my eyes. The grid of the pattern flicks past the periphery of sight like light poles

Barrenjoey Headland – where the old life ended, and the voyages begin.

beside the road at speed, as on the Norton, riding, some hours before the climbing and the fall. A deep explosion as my head hits hard white tiles . . . The thud sweeps all before it, darkness falls . . .

I am being wheeled away. I seem to notice travel, then am wheeled away again, through new corridors, new spaces, faces, rooms. I do not understand. I think a female doctor appeared here . . . Time passes. I am barely conscious, then I am returned to Mona Vale, intact. No surgeons' knives have sliced inside my skull. In hindsight, what joy, what relief.

After this second fall, in the Intensive Care Ward itself, several new disabilities either appeared for the first time, or only then registered in my consciousness, the most devastating being that I could no longer move my left hand at all. It had only been a fall of a few feet as I tried to climb out of the bed, but since I could not defend myself due to my slowness of thought and left-side paralysis, it had been a very heavy fall.

For a right-handed person, the loss of the use of the left hand may not seem serious. If you tried coping for even one day with your left hand tied behind your back, however, you would see life becomes very difficult single-handed. A myriad of normal tasks become almost impossible – tying shoelaces, dressing, eating with a knife and fork, even washing. Right through to more complex tasks, such as driving.

To be transformed in one instant from an agile and intelligent person to a dependent, virtually hemiplegic zombie was devastating, to say the least, but all I could do was accept my situation for the time being and see what happened. Every morning I was taken down to physiotherapy for my 'morning cup of coffee': metal plates were strapped to the front and back of my wrist and current applied to make the left hand jump up and down at the wrist, waking me if nothing else! However, this never taught me the pathway of voluntary control, for triggering movement at *my* command. Nor did it trigger any movement at all in my fingers, either individually or en masse.

I cannot remember if anything was tried to get my left eye mobile again, from being jammed with its pupil towards my nose, but apparently it showed no signs of improvement after about three weeks, nor did my hand.

By this stage I was starting to be able to think again, and take note of the continually negative comments from the neuro experts. They seemed to be telling me that since no recovery had occurred by now, it was very unlikely to occur at all and I should learn to accept life the way I was . . .

The hospital at Mona Vale was situated in a beautiful position, shielded from the main road a quarter of a mile or so to the west by an arm of the local golf course and a band of bush beside the road. To the east, grassy slopes led down beside the diminishing cliffline to the beach and ocean beyond. A location well suited to my recuperation, I thought. Pleasant strolls in the sunshine across the grass to sit atop the cliffs and contemplate the sea below, the horizon beyond, the ever-changing skyscape above. And, of course, my situation and what to do about it. *But* . . .

'No, we couldn't allow that – not unsupervised.' 'We don't have sufficient nurses etc., etc., etc. I was restricted to the lino floors and corridors, the peopled wards, surrounded by the really ill, and a lack of health so palpable it over-shadowed happiness. I had to leave this 'town' . . .

Luckily I have never been a doctor worshipper, so I chose to ignore their negativity, escape from hospital, take myself off their medications despite their warnings of post-traumatic epileptic fits, and devise my own exercises to recover the use of the impaired functions.

I could not truly 'run away' while still paralysed down one side and seeing double, but with an early start I could stagger away and hopefully make it to the bus stop for a ride home. Unfortunately, my only clothes to escape in were a dressing gown, pyjamas and very dark optical sunglasses, my clear ones having been broken in the fall. This outfit did not impress the local constabulary, cruising past at 5 a.m. They picked me up and took me back, a bit premature in leaving as far as they could tell!

Had they been capable of believing it, there was considerable method in my 'madness'. I had been brought up for the first ten years years of my life aboard a yacht moored in Mosman Bay and had been rowing dinghies almost from the time I could walk. My plan had been to get home and try going for a row, since all my hand could possibly do with an oar would be to grip it. This would trigger voluntary movement in the hand itself, and some movement at least in all fingers. Such was the theory.

Meanwhile, back at the hospital, they decided to keep me only another week. They were absolutely amazed that a patient would try to escape their help, and also that I had made it so far. For this final week I was allowed visitors at any hour. Initially, I thought, out of kindness. Really, they were terrified of the consequences should I escape again and be knocked down crossing the main road, hindered as I was by vision and mobility problems.

Time to go at last! But first I reminded them that I still had a headful of twenty-three stitches under my hair. They had been forgotten, I suspect, because somehow they had been put in without shaving my head. The stitches had very thoroughly healed in by this stage, so ripping them out was almost as painful as it would have been to place them without anaesthetic. This last obstacle overcome, I was free to leave . . .

At this stage my main source of inspiration to restore my hand to usefulness was Solo, my supremely beautiful cream German Shepherd. She had the most expressive large brown eyes and ultra-alert ears that gave her face a range of expressions greater than that of most humans. Two of her favourite pastimes were running, racing, chasing after seagulls along the beach and out into the water, or, if I were out rowing, going for long swims following behind the dinghy. Hence the necessity rapidly to restore my left hand and arm to useful rowing tools, and the need to practise walking again, so that I could take her for long walks to 'Seagullville', the Pittwater side of the beach just inside Barrenjoey Headland.

I arrived home, and with the aid of a walking stick to help me gauge distance due to my seeing double, worked my way down the steps to the water, the dinghy, and oars . . . Nothing!!! No movement in my wrist, hand or fingers at all! Despair! Devastated, I reclimbed the stairs, my theory of recovery in tatters. The future more bleak than ever, and for Solo, no new joys to share, no fun, no swimming everywhere.

I lay on my bed thinking, and while I was doing so an eye exercise occurred to me. The ceiling and walls of my bedroom I had painted black years before, a black background being an excellent 'frame' for photos, paintings and drawings; but I had left the cornice white to give the illusion of the lid just being lifted. This strong white line wending its way around some irregularities in the plan shape of the room made a complicated path for my eye to try and follow, with the good eye covered as I lay. It necessitated a lot of lateral movement and considerable up-and-down movement, so I set to work forcing my eye to follow circuit after circuit, hour after hour.

A couple of weeks later friends were starting to renew contact, and despite the beginnings of reclusiveness due to feeling flawed, there were some I still looked forward to seeing, to share a laugh and swap ideas. One such sunny morning, warm for early spring, I was balancing a rubber ball on the palm of my hand while a friend and I talked, trying to encourage my fingers to bend and squeeze, to grip the ball. In fact I could hardly bend my wrist, let alone move my fingers. We talked on about this and that until my friend said, 'Imagine that is McMahon's head in your hand' (Billy McMahon was Prime Minister at the time). I went *squeeze*, and just like that regained gross control of my 'dead' hand.

Amazing! Absolutely amazing! As if a whole cluster of circuits had been reconnected. As if a switch had been turned on again after being turned off since I fell.

Later, prompted by Solo herself, it was time for the real test. Down to the waterfront and into the dinghy for me, Solo into the water astern. We rowed for miles up over the sand flats, Solo smiling, chasing gulls and soldier crabs; I, still amazed, sitting and watching. Oh happy day!

The lateral movement in my left eye was improving, but I still couldn't co-ordinate up-and-down movement between my eyes, so I saw double at top right and lower left. I found reading too mentally exhausting to be able to cope with more than part of a page at a time, but things were on the improve, all was fine . . .

'Solo! Solo!' I called. She was lagging way behind as we came back up the stairs from our morning row. Normally she bounded up ahead. I had to carry her today . . . Ticks! Frantically I began to search. With ticks, the hind legs always seem to be affected first, so as long as I could find them in her thick fur and remove them promptly, she should be all right. But it was very difficult to search one-handed. There was still virtually no feeling in my left hand – only gross movement had returned. I remained dependent on my eyes to 'feel', and still do.

Had I been firing on more than one cylinder mentally I would have been able to think through all the options better, and Solo, I am sure, would have survived. After finding three ticks and believing that these were all of them, I waited for my father to get home to see if he could find more and to take her to the vet. Believing she would be back next day, I bid her only a casual farewell and the vet duly gave her the antivenin. None of us worried further. The next morning, however, the vet phoned to say that she wasn't responding well and asked to keep her longer in order to keep an eye on her. At this point I should have insisted she come home as there was nothing further for him to do. However, I bowed to 'medical' opinion and he kept her, phoning a day or two later to say that she had died.

Fretting for me and home was what broke her spirit and will to live, not the ticks, I have thought ever since. I was almost demolished by her death. No longer did I have reason to recover the use of my hand, having lost my only real friend. She had been always willing to share an adventure, always ready to play and cheer me up, through her mere existence. She was so aesthetically pleasing an animal and so sensitive. Lacking her weight on the end of my bed at night it became almost impossible to sleep. My hand went backwards in its recovery, my eye also. I lost the will even to live. Feeling more flawed and alone than ever, I began to avoid contact with old friends and started to become a definite recluse.

Alarmed at this accelerating backward trend, my parents thought to cheer me by suggesting a trip down to Port Davey on the south-west Tasmanian coast aboard the *Wraith* (full name *Wraith of Odin*), aboard which I had been brought up. As I was normally in charge of one watch and my father in charge of the other, this would be a good incentive to restore as many faculties as possible before we set sail. If it proved too much my mother could take over from me, as she was a competent helmswoman also. Two old university friends of mine and a new friend from Tasmania, who intended going ashore at Port Davey and walking back to Hobart via the South Coast track on her own, completed the crew. Of course the medical profession advised against the trip, owing to lack of emergency facilities should I have a post-traumatic epileptic fit, but I was keen and prepared to take the chance. We decided to go.

Initially the mental strain was a bit too much – I was exhausted after only two hours at the helm and had to do a lot of sleeping. This, coupled with my slowness of thought at that early stage only three of four months after my fall, made me poor company for my friends. They tended to talk and laugh away by themselves, leaving me alone more and more to cope with my own problems. This was not obvious to me at the time and I don't remember it bothering me. At least not until after Helen left us at Recherche Bay, the weather having forced us to retreat when we were well south of Tassie. We were unable to make the necessary westing to get around the corner and into Port Davey itself.

All the way up the New South Wales coast, and from back in Bass Strait itself, we had to work our way to windward, earning every mile the hard way against the southerly set. Prior to my fall, I had raced VJs and Skates with considerable success, the windward legs being where we could count on making our greatest gains, especially in large fleets. I had retired from racing in 1968 after running out of local competition and with university occupying more and more of my time and interest. Suddenly, watching the mistakes the others were making in trying to make ground to windward fired off something in my old 'racing' brain. I decided it was up to me to get us there and so took over. I extended my watches to sixteen hours straight at the helm, and soon we were knocking off the miles, close tacking up the coast never more than a few hundred yards off the rocks during daylight hours. This was a definite leap in my mental progress and boosted my self-esteem back to a reasonable level.

But the best news was still to come. On having my eyes checked after our return, there was no discernible difference between the movement in my right and left eyes – and this was only months after the experts had told me that the left eye would never move again! The totally unconscious exercise of keeping an eye simultaneously on the sails, the sea and the compass card had achieved in a few weeks what those experts had pronounced impossible.

I still had very little fine control of my left hand and could not tie shoelaces or use a fork without becoming exhausted at the mental effort. And my thinking was nowhere near 100 per cent of its previous capacity, but I was able to read more at a time without strain and tiredness overwhelming me, and definitely felt on the improve.

Autumn arrived and with it the morning mists – flowing over the hills and out of the bays opposite at dawn, then later giving way to the sparkling clarity of crisp and sunny days. All these changes were suggesting to me that maybe greater activity was called for, but I couldn't quite decide what . . .

I needed to restore greater confidence in myself and my ability to cope again on my own. One of my great wintertime loves, ever since I was introduced to it in early childhood by my parents, was bushwalking in the Blue Mountains. Long multi-day walks, sleeping out under natural overhangs and caves or in the open under the stars if the weather was fine. It seemed to me that if I could regain the confidence to enjoy these long solo walks, far from possible help or civilisation, it would go a long way towards restoring the faith in myself necessary to feel confident about rejoining the workforce. Over the next couple of months I set off on ever longer, ever more ambitious walks until they averaged about five to ten days per trip.

At around this time the possibility of a job as trainee keeper at the zoo came up, so, feeling capable of handling that, if not a return to my profession as an architect, I took it on. Conflicting opportunities always seem to arrive simultaneously and just after I had started work at the zoo I was offered a chance to attend Mount Wilga Rehabilitation Centre to receive speech therapy for an inability to express myself clearly when stressed by some situations (a thing as simple as asking the fare on a bus could render me speechless) and to receive concentrated physiotherapy on my left hand in an attempt to bring it back to more useful life.

This in the long term was a far more valuable opportunity, so I regretfully handed in my resignation at the zoo and became a day pupil at Mount Wilga, staying with a friend in town while attending. At Mount Wilga two things quickly became apparent. Firstly, 'speech therapy' is almost a misnomer for that profession, as they are equally adept at working on problems in the visual/perceptual area as at treating difficulties with speech and verbal expression. It also became apparent that most of the restoration work I needed was in the visual/perceptual area, particularly if I wanted to go back to work as an architect. The second major discovery was that of all the patients I met there recovering from a head injury, I appeared to be the only one to have retained a sense of humour and who still seemed capable of laughter. Most of the amputees waiting for new limbs and a surprising number of the paraplegics and quadriplegics were of a very cheerful disposition, but not the ones with damage to the head.

All the head injuries except mine turned out to be from car accidents, and this made me theorise a bit about it. It was not possible that all car accident injuries wiped out exactly the same parts of the brain. Could it have been due to having little sense of humour to start with; or due to getting below a threshold level of working cells where it was no longer possible to recognise or appreciate the ridiculous, the outrageous, the wildly eccentric? Of those most well adapted to their injuries, many seemed to be the paras and quads, one of whom had been a top VJ sailor who crashed his car on the way home from an interclub regatta. How sad it made me to be brought face to face with the transformations necessary in these people's lives, and how lucky I felt at my own 'landing'. A landing just a foot or so different in any direction, or a slightly different landing posture, and I would certainly have ended up either a para, quad or dead.

Again, a totally unexpected conflict of opportunity arose after only a month or so at Mount Wilga. On arriving home from Glebe one weekend, a most unlikely apparition appeared before my startled eyes. A 92-foot schooner, never before seen on Pittwater, lay at anchor directly in front of home. The *Tau* (Fijian for friend) turned out to be the latest creation of Colin Philp, an old Tasmanian acquaintance of my parents. Colin was an architect who later took up yacht design, then moved to Fiji, where he worked again at architecture and setting up tourist developments; one of his most renowned creations was the Tradewinds Hotel where visiting yachts could literally tie up to the veranda of the bar!

Having built the Tradewinds himself and seen it through to running success-fully, at the age of sixty-six he was bored with the predictability of it all, so designed the *Tau* and built her with the aid of only two Fijian helpers, at one end of the Tradewind site. She was a 92-foot twin (bilge) keel schooner with two equal-height masts. They had motored her out to Sydney from Fiji, without masts, then masts and rigging were added in Sydney, with her sails flown out from New Zealand.

The upshot of all this was that they were leaving the next night for her maiden voyage under sail, back to Suva. Via Noumea, the Loyalties and the New Hebrides, then on to the Lautoka side of Fiji, visiting various resorts of Colin's friends along the way, then finally to Suva. They needed another experienced crew member to help take her there . . . would I be interested? Talk about the crazy upheavals in life – here was an opportunity from heaven itself, but I didn't even have a passport. We agreed that if I could get down to the ship by dinner time the following night with passport and sea gear, we would leave immediately. Otherwise they would leave anyway and reorganise watches etc., to make do without me.

Chapter Two
Tropical Realworld

As soon as the doors to the Commonwealth Centre opened next morning, I raced in to explain my case and see if I could get myself a passport at such minimal notice. I was lucky in talking to someone sympathetic. She promised to do all she could and told me to return with photos later in the day. Things were looking good. Now to find the time to return home, pack and get back to North Sydney before it was too late. I phoned Mount Wilga to explain – we were away!

Sydney Heads and the lights of Sydney gradually receded in the night, and morning found us in a totally sea-girt world, with lumpy grey seas and rain. A strong easterly wind necessitated us being hard on the wind. It was a very uncomfortable start to the trip. Day after day, day after day, bashing into strong headwinds virtually all the way to Noumea. Not the imagined pleasures of 'tropical' sailing at all. More like Bass Strait in the throes of a southerly gale. Eventually our northing won us through, and with the wind swinging further into the south we started to enjoy more typical trade-wind conditions. Making our landfall to the west of the main pass into Noumea Harbour, we dropped anchor off a small beach and went ashore for a swim. This was my introduction to the tropics, and what a disappointment this first taste was! The air was hot and humid, the sky overcast and, on diving into the water, I felt no burst of refreshment. The water was almost as warm as the air.

Moving in toward Noumea itself on the following afternoon, however, the feeling of tropical magic, of entering a different, more exotic world, did take hold. I marvelled at the height of the steep, jungle-clad mountains of the hinterland, the emerald-green lushness of the foliage near the water, and the sparkling whiteness of the architecture – like jewels scattered amongst the greenery. Moored alongside a wharf near the Cercle Nautique we were a longish walk from town, but all of it interesting. Whether sitting at a streetside table by the Baie des Citrons soaking in the ambience of a sunny afternoon, exploring the hilly streets and colonial architecture of older portions of the town, or discovering a great blues piano record being played in a downstairs hotel bar near where *Tau* was moored, everything was new.

From Noumea we made our way toward the south-eastern tip of New Caledonia, keeping inside the surrounding barrier reef until we branched northward toward the Loyalty Islands between Cap Ndoua and the Ile des Pins. The silhouettes of the surrounding hills were dark and mysterious in the fading night. The clouds after sunset grey tufts edged with fire, floating beneath an overall pink from the cirrostratus above . . . The descent of a tropical night at our last anchorage before returning to the open sea. Romanesque churches indistinguishable at a distance from their Mediterranean antecedents poked their whitewashed towers above the enveloping palms, an incongruous sight as we sailed past the island of Lifou, Uvéa bound. It was sad to see evidence of foreign domination so widespread, with the indigenous traditions and beliefs devalued by imports unrelated to local conditions.

Disappointing to me also was the continued use of autopilot to steer the boat, even in these ideal sailing conditions when the joy of helming such a large yacht manually – weaving a constantly changing course to take advantage of each gust of wind and each nuance of swell shape – would have left a sparkling and indelible memory.

Uvéa appeared, low, palm-covered and very seductive in its sun-drenched tropicality. I had always envisaged a tropical atoll with its enclosed lagoon as a relatively small and finite world, but Uvéa blew all such preconceptions away. So large that all but the immediate shoreline lay over the horizon, the lagoon was almost an inland sea in its own right. The ubiquitous village church lay some way back from the beach with only its octagonal towers visible, but very audible at dawn with the peal of its bells

The beach of pure coral sand set off for the horizon, vanishing in the distance as a thin white line between the green of the palms and the blues of the sea. This was as warm and transparent as the air itself, grading through all shades of turquoise on its way toward blue. The water was a visual and tactile delight, soothing as it echoed the sky. Near the top of the beach, grasses and fine creepers sprinkled the sand, filigree outliers of the palm forest behind. As the tide went out further than expected, the *Tau* sat sedately in balance on her twin keels, a wonderful advertisement for them when shallow-water cruising, although I suspected them of creating considerable drag when sailing at speed.

All things come to an end, and, with the sun past its zenith, the wind and tide on the rise, and the horizon calling, it was time to get back aboard and leave. Immediately on clearing the lagoon the autopilot was again turned on to handle the steering, but this time I was in luck. It refused to work and repelled all attempts at repair, so at last I had a chance to steer by hand.

Having raced small centreboarders successfully for many seasons and having hand-steered the *Wraith* through all conditions, sitting idly by while a machine blindly followed a course was to be reduced to the status of a mere passenger, both irratating and boring. Seizing this chance, I sailed us the whole way from Uvéa to Port Vila in one long watch. Approximately eighteen hours at the helm from latish afternoon until mid-morning the following day.

The wind blew steadily but gently, and the night was warm as we surged on through. Familiar constellations rose in the east, evoked wonder in their travels and dipped into the west. The band of the Milky Way blazed all night, spanning the heavens until lost in the dawn. Sefo and Naca, two Fijians in the crew who had kept me company from time to time overnight with coffee and conversation, emerged again at daybreak as fishermen. Soon a large mahi-mahi was brought aboard to boost our supplies. By the completion of breakfast the island of Vaté lay close at hand, impressive with its green-clad heights and luxuriant shore. In the morning light it seemed to glow with radiant tropicality, a combination of colour, temperature and the gentle caress of land-scented air.

I was not sorry, though, to hand over the helm to those in the crew with local knowledge. It had been a pleasure to hand-steer a good stint at last, but over-complexity again diluted the pleasure. The *Tau* had been set up with hydraulic steering and there was almost no 'feel' getting through to the wheel, no sense of the vessel as a living being. Maybe this was only a matter of adjustment, to cure the sense of lifelessness, but it had a lasting influence in my leaning toward simplicity when creating my own vessel.

By the time we arrived at Port Vila overcast skies had returned, and this predominance of cloud, combined with constant heat and high humidity, led me to question whether the tropics were a cruising ground compatible with my nature. My land-based activities of rock-climbing, running and bushwalking demand a high level of physical fitness, but the combination of heat and humidity in these parts could easily lead me to lethargy. At sea the warmth was a pleasure when working on deck, but once on land the trend was towards sloth.

As far as sailing was concerned, the voyage ended for me at Vila. Although I remained with the ship until we reached Suva, the remainder of the voyage was completed under power, motoring the entire way for some unfathomable reason – perhaps a lack of windward ability as we had headwinds from here on.

Disappointing though this trip was proving from the sailing angle, I was gaining valuable insights into what was important to me for the creation of my own vessel. One final burst of 'sailing' did occur, most unexpectedly. While we were anchored off an island near Lautoka, a speedboat arrived from a resort nearby with an invitation for Colin and crew to come ashore. Speedboats had been my arch enemies since starting to race VJs as a boy, so I was utterly unimpressed as we all piled aboard and idled clear. Wham!!! With full throttle applied to twin 140 hp Mercs, the catamaran was instantly up on the plane and it was like Skate sailing revisited as we hurtled off at an amazing rate of knots. What a glorious change from slow displacement sailing, what a complete surprise! If I were an engine lover I could have been converted.

Chapter Three
Return
to
Ground

On returning to Sydney I found I had lost my 'day pupil' spot at Mount
Wilga, there being a long waiting list for patients trying to gain entry.
Re-admittance did not look very hopeful for a while. Then a friend on the staff
mentioned the possibility of a live-in place becoming available soon and would I
be prepared to take that?

Every morning I was awakened by the coughing spasms of the smokers in our
dormitory cottage and immediately stopped smoking the little that I did. It was a
most depressing start to each day, but the natural surroundings of Mount Wilga
came to the rescue. Originally built by Marcus Clark in the middle of natural
bushland, the suburbs of Hornsby had not yet encroached on all sides. I could go
for wonderful walks before breakfast, across the rifle range and into the bush
beyond. This fell away towards Galston Gorge and a little creek that was a
tributary on its way to Berowra Waters. Out here, surrounded by untouched
bushland in the crisp of early winter mornings, I could regain my equilibrium and
return for breakfast uplifted and enthusiastic to start the day's work.

I threw everything into those months as a 'live-in', my ability to register and
interpret sensation in my left hand coming along in leaps and bounds. I brought
my drawing board and T-square up from home to practise draughting or to find
out if I still could. It quickly became apparent that I would have serious problems
using a T-square due to lack of joint sense (the ability to know a limb's position in
space by the unconscious messages received back from the joints) in my left arm.
But this was not too much of a problem, as no commercial offices still used T-
squares. They used parallel rule machines or full drafting machines. Of these, I

could only use the parallel rule/paraline machines, but this posed no serious difficulties as I could provide my own equipment if necessary.

At around this time, remembering my experience in the real world of architecture, and noting also the experiences of other university friends, I was beginning to feel that I no longer particularly wanted to work as an architect anyway. There were so many things that interested me and that I wished to express, and architecture satisfied only a very small proportion of these desires. Also, the hypocrisy of many architects in the way they sacrificed design principles in the pursuit of their work made me rather ashamed to be associated with the profession. I decided to try and concentrate on my painting and writing, working towards making a living out of these on my return to the outside world. How I would achieve this, though, was less than clear.

With no warning at all, change was forced into my life from outside. Not realising the magnitude of my left-hand impairments and their repercussions on almost all facets of everyday life, the controllers told me my time at Mount Wilga was up. I had to get out at the end of the week to make way for others. I had succeeded in re-educating my brain to differentiate between a whole host of sensations in physiotherapy classes by now, but had not been doing it for long enough for the re-education to have become permanently imprinted. I feared greatly that I would lose all the benefits of the past months concentrated effort once the facilities to keep at it were removed.

> Burning schisms, splits and fire,
> boiling hatred, quagmire . . .
> Shattered, scattered mental pain
> as 'TRUST IN PEOPLE''s edges go brown,
> curl over, and dissolve in flame . . .

. . . part of a poem written that very afternoon after being notified I had to leave. I was very unimpressed by the medical profession and their arrogance yet again!

What on earth to do next? I returned home with my box of tricks to try and keep up at least a reasonable selection of physio exercises alone, and started going for long rows again while pondering my future. I seem to think best when either rowing or walking. One such day, while weaving in and out amongst the moored boats at the end of the bay, observing and absorbing, but not really looking for anything in particular, I saw her. It had not been long since my experiences of sailing tropic waters and living the tropical cruising life, so my mind was very open and quick to spot a possibility of achieving at least some of my sailing dreams – the fine-weather ones. I circled around her. I drifted past again and again, observing from every angle. This was love at first sight! She appeared to be a 16- or 18-foot skiff hull, hard chine aft, transom hung rudder, that had been decked with prodigious camber to gain a miniature windowless cabin with seated headroom. She had a trapeze and long tiller extension, so was obviously created to be sailed like the centreboarders I used to race, with my head way out from the gunwale, watching the bow slice through the water and anticipating her every move. Her spinnaker pole stowed alongside the boom, and with a little sculptured ship's cat at the aft end of the cockpit, what more could one want?

I asked the boatshed about her but they knew little and the contact number rang but never answered. Maybe this was for the best – my funds were minimal.

Being so small and simple, though, she couldn't possibly cost that much – if she were for sale. Inspired into action I set out to find work with a vengeance. I had to get that boat and be off. Pronto!

My vision was of myself lying out on the trapeze, tiller extension in one hand, mainsheet or spinnaker sheet in the other, with sunsparkle on the water ahead, ribbon of wake astern and talking to the ship's cat as we sailed. This prompted a surge of activity and directed enthusiasm I had not experienced since the fall. I was alive again!

A friend who had recently completed his architectural degree and was now contract draughting for good money in the State Public Works suggested that I could almost certainly handle that type of architectural work. I wasn't nearly as confident, but being desperate decided to try. In those days some Departments of State Public Works were doing far more adventurous and innovative design work than almost any firm in the private sector, who were obsessed with flats and office buildings and boring repetition of solutions. It was thus with great joy that I joined the Schools Division, where I found the work ridiculously easy after all.

This was because they considered me just another contract draughtsman on the team. I was not very talkative and still unsure of myself, so allowed them to believe this for a while. Gradually the truth came out that I was a qualified architectural graduate like my bosses. From then on I was given more and more design work and responsibility and really began to thrive, mind alive, progress on all fronts.

After I had saved what I considered a reasonable sum to offer, I again tried to make contact with the owner – successfully this time. He told me quite a bit of her history. The original owner who had 'converted' her had also been an architecture student, had single-handed her to Lord Howe Island and return and had done well racing her. The current owner was asking an exorbitant amount for such a minimal vessel, and when I contacted the creator himself, he agreed. It had cost him only about half what this guy was asking to create her from scratch.

In my final year of architecture at Sydney, I had decided that landscape architecture was the field I would be happiest working in. To this end I had intended going to New Zealand after graduation to do a post-graduate course in landscape architecture at Lincoln College, Christchurch, which had been recommended. There were no landscape architecture courses at a local university then. Another option now occurred to me. The Westlawn School of Yacht Design course covered the design of both sail and power-driven vessels up to around 150 feet long, where traditional naval architecture took over. Why not do this? It was then the best course for yacht design in the world, and offered a correspondence course necessitating no great no changes in life while I studied. This way I could design, build, create my ideal vessel. Large enough to share a life afloat with a partner, but as small as practicable for the pair of us to live aboard happily in order to minimise both initial and maintenance costs. Off went my enquiry in the mail, off went my initial payments to begin the course. All sorts of new drawing and design tools unfamiliar to an architect started appearing in my 'studio' at home. I was away.

In every recession the building industry is among the first to suffer from cutbacks in people's ability to spend. Shortly after I had rejected the offer of a full-time position, all contract staff were laid off. I was jobless, along with many other architects in Sydney.

This called for thought. After rapidly completing my latest yacht-design course exam, back to the mountains I went for another ten-day stretch of solitude in my beloved bush. I needed to clear the mind completely of my period of work in the city and think out the next moves. Obviously I needed further work, and a lot of it now that I was intending to design and build my 'ultimate' vessel, but of architectural work there was none, and jobs in any other field were scarce.

At this point a slim chance opened up for a position as an architect in New Zealand, so I applied immediately, looking forward to a change in life and setting.

If the Department of Public Works Schools Division where I worked in Sydney had been a hive of innovative and experimental design activity, the Education Board in New Zealand was its absolute antithesis. Slavishly repeating standard designs and practices, with no money or room for more creative solutions, I found the work hellishly boring and dull. Countering this to some extent was my yacht-design course work which I continued at home, getting over forty hours work done on weekends alone. I averaged about seventy hours per week on it while still working the usual forty-hour week at the Board. I also prepared entries for some architectural competitions to try and keep my mind active and played blues harmonica with a Maori band several nights each fortnight to keep my musical interests alive. Mainly, though, the year was spent trying to cover as much yacht-design course work as possible. By the time I returned to Sydney I wanted the dream sufficiently designed to be able to commence construction. My social life was minimal, my existence frugal.

It was necessary to score 75 per cent or more in each exam before the next exam and text were sent. This was no problem, but the delay in return mailings was serious. I felt that time was running out and when an almost suitable exam question arrived I bent the design parameters to use it to draw the hull lines of my own vessel, even though the design of hull shapes for sailing vessels had not been covered yet. Sure that the years of racing, reading about and observing yachts had given me a good intuitive feel for what worked and what didn't, I went ahead with giving birth to my dream.

Having been brought up aboard a beautiful sea-going timber yacht from birth to the age of ten, and having grown to love and trust her over many thousands of ocean miles and suffer with her through the pains of shipwreck, dismasting and the loss of a rudder at sea, I have always thought of wind-driven vessels as alive, each with their own idiosyncrasies and patterns of behaviour. Never could they be considered mere possessions, status symbols or investments.

One night I was working late on my hull lines while listening to a song called 'Little Wing' by Jimi Hendrix. It occurred to me that the lyrics of the song could apply equally to one's vessel, one's lover, or both – as combined in the 'original' dream of sailing wherever we desired, myself, my love, and *Little Wing* – the perfect name for my creation. A gentle name, unlike the aggressive names adopted by most modern yacht owners, and always a reminder of the dream.

At the time I was in hospital, two Frenchmen in a little yacht called *Damien* were cruising Antarctic waters and their articles were published in the local magazine. At one point in the Southern Ocean, when completely rolled and dismasted, they remained upside down for so long that they thought they were going to drown as water found its way in through places not designed to be immersed for long. Eventually *Damien* righted herself when hit sufficiently hard by another breaking wave, but this episode stuck in my mind and became the only conscious design influence from another vessel in the design of *Little Wing*. I designed her to be unstable in the upside-down position so as to right herself rapidly and once more be an operative means of transport. Everything about her rig I made overly strong with a view to retaining that intact if and when rolled. I say 'if and when' because tropical trade-wind sailing was not what she was designed for.

In childhood, Felix Riesenberg's book on the Cape Horn region had fascinated me, and a great desire to cruise the Patagonian channels/Tierra del Fuego region had been born. If *Little Wing* were to do this she would need to sail a lot of Southern Ocean miles in her time, with the ever-attendant risk in those waters of being rolled or pitch-poled. The mountains of Antarctica, sweeping many thousands of snow- and ice-clad feet directly into the sea, were only a hop, step and jump further south. It seemed only sensible if cruising these waters to gaze in wonder also at these gold and pink-tinged giants, and the legendary blues, blue greens and whites of the bergs. This side trip would demand the ultimate in strength and seaworthiness and reinforced my 'keep it simple and strong' design philosophy.

By spring I had made up my mind to leave Dunedin at the end of the year and return to Sydney to commence construction, although I had yet to make a final decision on the material to be used. I had completed a contracted set of lines and offsets for both the round-bilge and multi-chine versions, plus a tentative sail plan and heaps of calculations covering the most relevant performance characteristics. I felt confident about being able to proceed once this decision had been made.

At this stage there were two main contenders for construction material, bearing in mind my skills or lack of them at yacht construction, and my bank balance. Another consideration was the fact that I had no site on which to build, and this lack was obviously going to complicate costing considerations. The two contenders were (i) the round-bilge design in one to two inch foam/fibreglass sandwich for its insulative and buoyancy/unsinkability attributes, and (ii) the multi-chine version in steel for its strength, relative lightness if its strength were fully taken advantage of, and comparative cheapness of material. Against steel were my lack of steel construction skills and the cost of necessary equipment before building could commence.

The year at work dragged on, and a new boss architect arrived, but one no more conducive to innovative thinking. I handed in my resignation for the end of the year. As if to reinforce my decision I walked to work through falling snow for most of early November and the cold that I hadn't allowed to bother me during winter when my muesli would freeze to ice if I let it soak overnight, now made me fed up and longing to get back to summertime Sydney. I had achieved almost everything I had set out to and now it was time to move on to the next stage in my evolution.

Several important lessons had been learnt from this year, more or less unintentionally, but no less valuable for that. Firstly, concerning cold and physical discomfort: despite the fact that all but a month or two of the year had been colder than Sydney virtually ever gets, it never bothered me until after I had made the decision to leave. I wore almost the same clothes as I did in Sydney with few concessions to the temperature, and lived all year without a heater at home, keeping warm by exercise instead. I think this was because I fully expected it to be cold and it had been my decision to live there. It would have been foolish to complain. Secondly, despite my extraordinarily long hours at the drawing board each week, I managed to maintain my complete exercise discipline started while a live-in at Mount Wilga. Running several miles pretty flat out and about half to three-quarters of an hour on other assorted exercises on average four to five nights a week. This despite doing all my work at the board standing and bending over it. Thirdly, I discovered I could live a perfectly satisfying life while observing an utter frugality in living expenses in order to realise the 'dream' as quickly as possible. It worked out that after rent, my total living expenses for the year for food, grog, entertainment, electricity, gas and water etc. averaged only $10 a week! And it could have been less had I not decided to try living as a vegetarian in a meat-eater's heaven.

One thing I let slide was my discipline with the box of tricks for left-hand exercises. I decided that daily life now offered a sufficient variety of fine-control tasks at least to stop deterioration. To test this I had brought my sextant with me, even though I could not use it when I left Sydney. I aimed to return by ship and test my hand on its ability to turn the micrometer screw during the voyage. I had to go up to Auckland to catch a ship back to Sydney, since no ships left the South Island Sydney-bound. The experiment worked. Each day I would practise taking sights whenever there was a sun to shoot, and although not exactly with dexterity, I could use it. Some modifications to the screw itself and more practice were all that were needed to achieve fluency.

Chapter Four
Taking on Form

While still in Dunedin designing, I was interested to read in an Australian boating magazine an article on three young Dutchmen who had just built themselves a 72-foot steel version of the famous Herreshoff ketch *Ticonderoga* and finished her to highly professional standards. As I was still in the throes of trying to decide the most suitable material for construction of *Little Wing*, I resolved to pay them a visit on my return to discuss my situation and gain some first-hand insights into the pros and cons of building in steel.

To the end of Glebe Point Road I walked one grey and humid day, to find them all at work on a double-chine yacht hull they had nearly completed for another client. At the end of the day they took me over to look at *Batavier* and as I looked and looked again, out came a flood of questions. We talked and talked over coffee, with me deciding to come back and see them again in a few days when I had had time to fully absorb and consider the ground we had covered.

It had become apparent looking at their set-up, with sheds covering their work and protecting their many thousands of dollars' worth of tools collected during the years of building *Batavier*, that all my savings would barely cover the cost of tooling up. That is, if I were to do a professional job of building. And then there would be the costs of materials, building, site rental etc., etc.

It was very important to me, since I was putting my entire resources and soul into the creation of *Little Wing*, that she should end up looking a thoroughly professional and well-built vessel. She was, after all, going to be the sample of my yacht-design work most likely to attract further commissions, so I could not have her looking like a poorly built amateurish hulk. Bearing in mind my disabilities, the lack of a site to build on, and the lack of tools and equipment in my possession, building in steel seemed an insuperable obstacle. Despite this I was becoming more and more convinced that steel, with its great advantages in strength and watertightness, was the ideal material for my purposes. This construction method decision was the first of the no-latitude-for-error type which would continue surfacing until after completion of the voyage.

Of the others considered: (i) foam-sandwich construction loses its strength once the outer layer of the sandwich is breached, making it more susceptible to impact damage – I was thinking of ice damage at the time. (ii) cold-moulded timber would have been a distinct possibility, but I felt that I would need to build under shelter – an impossibility given my finances – and I was not at all confident I had the skills or ability to overcome my hand impairment and create a professional job.

Having successfully raced chine-built planing centreboarders all my youth, I was partial to a multi-chine design, with the lovely shadow lines you get under the chines if they are designed well. The round-bilge version, pretty though her strong, sheer line would make her, would still resemble any one of a host of mass-production round-bilge yachts of around her length and I wanted her to look more distinctive than that.

I decided, largely on aesthetic grounds, that I would opt for the multi-chine, as the performance co-efficients calculated for both had been almost identical. This brought the realistic choices of material down to either steel or possibly plywood. For strength and watertightness, and even for weight once equivalent strength were considered, steel became my choice. But how was I to carry it out?

At this point I should explain why I did not consider Ferro-cement. Even bearing in mind the total failure of Ferro under severe impact load, this was not the main reason for rejection – it was on weight grounds. For a yacht of my size, the proportion of total displacement made up by the hull and deck structure would be too high to allow for good performance, and I had been racing too long to put up with a boat that didn't perform to my satisfaction. I had helped build a 60-foot Ferro yacht while a student at university, so I knew that the construction would offer me no problems.

Back I went to the Dutchmen to see if there was any way we might prove of use to each other. We pored over my drawings, talked over a coffee or two and finally arrived at what seemed a satisfactory decision for all concerned. I had enough money to cover the cost of them building the steel shell of the hull without decks or deckhouse, and I was sure that by then I would have worked out a way to complete *Little Wing* myself. Two of them in particular seemed to like her design and were keen to give it a go, so we hastily scribbled out a contract. All signed, we bought a few beers to celebrate, and were started. They needed some money immediately to purchase steel, so with my first withdrawal of funds next day, *Little Wing's* physical creation began.

By this stage I had bought myself another motorbike, second-hand from a friend. I rode down to Glebe most days to help with the lofting and other decisions that had to be made about framing sizes, plate thicknesses and such. All structural sizing in fact was arrived at initially through discussion in the Dutchmen's shed, the checking calculations done later to avoid holding up proceedings.

The motorbike taught me a very interesting thing concerning my left hand. Because I had been riding motorbikes for a long time before my fall, the use of the hand in riding manoeuvres was virtually instinctive, not a matter of conscious thought. I found the impairment in the use of my hand no problem, no problem at all to fast yet safe riding, even through city traffic. This has turned out to be true of many other things. Those that were instinctive before the fall have been no trouble to resume at a similar level of proficiency. Whereas those that depend on joint sense in the left arm, that have had to be learned from scratch after the fall, have remained quite a problem no matter how much practice I get. The changing of gears in a manual car, for instance, is still difficult.

By the time we had finished the lofting and fabrication of transverse frames and had set them up in their correct positions, it had become apparent to the Dutchmen that my offsets (the actual measurements used to set up and build the hull) were far more accurate than those of the other yacht designers whose designs they had built. Late one afternoon, therefore, they made a suggestion which could possibly help all of us in the different ways we needed. The accuracy of my offsets enabled them to fabricate the frames and set them up to produce a fair hull with a great deal less time spent on fiddling and adjusting than what they were used to. This saved them construction time, and as a result saved the client money.

It may have been just a test of my ability to produce the goods, but they mentioned a fellow coming to see them the following Tuesday, who had seen *Little Wing* in frames, and was interested to see what I had in the way of a round-bilge design of around 45 feet. Wow! It had taken the better part of a year to reach the same point with *Little Wing*; now I had three days to produce the same for a completely new design! A quick can of beer with them while I reviewed this outrageous offer and I was away.

On the following Tuesday there I was, with tube of drawings in hand to meet this imaginary client. Because the considerations in the design of *Little Wing* were so fresh in my mind, and because the ongoing yacht-design course work had kept me fluent in the preparation of hull lines, after seventy hours at the drawing board over three and a half days, I had produced a reasonable set of preliminary drawings. Hull lines, sail plan and accommodation layout had been completed, with sufficient calculations to indicate that they would be workable as a final design. I think they were a little amazed! A fellow did come down to visit that afternoon, but he was not interested in a 45-footer – too big, too expensive. After talking to the Dutchmen at length, however, he decided that he might be able to afford a 40-footer, again a round-bilge design. He would be back Friday afternoon to see what we could offer!

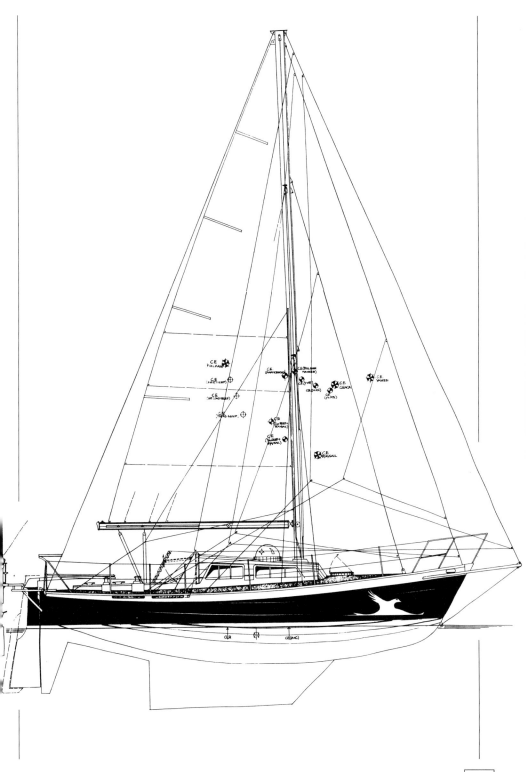

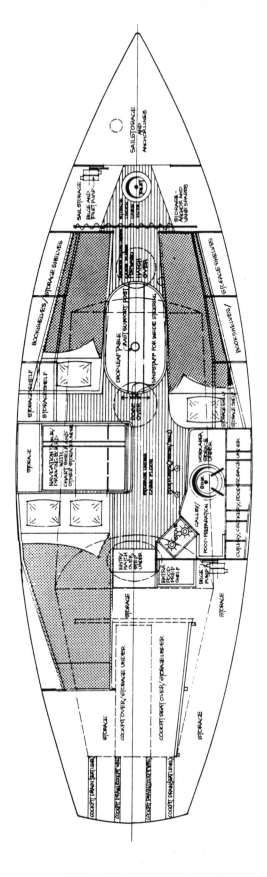

No time for a farewell coffee. This bite could be the real thing, so I drove straight home, back to the frenzy. It does not work well in yacht design merely to scale a set of drawings up or down to make them fit a desired length. Unless the difference is a very small percentage, various attributes of the design and various design ratios become out of proportion and performance suffers. Also accommodation layout possibilities vary greatly with only small variations of interior volume, so you can easily find yourself unable to fit the drawn arrangement in, or leaving too much interior volume wasted.

Through sheer excitement and enthusiasm I continued my twenty-two-hour unbroken design shifts (New Zealand weekends had been good training for this!) and duly appeared on Friday with the drawings and some spare sets of prints to show any other prospective clients in my absence. Our client duly appeared after work; he liked what he saw and took away a set of prints to compare with existing designs that he had looked at. We, the Dutchmen and I, had a few well-earned beers and I drove home to sleep, having taken the first steps towards a new profession.

A few days later I received an excited phone call from Glebe – he had signed. Now a new frenzy began as we needed a table of offsets, thus, also, a contracted set of lines to take them from. While construction proceeded I followed up with a more final sail and rigging plan, revised cabin layout, the necessary calculations for trim, stability and various performance ratios, plus recommendations for auxiliary power and other equipment. Structural sizes for the hull were again decided initially by discussion in the shed, then checked later at home. My new profession had begun.

At this stage, despite the need for money to complete *Little Wing*, the amount I received for design fees was a very secondary consideration. What was important was the chance to get a few of my designs actually built and sailing; only then would my name become known as a designer. I worked hundreds and hundreds of hours at home alone on these designs, checking, checking, checking, for a virtual pittance in fees. But they were getting built.

Construction of *Little Wing* was put temporarily on hold while they started on the 40-footer, as we hoped to sell many of these as an almost stock design. This delay in progress on *Little Wing* was acceptable as I was fast running out of money to pay the Dutchmen for further work. More fees would help. At about this time they suggested completing my deck, deckhouse and cockpit all in steel for a reduced price. This rusting shell could then be moved to where I could take over – revising, modifying, and completing until she became a home.

Even this lesser price, offered in acknowledgement of our partnership's success, was beyond my ability to pay. I hated to borrow, to be in debt, but if I couldn't find the money what would happen to *Little Wing*? Like so many others who started to build their dream ships, would I be forced to abandon her as an unfinished shell, dream shattered?

Just as yacht design itself is a discipline involving compromise between many conflicting characteristics, all desirable to a greater or lesser extent depending on the ultimate purpose of the vessel, so I discovered life now to be a situation where compromise in my ideals was necessary if further progress was to be made towards my primary goal. Optimistic that I would soon find regular work once my current yacht-design commitments had been completed, I relented and allowed myself to get in debt. Work on *Little Wing* resumed and another of my 40-footers was commenced. This one had some construction variations on the first, but was otherwise identical; we also began work on a 36-footer to complete the family. I had designed the latter to fill a gap I perceived in the smaller end of our range, which now covered from 55 to 33 feet LOA (Length Over All). Things were busy at Glebe.

At around this time I was also illustrating a children's book and hunting up further illustration work with a variety of magazines. At the end of one particularly heavy day of visiting about a dozen magazine publishers, I found myself in the editor's office of a well-known boating magazine. He turned out to be an acquaintance from back in my VJ racing days. He had no illustration work to offer, but did publish an article several pages long about me and my designs in their design section.

I thought I had it made, that offers of further design work would pour in. How wrong I was. Apart from a few crank letters and one tentative bite that came to nothing after months of correspondence, nothing! I was amazed. I was also very poor and now in debt, so when an offer came from two old university friends to move to Blayney and work with them on the documentation drawings for a few million dollars' worth of hospital additions, I jumped at the opportunity.

By this time *Little Wing* had been launched – 6 October 1977 – and placed on a mooring I had put down a couple of months earlier. The launching followed removal from Glebe and several months working alone at wire brushing, priming and painting the interior, which I had not been able to afford to sand-blast, then finish coating and anti-fouling the exterior, which had been sand-blasted and primed while still at Glebe.

For a long time she remained like this, floating on her mooring and looking pretty, but remaining an unfinished mastless hulk until my savings grew enough to enable me to work on her some more. The Blayney job, another compromise in that I was returning to work at my original profession, was ultimately to prove the key to her completion, and in the long run, my own fulfilment derived from her and her success

* * * *

Dry and rolling hills stretched off into the distance, the air redolent with the smell of parched, moistureless soil and withering, desiccated eucalypts, the few that remained of a once life-supporting and moisture-retaining

From astern – shadowlines and the beauty of the chines.

skin that clothed these hills. The dry dams and numerous deep erosion gullies were mute testimony to the failure of white man's efforts at trying to force the original landscape into subservience. To suffer his narrow designs. Imposed, unfortunately, in an era lacking knowledge. It wasn't realised that in reducing the natural diversity of life to such an extent, all they would create in the long term would be marginal desert country and lifelessness for all.

But not all plant life managed only a stunted caricature of its healthy form. The Scotch thistles that surrounded the little abandoned farmhouse we rented had assumed the proportions and density of a forest, with stem diameters at the base of around 3 inches. The crimson rosellas seemed to enjoy eating their flowers and would perch delicately amongst the spikes, holding a blossom in one claw while daintily dismembering it with their beaks. I chopped the top 8 feet or so of one particularly choice specimen to put in the empty bath as our Christmas tree. There was no rainwater in the tanks, so we showered in town. We tended to work in the office for an average of twelve to sixteen hours per day (approximately twelve at the start, nearer sixteen to twenty at the end, sleeping on the office floor) since it was a contract job with meetings and time schedules to meet. Our home base was scarcely used. Some days we would deliberately take a break at around sunset and go for long, exploratory drives through what was, to our city eyes, a beautiful rural area. Thus we discovered the Neville pub, a magical little spot for an evening beer or two. Other evenings, when the moon was full, we raced around the paddocks on our push-bikes by moonlight, rounding up pockets of sheep or just hurtling around at speed, with the excitement of not being able to judge what was a rise and what was a hollow, with unexpected and sudden results at times.

For this country escapade I bought running shoes for the first time, since my feet were too soft for running barefoot on rough country gravel. What a revelation after eight years of running barefoot on hard road surfaces. It was like floating on air! Amazing! The barefoot years must have taught me to tread lightly, though, as I have never suffered joint problems from a life of barefooting, and these first cheap running shoes lasted for over 10,000 miles of road-running before the stitching gave out and the soles wore through!

The money saved from the Blayney period enabled me to buy the bare sections for my mast, boom and spreaders, which I assembled in a friend's backyard, putting in the electrics for the masthead light and some extra wiring to allow for future changes at the same time. I also sealed the mast and boom sections near both ends with wooden plugs fibreglassed in place so that if I lost the entire rig overboard when rolled, being a deck-stepped mast it would probably survive intact and float instead of sinking and needing to be cut away. Thus, also, my external halyards. The openings required for internal halyards would mean the mast would sink quickly. Sealed as it was, it should float long enough to lash aboard somehow and set up again after making port under jury rig.

While working on the mast during the day I was doing bits of design work for various boat manufacturers, and illustration work for others, at night. This stretched my savings to include money for standing rigging as well. I tested the mast plugging by towing the mast behind the dinghy from the beach near my friend's place to the shore near my mooring for attaching the rigging. It floated beautifully for a quarter of a mile or more, no leaks.

One weekend morning at high tide the local lighter plucked it from the waterfront rocks and after an hour or so of frantic juggling, there sat *Little Wing* at long last looking like the vessel she was supposed to be.

There was still a long way to go. I had no sails, no ropes, blocks, winches or deck fittings of any kind, except the mooring bollard fabricated and installed prior to launching. I did not even have any framing in place inside the hull to install a floor, however temporary. She was still an empty hulk, but at least she was one with mast and rigging.

My mooring bollard was the first of many fittings I would have to design and fabricate. Because nearly all stock fittings were pared down to the minimum size and weight for the racing market, almost everything available was useless for my 'keep it strong but simple' aims. Many aspects of *Little Wing* were unorthodox – for example, the large elliptical submarine hatch aft and circular submarine hatch forward. It was therefore necessary for me to design from scratch nearly everything aboard the boat except for winches, oversized yacht blocks, the stove and the toilet. The cost of most standard gear of the strength I was after was prohibitive, another reason for designing and fabricating my own.

Very soon there was no more money in the bank. No more progress. Another full-time job was necessary. Because I was doing all this design and fabrication work on my own, things took me many times longer to complete, and my extended bursts of concentrated boat-work gave a very erratic-seeming record of employment. By now it was almost impossible to get work in my own profession, and most other jobs I applied for regarded me as being either overqualified or lacking in experience – even though anyone with a modicum of intelligence could have adapted themselves speedily enough.

To complicate matters, I had learnt that the only means to amass real funds, in quantities sufficient to buy both time and materials for boat progress, was still contract draughting and architecting. With another recession coming on, there was very little of this, and there were a great many architects around with vastly more experience than me. Luck, however, was on my side, and I landed a job with a predominantly industrial architecture-based group of designers and builders, and basked in the happy glow of being a regular employee, although on a contract basis, for a full year. Because they could see that I produced the work and didn't falsify my time sheets, they willingly paid for hours spent on design and draughting completed at home, so when the opportunity arose during my final months, I started putting in hundred-weeks, staying with a friend in town whose drawing board I could use at night, thus saving on travelling time.

I managed to get most of my deck hardware at wholesale prices from a yacht manufacturer I had done work for, and many other important items at a good discount owing to the quantity of gear that I was buying. I was impatient by now to take her sailing, so decided against making her first set of sails myself. It was now nearly five years since she was launched, so in went my order with a sail-making friend and, as I slipped once more into joblessness, the reality was an unprecedented period of productivity aboard *Little Wing*. This culminated in her first sail one late spring/early summer nor'easter of about 10 knots, perfect for a trial. It was a very satisfied Creator and his Creation that drifted back to the mooring that evening when the nor'easter died. In fact I towed her behind the dinghy for the last few hundred yards. She remained an empty shell down below, however, with no floor framing, no temporary flooring, not even a level surface on which to put things. Everything was loose in the bilge, a mess.

Chapter Five
Problems, Solutions

I don't recall consciously having learned anything about sailing during the years of living aboard the *Wraith*. Despite doing four Sydney to Hobart races and return by the age of seven (my first was at the age of three which would make me the youngest to sail in the race), and despite thousands of miles of coastal cruising. I was too young. I only began to learn consciously when I started racing my own VJ, at the age of twelve. We had built this in the living room at home. Racing as skipper in the planing centreboard classes is the only way that I have seen truly to learn to sail. I did try working as a sailing instructor in keel boats for a while, later, but found them far too forgiving of error to be a useful teaching tool. Even though I may not have learned consciously from those live-aboard years, the people who sailed with my parents were virtually all competent seamen, so I suspect I learned quite a lot about matters of seamanship by osmosis.

My father had been brought up at Leura, in the Blue Mountains, but both his parents were dead by the time he reached his early teens, so he completed his secondary schooling as a boarder in Sydney, remaining there for his university years. Finding life in the city unpleasant after his mountain youth, he bought a little second-hand yacht as soon he could, living aboard from then on. After meeting my mother they continued living aboard the *Connella* until I was born, at which time they decided to build a larger yacht instead of a house, and continue life afloat (my parents, my sister and I). The land they eventually built on at Palm Beach was at the time of purchase the cheapest deep-water frontage land they could find in Sydney, and the house they built basically the cheapest square box. Really just a larger sailmaking loft than the deckhouse of the *Wraith*, with some bedrooms attached!

In those days of the early Sydney-Hobart races there were no compulsory life-rafts or radios to call for help. Safety gear to be carried was left largely to the discretion of the skippers. No responsible skipper would embark on a voyage putting his crew at risk, however, so only those who felt confident of being able to complete the voyage safely tended to enter. No one was lost, no vessels came to grief and rules to protect fools from themselves were not needed.

Common sense and good seamanship were, and still are, the most reliable safety equipment, but they can cost a lot, in terms of time, to acquire. Not to mention the enduring of fear and uncertainty. Hence the modern tendency toward short-cutting and becoming dependent on all sorts of safety equipment which only costs dollars instead. Hence also the increasing number of fatalities, serious injuries and serious damage to vessels themselves.

I had plenty of time to ponder such matters during a few yacht deliveries I did after the *Wing* was sailing, in search of more boat-building funds. One voyage, from Sydney to Adelaide non-stop, was enlightening in this regard. Particularly gruelling, but very satisfying also. I had insisted on the voyage being non-stop after trouble on another delivery when the owner had insisted on a stop en route, lost his nerve about continuing despite favourable conditions, and had later been forced to sell his stranded yacht as a result.

The yacht in the Adelaide saga was a 37- or 38-foot hard-chine plywood design that the owner had built himself and sailed up to Sydney from Melbourne. Having now moved to Adelaide to live, he wanted her down there. Since they had sailed her up from Melbourne, I assumed that certain basic navigational needs would have been attended to. Wrong!

Already three days of perfect nor'east sailing weather, which would have got us around Gabo Island and heading west, had been wasted while a so-called radio expert wired a radio up, and I was becoming furious at the waste of ideal conditions and overlooked checking some basics. What a waste of enjoyable miles! Wind-ships set sail when the conditions say, 'now', not when their human occupants find convenient, but these landsmen hadn't learned that yet.

Having just got out of Botany Bay, I discovered we had no deviation card for compass error, no charts other than the front page of the East Coast Pilot that I had brought along, no useful sextant or tables, and that the radio had been wired up in such a way that the batteries were now flat. And there was no hand-start on the engine, so we had no navigation lights, no compass light, no radio after all, and no way of using the engine if we needed it! Whoopee! To say that I was annoyed would be an understatement, but I reckoned I could still do the job. As soon as the southerly came in and we started bashing into it, the owner and the radio expert retreated below, feeling sick, and leaving me free.

Alone, I got on with the task at hand, getting the boat to Adelaide as quickly as possible and for all practical purposes single-handed, since neither of them could hold a compass course and our only navigation now was the dead reckoning computer in my head.

I had three hours' rest in the first fifty-one hours at sea, then an easterly gale came in just after passing Gabo. I took the helm for another forty-two hours straight before a calm patch near Wilson's Promontory enabled me to get a little sleep. This forty-two hours straight, after the initial long stint at the helm, was only possible because surfing westward on the swells through Bass Strait so reminded me of sailing the Skate. It was like a long reverie through happier times! The only thing that spoilt it was that there had yet to be a clear sky to the west for me to get an idea of our compass error on a westerly heading. Knowing how many unlit rocks and islets there were in the region we were approaching made the nights very long. The dawns were welcome as saviours. The 'crew' at least stayed down below and out of the way, seasick, so I didn't have to worry about losing them overboard as well.

Tacking into the Adelaide Yacht Basin with yachts motoring out for racing and us with no engine and almost no room to manoeuvre, yet making it to a berth at the far end, was one of my most satisfying sailing experiences. It proved to me yet again that with skill and a little luck one can get virtually anywhere without the need of an engine.

For navigation, the system I worked on for my dead reckoning (DR) was to aim for certain key lighthouses along the way as checking points, and to stay at the helm myself all the time we were moving in order to estimate our speed and course with some accuracy. The lighthouses I chose to sight between Sydney and Adelaide were Gabo Island, Wilson's Promontory, Cape Otway, Portland and Backstairs Passage.

The only hiccup in this plan was the landfall at Deal Island instead of Wilson's Promontory, prior to me being able to ascertain our compass error (some 15 degrees on westerly headings). This landfall was also due to choosing the safer surfing course option through my long Bass Strait watch instead of an ideal compass course.

This voyage, although it earned me no more than my return fare from Adelaide in financial terms, did wonders for my self-confidence – I found I was able to improvise my way successfully out of a whole succession of unforeseen problems as they arose. It was thus one of the turning points in both my recovery and my sailing education.

Returning to Sydney, I found myself another short contract draughting/architecting job and at nights worked toward finalising the interior layout for *Little Wing*. Happy with this latest version, I fabricated then installed the steel and timber sub-floor framing in readiness for a livable interior.

But first, a job that I had been putting off for years needed doing. Where the sides of my keel taper in towards the aft end to form a point, no surface treatment, sand-blasting or cleaning of any kind had been possible after construction because of the shape. I had left it too late. I had filled this space by pouring in closed-cell foam which expanded to seal the untreated surfaces from air and water. After only a year or two it became apparent that closed-cell foam does not remain very closed-cell for long. In fact it ended up absorbing water like a sponge, invalidating its presence. I had come to the conclusion that I would have to remove it all, but how? Once removed and cleaned, I had decided to refill the space with molten pitch. But some jobs you build up in your mind to be so difficult that you put them off and put them off forever, the difficulties being magnified by the avoidance.

I no longer had transport of my own and the search through distant industrial areas of Sydney to purchase materials and hire equipment was daunting by public transport. For instance, it was illegal to carry bottles of gas for the burner to melt the pitch on public transport, and the pitch itself too large a load to move without a vehicle.

I had recently met a girl who seemed to share many of my interests, namely sailing, scuba-diving, bushwalking, even rock-climbing! Inspired by this friendship I set about attacking the foam with crowbars, reinforcing rod and all sorts of tools to break it up, then removing it with other improvised tools. The void was then sponge-dried to remove water.

At last I had all the material and equipment ready, and Jane came over to help. At midnight I started the burners and for the next thirty-six hours they ran continually as we melted barrel after barrel of pitch into steel drums, ran them down the hundred or so stairs to the waterfront, rowed them across to the *Wing* and, having got them aboard, poured the molten pitch, still at a temperature of a couple of hundred degrees centigrade, into the confined space of the keel. The first pours were somewhat exciting with the remnants of moisture forming explosive pockets of steam, but we completed the job by Sunday evening with no serious burns to either of us, nor any damaging spills. This was a job I had put off for years because it had become 'impossible' in my mind. Yet just the two of us, working as a team, had completed it in under two days. I had spent about ten days on the preparations alone, but the whole thing had proved to be no big deal after all.

Jane was to be indirectly responsible for me completing another impossible job on the *Wing* that winter, this time on my own. The job was to install more permanent and waterproof cabin windows than the temporaries I had put in years before. This involved drilling and tapping well over 300 holes through the steel of the cabin and matching holes around the perimeter of the polycarbonate windows themselves. Holes which could only truly align when the windows had been force-bent to match the curvature of the steel. Force-bent by the fastenings that the holes were being drilled for! This took some thought, sequencing the work, as there was no second chance once I had built up the silicon bed for the final fitting.

Jane was the first climber I had come across since working in Dunedin nine years before, and now that the *Wing* was actually sailing I figured I could afford the time and money to see if I could still climb. I decided to try a commercial rock-climbing course and if I found I could cope, join the Sydney Rockies

(Sydney Rockclimbing Club) for further climbing. I booked myself a place on a course starting in a couple of weeks and this was my spur to activity. I wanted my mind free of boat job worries by then so that I could absorb the climbing experience fully.

The first clear spell of winter's westerly weather arrived one Monday, and I set to work. Chancing all on the feeling that the clear spell would last a few days, I removed all temporary windows at once, leaving the boat open to the elements, and drilled and drilled and tapped and drilled and primed the holes and finally, in one afternoon of fitting frenzy, had all four windows firmly bedded down, having taken on the curvature of the cabin itself. The reflections of the evening light appeared in them as flashes from perfect gems. It was done, and I had learnt again . . . just get started, kiddo; once you are underway you can overcome all obstacles – just get started.

Chapter Six
The Heights Rediscovered

We started from scratch. The knots that were used in climbing, various ways to belay, various ways to abseil, and the calls used to communicate clearly with one's climbing partner on a climb. All this in between sporadic heavy showers of rain, which made the thought of climbing wet and slippery rock somewhat daunting. We decided to boil a billy and have lunch, the weather looking as though it might clear soon.

Yippee! Although my hand showed signs of creating problems out of some types of climbing moves, my natural climbing ability and balance from before the fall had not deserted me after all. I could mostly figure out ways around the problem moves not by doing things as my leader had, but by working out my own often quite different sequences.

From day one it was blatantly obvious that one thought one's way up a climb, each sequence of moves a creative work in its own right. It was definitely not a purely physical activity based on strength alone. The strength was needed more in the mind. To stay calm in unnerving situations and still be able to think clearly, to problem-solve one's way out of trouble. This is not to say there was no physical aspect to it. Muscles unused to those types of moves and strains felt as though they had really done some work when I woke next morning. But the memory of the sheer physical delight in some sequences lingered, and far outweighed whatever pains were there from lack of climbing fitness.

Up early after I stayed with friends in Katoomba, we met next morning at the climbing shop, then set off quickly, our aim being to do the West Wall of the Three Sisters and then, if time allowed, the Mantel Shelf, a climb on one of the

Sisters. The most visible climb in the mountains probably, with up to 100 tourists on the path to the Giant Stairway watching every move.

How entranced I was, how impressed by the beauty of it all as we rapidly descended the Stairway, overtaking tourists willy nilly as we hurtled by, our climbing gear jangling as we went. In places the early morning sun caught fronds of fern in its beam, lighting them an almost luminous pale green, with drops of moisture from the previous day's rain like crystals, lending sparkle to the scene. Branching off the track, we ascended an initially almost invisible side track until we came to the foot of the face itself, still cold, wettish and in shadow. Sun was bathing the upper regions of the face in an enticing glow of warmth, so we rapidly sorted gear, went over the knots and calls I had learned the day before, then we were off.

The first pitch, damp and cold but relatively straightforward, did little one way or the other to my enthusiasm for the climb. I was thrilled actually to be climbing one of the classics of the mountains. Struggling to retrieve my leader's runners as I ascended the second pitch, a corner all the way requiring foot jams, hand jams and some bridging here and there, introduced me to the bane of my seconding career, and one of the prime motivations for my rapid switch into the leading of climbs a couple of months later.

The problem was, of course, to do with my left hand. I lacked sufficient fine control and feeling in it (and still do) to remove runners, or place them, left-handed. Since a well-placed runner is not an easy thing to remove, especially while trying to maintain balance on marginal footholds with maybe nothing for the left arm to contribute, I would often exhaust my good arm to the point of uselessness trying to remove just one runner near the very bottom of a pitch.

With the aid of a few rests on the rope (allowing it to take my weight), however, I struggled to the top of the pitch and almost immediately my efforts were rewarded. To such an extent that a new addiction had been born on only my second day at it. The third, fourth and subsequent pitches of the climb introduced me for the first time to the absolutely delicious – I can think of no better word to describe the almost physical feel of what was really mental bliss – sensation of thinking through then carrying out sequences of moves to overcome problems in high and exposed situations. I was hooked.

Whereas the one- and two-pitch climbs of the previous day had a sufficient height gain to prompt fear and the taking of care to ensure a successfully completed climb, they lacked the dimension of being overwhelmed by an almost spiritual high that the added exposure of far greater height seemed to bring. From here on I preferred long multi-pitch climbs that were an adventure in themselves, and gained far less pleasure from one-pitch problem climbs. I was only a beginner, however, and all climbs had their lessons for me, so I climbed every weekend for the following months, despite the fact that it rained at least one day of nearly all those winter weekends.

Shortly after my climbing course I chanced upon some members of the Sydney Rockclimbing Club mid-week, before a long weekend they were planning away at

Booroomba Slabs – the view across from about 110 metres up on 'Equilibrium'.

Booroomba, south of Canberra. It was here I discovered firstly, a group of friends who were to become the best friends of my adult years, and secondly, my favourite style of climbing. Long run-outs over granite slabs with so few hand-holds as to be no problem for my left arm and so few places to put runners that my right arm couldn't get tired when removing them. When I began leading this style of climb a while later, I was immediately at home. Long run-outs over virtually holdless rock made faith in the friction provided by one's feet about the only security there was. Often a pitch of 100–150 feet had only one or two possible runner placements, if that. These climbs demanded good balance, both mentally and physically. When feeling good, that sensation of total commitment was sheer heaven. When lacking in confidence the terrors struck and made upward motion virtually impossible.

My new friendships grew steadily in strength as time progressed. Climbing friendships have proved very good in this regard. There is no room for pretentiousness or fraudulence on rock, where our lives are in each other's hands at all times and where the ability to see the ridiculous in any situation is so helpful in releasing tension.

As summer came around, some of my friends were planning their own rafting expedition down the Franklin, something I had longed to do for years. Since 1972, in fact, when it was part of my south-west Tassie plans. Another of these plans, unforgivably lost for all time it would seem, was to walk into and spend time around the real Lake Peddar before it was drowned and gained its currrent status as a monument to the all-time stupidity and mindless destructive greed of rampant moronity.

I suggested that if they could get enough time off work we sail down in *Little Wing* and they return by air to save time while I spent some time visiting friends around Hobart and maybe doing some climbing down there. Then finding a crew or single-handing her back to Sydney. This idea was jumped upon with enthusiasm, but *Little Wing* was still an empty shell except for framing, more suited to day sailing than an ocean passage. I explained this and they kindly offered to lend a hand over the next few weekends to get her to a spartanly habitable stage. I really was committed to my latest accommodation layout now as there was no time to waste on indecision.

Hundreds and hundreds of lineal feet of various size radiata pine were bought for the framing I had estimated to be necessary, and dozens of sheets of ⅜ and ½ inch-thick plywood to be cut into bulkheads, bunk tops, floor panels and so on. It was impossible to imagine, seeing all this timber piled in one spot, that it could possibly fit inside the boat in any form, let alone as finished joinery with everything in its place. I pre-cut as much as I could in the house, then with the boat pulled over to a neighbour's jetty so that we could use shore power, and thus power tools, I improvised frantically around my latest accommodation layout. With no time for referring back to the drawings I was making a continual run of snap decisions as fast as Chris, Heather and Ron could jig-saw, drill and assemble with bolts and screws.

47

One morning this haste was almost my undoing. The *Wing* was pulled towards the jetty in order to use shore power, and I used to row the lead out before starting work. To save time I had turned the power on at the house, and with my hands full of oars, held the lead between my teeth as I rowed. This was all right while my feet were lying on the dry aft seats of the dinghy, but I had forgotten how badly it leaked. And there must have been a break in the insulation covering the wires. As I stood up to pass it to Ron . . . Wham, wham, wham. 240 volts coursed through my body along the most direct route from teeth to feet. It echoed around inside my chest like a series of explosions, and if Ron hadn't spoken at that moment, snapping me back into activity, I think my poor heart might have decided I was already dead and not still poised on the brink.

It was a frantic three weekends, but at the end of that time we had a toilet, sink and stove in place, three bunks and a basic framework for storage.

Ron, a CSIRO research scientist working mainly with sheep and deer, was not yet thirty but had been climbing since his teens, as had Chris and Heather, who had been bushwalking, rock-climbing and ski-touring together for almost twenty years. Chris was still a high-school teacher and Heather a social worker when I met them. After taking their long-service leaves to climb together through the British Isles, Europe and North America, however, the lure of the hills was too strong. They had left the city to live in their Blue Mountains home, working at whatever became available. I had met them all on my first trip with the 'Rockies' to Booroomba, and we have been friends ever since.

Late afternoon of the final weekend, in a perfect 10–12 knot summer nor'easter, we had done enough to take her out for a celebratory sail, but it was to be our last. Even in these mild conditions one friend felt so devastated by seasickness that it was apparent that after a relatively long voyage he would be in no condition to cope with the Franklin. Another had a pressing problem with timing, so reluctantly my crew departed to fly down to Tassie. I set out to boost the strength of the work we had done and carry out a few more things I felt relevant if I were to single-hand the *Wing* to Hobart and meet them.

As I worked on alone, time flew. It flew so fast that it became apparent that all the new work I had decided to do, along with redoing most of the plumbing on my own to eliminate some problems, would take me beyond rendezvous time. I would have to miss the Franklin trip after all. I was bitterly disappointed, but *Little Wing* was a representative of my skills as designer, constructor, creator and sailor, so I wanted her to be in a truly seamanlike state when I went 'foreign'. I stopped rushing and added a host of finishing touches to satisfy my aesthetic and practical senses. I didn't get around to leaving on this, her real maiden voyage, until mid April 1986, with winter well on its way.

Chapter Seven
Maiden Voyage

Possibly it was the subconscious influence of the wooden boat seamen of early childhood that shaped my outlook on radios, engines, calling for help at sea, abandoning ship and related matters. Perhaps also it was derived from my renewed interest in climbing, and the inevitable discussion of climbing ethics. I was certainly too young to have consciously absorbed much that I heard as a child. Anyway, from her maiden voyage, and unproven though she was at this stage, I decided that *Little Wing* would be representative of my thinking on such matters and we would not commence our partnership as hypocrites.

There are times when the ability to communicate rapidly with harbour authorities and shipping at close range (line of sight) proves necessary. For such purposes I bought a hand-held VHF radio transmitter. Since I would probably be returning from Hobart with a crew member, I would then have responsibility for another to consider, so I bought an EPIRB (Emergency Position Indicating Radio Beacon – a beacon set off only in emergencies such that the exact position of the EPIRB, and thus the emergency, can be rapidly pinpointed and help directed to it with minimal waste of time) to cover extreme emergencies in that regard. A life-raft is a non-navigable craft and almost useless for self-rescue, so I took an unsinkable dinghy and, being an experienced rower, thought this sufficient for safety. I had (and still have) no engine, having decided that my money was better spent on spars, rigging, sails and deck hardware. With these she could perform as she was designed to, sailing from A to B in nearly any conditions without artificial aids. I had a large sweep oar to scull her forward in calm windlessness in harbour if necessary, or I could tow her behind the dinghy. Otherwise, we would get there under sail, wherever 'there' happened to be.

The word 'voyage' suggests a reasonable distance component. No matter how exciting, instructive, pleasantly successful or troublesome were my trial sails between Sydney Harbour to the south and Cape Three Points to the north, none of these could be classified as a voyage. This honour went to my single-handed, non-stop trip from Pittwater to Hobart during the latter half of April '86. It was my first totally single-handed ocean passage of any length, and also *Little Wing*'s. We would be learning together.

In line with my 'try the simplest system first' attitude – both for saving cost and having nothing aboard that I could not, with patience, fix myself – I as yet had no self-steering gear. I intended experimenting further with various sheet-to-tiller systems that I had been trying out during recent trials. Hopefully I would work the bugs out of these rather rapidly. If not, I would be spending many sleepless nights and never-ending days at the helm. Naturally I was apprehensive on several fronts, but I had covered the route many times before, and everyone kept telling me what a strong little boat she was. I chose to believe them and stopped worrying about her falling apart, at least.

What still did worry me prior to setting out was the thought of hitting a semi-submerged shipping container in mid-ocean. Tales were rife of sinkings and near misses. With our steel hull (⅛ inch plate) and myriad of chine bars running fore and aft, I reckoned we would have to hit one corner-first for it actually to hole us, but anything is possible at sea, so this became my greatest worry prior to casting off. Once at sea, however, my mind was fully occupied with problems of reality, such as the weather, navigation, tactics and efforts to get her self-steering on all points of sailing, and I don't think I gave the idea more than a moment's thought for the entire voyage.

The morning of departure dawned fine, with a strengthening nor'easter forecast to swing into a gusty north-westerly before the south to south-west change behind. A typical summer sequence, and unusual so far into autumn. I departed my mooring in a lively 10–15 knot breeze with one reef in the main in anticipation of things to come, and Yankee set, streaming the log off Barrenjoey at around 1.45 p.m. Hobart here we come.

So far I had not been able to get her to self-steer satisfactorily downwind with sheet-to-tiller systems, although I had not yet tried under headsail alone or with the mainsail reefed at the third reef. A full afternoon of daylight lay ahead, in conjunction with an ideal breeze to experiment with. It should have been the time to work out a satisfactory system. A southerly change would soon be here judging from the sky and wind progressions, and I knew I could get her to self-steer to windward when that arrived. Instead of experimenting, I opted for covering the maximum number of miles southward that I could before the change. This was my first error of judgement for the trip.

As the nor'easter strengthened, I took in another reef in the mainsail to make steering a little easier, finally dropping the mainsail completely later that night.

We hurtled south under Yankee alone until I felt that my tiredness might lead to a serious error of judgement as the wind continued to freshen. The wind swung into the north-west, and I dropped the Yankee after quite a struggle in the now 25–35 knot wind and total darkness, continuing under staysail to try and cover as many miles as possible. I could rest once the southerly arrived. The night passed ever so slowly and it became hard to stay awake. I couldn't leave the tiller to eat or drink so was imprisoned in the cockpit indefinitely, a captive of inflexible aims! Gradually the sky lightened in the east, revealing a landless and windswept horizon on all sides. The wind was now a steady 35 knots or more from the north-west and still no southerly. The hours really began to drag and all sorts of fears started surfacing as exhaustion set in. It was time to stop, to rest, to wait awhile and regather the strength and optimism of the previous day.

I dropped the staysail and for the first time tried lying-a-hull, thinking that the strength of the breeze acting on my rigging would keep her motion slow and easy. In the swell/sea combination due to the nor'wester across a fetch of about 50 miles? Never. The rolling was so uncomfortable that I resolved never to lie-a-hull as a means of heaving-to again. But I was exhausted and even the ungodly rolling ultimately could not keep sleep at bay. I slept for twenty-four hours, my radar detector probably blipping warnings frequently, but I was too tired to notice. I did hear the first, though, immediately after lying down, and rose to find a large Nauruan ship with bulbous bow cross our path mere boat lengths away.

While up and frightened into wakefulness by that first ship, I watched what seemed a natural tragedy in the making: a white heron vainly flapping, flapping, flapping, trying to make headway in towards the land but unable to progress against the strong wind. I hoped it would see *Little Wing* as a haven in all that ocean and land aboard for a rest. I even talked to it gently in mid-air to try and soothe it down, but on and on it went, flapping its way to what appeared certain exhaustion and drowning. I felt so sad.

Next morning found us underway again in a variable 15–20 knot northerly, at times moving back into the north-west. It became blatantly obvious what a stupid position I had chosen to lie-a-hull and rest. As I struggled to get her self-steering under Yankee alone, ships were passing both ways, on either side of us. Admittedly at a distance, but close enough to indicate that I had chosen the centre of the shipping lane to and from the corner at Gabo Island as our resting place. The steel hull, deck and deckhouse rolling madly in the waves must have given a good radar image for other ships to avoid, as I was certainly unaware of their presence! Radar reflectors of my own making were high in the rigging, and perhaps these helped.

I had some success in the self-steering department, but not sufficient to make her self-correcting in the stronger gusts when she was also swung off course by following seas. Still intent on making as many miles as possible before the overdue southerly, I hand-steered for most of that next night under Yankee alone. A glorious swooping ride, broad-reaching down the moonsilver and shadowblack swell faces for hour after hour. Sheer heaven! In the early hours of the morning, surrounded by distant lightning displays that were too distant for me to hear thunder, but close enough to provide visual atmospherics, the southerly eventually arrived. With her steering herself comfortably to windward under Yankee alone, I could sleep.

It had been surprising to me earlier, when watching passing shipping during the night, how inconspicuous their port and starboard lights were. Impossible to distinguish at a distance with the naked eye. This made the gradual opening up or closing of the distance between forward, masthead and stern lights the only clue to their courses relative to ours. Not easy, and there were some tense times that night. In the morning, after sorting out the halyard tangles from my first night-time mainsail drop, I rehoisted it at the second reef and again she self-steered perfectly, hard on the wind under Yankee and double-reefed main. I went below to read and rest through a basically calm day punctuated by rain squalls. I had to reduce sail before dark in one of these squalls, eventually getting her to self-steer again under staysail and triple-reefed main, plodding slowly to windward all night. The masthead navigation light chose this time to die. It was not the fuse, so the damage had to be at either the masthead or the deck plug (perhaps kicked while sail-changing at night). Either way there was nothing I could do about it until I was in smooth water, so I decided to use my lower port, starboard and stern lights (three times the current draw) only when a collision possibility was there, relying on a radar detector (brought along as an experiment) to alert me.

The following night a locking-pin shackle undid itself and the Yankee halyard was lost aloft, preventing me from setting my most useful sail. Luckily, it became entangled in one of the shrouds near the lower spreaders, so despite the big seas running I tied a set of ratlines with thin terylene cord between my lower shrouds, climbing as I went, and soon had it retrieved. I was learning, admittedly through errors of judgement, but all minor and with plenty of sea-room to set things right. All halyards not in use needed to be separately and securely held taut, or the violence of motion aloft soon had them on the loose, then tangled and unusable.

The thing that had become an almost unbearable annoyance, however, was the almost continuous waste of good sailing breeze through not being able to make use of it fully. Single-handing without adequate self-steering on all points of sail was proving very painful after so long making use of every tiny change during my racing years. It seemed almost criminal to waste these favourable conditions, but I could not stay awake forever.

The other thing that surprised me, particularly after all the ocean sailing I had done as a child, was the difficulty I had in getting used to sailing at an angle of heel. I was now so used to planing centreboarders which we kept almost dead level in order to plane both upwind and down, that all this heeling struck me as dreadfully inefficient.

Wind changes came and went, sail changes likewise. The sea and sky were at times truly beautiful, at others the cause of great anxiety. Slowly we worked our way south, then back to the west once my navigation indicated that the time was right. Finally, at 4 a.m. on 23 April 1986, between rain squalls, I glimpsed Cape Tourville light. Further north than I had wanted to make a landfall under normal circumstances, but considering my problems with self-steering and sleeplessness, and my inexperience at navigating from the deck of a small ship, not too surprising. At least we knew precisely where we were, were in no danger, and with a dying breeze I could even get a few hours' sleep.

Later that morning a light breeze took us down past Freycinet Peninsula and Schouten Island, a place of many memories, thence toward Tasman Island. I hand-steered all of this as a southerly change was due and I wanted to get around Tasman Island before it hit, having learnt the consequences of not doing so from Hobart Race experience. Under Yankee alone, between Maria Island and Tasman Island we averaged 9–10 knots for one two-hour period, the wave riding and surfing in the strong nor'wester keeping me thrilled and wide awake. A 50-knot squall necessitated me dropping Yankee and continuing under staysail, praying nothing would break and send me drifting out towards New Zealand.

Lit by intermittent strong moonlight – full moon, flying scud – we finally rounded Tasman Island. It loomed as a huge, black, silhouetted form, dramatic in the foreground with cloud-wreathed Cap Pillar behind, another silhouetted giant. At sea level it was a chaos of breaking waves, one of which came through as white water to boom height, drenching me at the helm. Although both wet and cold I didn't change as I (wrongly) remembered Hobart to be not far away! Working our way toward Cape Raoul, then across Storm Bay towards the Iron Pot, lifts and knocks followed each other in a bewildering lack of pattern. The steep and closely spaced chop, a by-product of a long fetch and shallow water, slowed progress dramatically. I had been at the helm for over twenty-four hours again, and my judgements were clouded by tiredness and cold. I felt the presence of an imaginary crew member whom I consulted before making decisions, and I found it impossible in the changing conditions to work out the best sail combinations. Eventually, by sheer trial and error, I hit upon Yankee plus triple-reefed main and this powered us beautifully. At last we reached the Iron Pot and thence into the Derwent.

How beautiful the rural scenery around the mouth of the Derwent was, with its trees and fields with homes set amongst the trees. Lit by late afternoon sun, after so long at sea it looked like heaven itself, but I still had to work my way up a long strange river in the dark. I had always told myself never to enter an unfamiliar port in the dark, and to wait until morning to enter. Tiredness had clouded my judgement, however, and I pressed on in the gathering darkness, handing over to my imaginary crew while I went below. I needed to find fenders for when we reached the dock, and to check some lights on the chart to ascertain our exact position. With thoughts of what an amazingly beautiful rural scene the mouth of the Derwent had been, so close to the city and yet so close to the sea, I sat down to think out where the fenders might be . . .

I was awakened by a gentle bump, bump, bump and then the absence of motion. We were aground. I launched the dinghy and rowed out a stern anchor on chain and rope to pull us off while she was still floating on the gentle surges. No use. The anchor, of a type known as a CQR, or plough, just skated over the bottom and refused to bite. I tried again, with the same result. Totally exhausted, and the night being calm, I decided to remain where we were, meanwhile trying to sleep on an increasing angle of heel as the tide went out. At first light I rowed out another stern anchor but this wouldn't hold either. I was about to flood the dinghy and winch it up under my boom to increase our heel and maybe sail off when a local fisherman rowed out to give me a hand.

Before we could get started, the local policeman also arrived, saying he had called the Hobart Water Police and that they would be there any minute now. Sure enough a large 'Powercat' appeared and with the help of two of us sitting out on the boom to make her heel more, all of a sudden she took off stern first and we were free. Having been warned of the weather expected at any moment, I accepted their offer of a tow for the final couple of miles. Once underway they received a radio call for help, so I anchored off Sandy Bay Point while they carried out a real rescue: a dismasted yacht drifting towards rocks. Having completed that job, they returned to take me the final mile to the dock. It was gusting over 70 knots now, so the tow was not unwelcome.

Finally, into Constitution Dock at 3 p.m., where some of the guys from other boats helped me secure bow and stern lines and springs, and to coil the hundreds of feet of wet anchor line and chain. After being ambushed, interviewed and photographed by a journalist from the *Mercury* for Saturday's paper, I was invited aboard another yacht for a cooked dinner. I hadn't had one cooked meal or hot drink since Sydney. How peaceful it was in the dock, but I could hardly sleep with such an unfamiliar lack of motion.

On reflection, the major lessons to be learnt from this maiden voyage were as follows: firstly, the worst enemy all along had been tiredness. Cold and tiredness from extraordinary long watches sapping my ability to think clearly and rationally and to evaluate rapidly the true nature of situations as they developed. For instance, apart from two hours' rest off Cape Tourville, I had been at the helm for fifty-two hours without a break, food or drink by the time I fell asleep going up the Derwent. In this time I had made eighteen sail changes, twelve of them between Tasman Island and the Iron Pot as my ability to solve problems suffered from thirty hours of being frozen in wet clothes, combined with extreme tiredness. It snowed on Mount Wellington below an altitude of 1000 feet that day.

Secondly, a more thorough and systematic method of tying down unused halyards and lashing sails not currently being used, was called for. In order not to lose anything aloft, and to make deckwork at night (when I can't see and therefore can't feel with my left hand) less dependent on precarious balancing of torches in order to work. I was yet to discover head torches, but the lesson still applies.

Thirdly, there was the unendurable inefficiency of sailing single-handed without a good self-steering system that worked on all points of sail and in most conditions of wind and water. Even the control lines necessary for my more successful sheet-to-tiller arrangements made the cockpit area almost unusable. Inadvertently I would lean back against one or more in finding a comfortable position, thus altering course. I decided to build a trim tab on my rudder, in conjunction with a wind-vane system, on my return. The rudder had been designed with this kind of self-steering in mind, but I had wanted to try the simplest and cheapest system first. In all, over 50 per cent of the passage time had been spent hove-to, lying-a-hull or resting due to this lack of adequate self-steering.

Fourthly, I should never again forget to eat properly. On this journey I had neither cooked nor heated one meal or drink – not through seasickness, just not being bothered with the extra effort while making continual steering adjustments. On a longer voyage this would have become a really serious problem.

I had not been able to buy a large Admiralty Pattern (Fisherman) anchor in Sydney before leaving. With one of these I would have been able to haul myself off at the first attempt after running aground, despite a weed-covered, hard sand bottom. I was able to purchase one in Hobart, thankfully, so returned fully equipped. There had proved to be no serious flaws in the design of *Little Wing* as an able and easily driven seaboat. I would later modify the cockpit drainage system and improve the hatch seals, but not before the 'long voyage'. All in all I was quite content.

Chapter Eight
Winter-time Hobart, Return North

Frost sparkled on the pathway up ahead and frozen leaves crunched underfoot when I was taking short-cuts through the bush. The air bit hard with cold as I ran shirtless through its bite, and how hard I had to push to maintain warmth. The 'pack' was far behind as I led on down the trail, singing 'North to Alaska' as the frosty ground flew by. What joy this frozen moonlight night.

I was running that night at Ferntree, half way up Mount Wellington, with the Hobart Hash House Harriers and Harriets, having come across them in one of the hotels where I played with local musicians. Being starved of good hard running since my recent arrival, this was a happy chance discovery. I had never heard of the 'Hash' before. Each week I would run the hills and dales of Hobart and surrounds with them. It was an excellent way to discover out of the way places throughout their running range, and a good complement to my daily long walks of discovery around Hobart.

Hobart had seduced me completely by now. The warmth and friendship of the people I met, whether in town, in the pubs, down at the dock or aboard other yachts and fishing boats, was a wonder to experience after the cooler reaction to strangers in a large city such as Sydney. It seemed to belong to my era, and I felt so at home. The sight of snow-capped Mount Wellington rising proudly above and visible from nearly everywhere, lent a feeling of security, of timelessness, to existence. It became a most comforting sight when I woke and gazed skyward each morning. While at close range, how impressive was the soaring architecture of the Organ Pipes, Mount Wellington's crown. A friend who was busy working to restore an old fishing trawler for the summer season shared a house with an occasional climber, and although I had left my 'rack' back in Sydney, I had brought my climbing boots, harness and rope with me. One fine day we headed up to the North Buttress area of the Pipes, since in mid-winter this would be the most sunny and warm.

It is always interesting climbing new places. The architecture, texture and frictional properties of rock vary widely, necessitating quite different approaches to seemingly very similar problems. The Organ Pipes were no exception. Very steep, mostly vertical soaring cracks and corners. It was strenuous and difficult climbing one-handed. The friction of the rock was better than expected from its fine grain, however, and there was the totally novel advantage of being able to return to ground level and eat a few mouthfuls of fresh snow to quench one's thirst. All this on a perfectly sunny winter's day, with visibility extending to Maria Island and beyond to the north.

A surprise event was the night it snowed in Hobart. Really snowed, the heaviest fall since 1922 apparently. I had designed *Little Wing* with the intention of an Antarctic voyage at some time, but never expected to have thick snow on my decks so far north! I was playing harmonica that night with a local bush band at a hotel in Battery Point and a few of the locals expressed surprise at its heaviness so close to sea level, but assuming it was an isolated shower, ignored it. We played on.

A friend of mine, Anne, had flown down to Hobart in order to sail back with me. By the time we rowed back to the *Wing* after dinner at a local restaurant, the snow lay approximately 9 inches deep over the decks and all the way down to the water's edge on shore. How pretty it looked on waking next morning to see all those areas of pure white where complexity had confused the scene before. Hobart was paralysed. The snow was about 4 feet thick at the top of the Hobart Bridge, so no traffic flowed between the two halves of the city, and a similar depth over most of the suburbs kept virtually everyone who couldn't walk (or ski) to work at home that day. A lot of Hobart spreads up the foothills of Mount Wellington, and several feet of snow over everything halted most movement.

One of my oldest friends, hailing from the days when I first started racing VJ's, had by now returned to Hobart from a few months lecturing in New Guinea. Andy and I had shared numerous mad escapades both ashore and afloat during our racing days through VJ's, Skates and Lightweight Sharpies. He had left the bank where he worked and moved to Melbourne where he became a helicopter pilot flying to the oil rigs of Bass Strait and doing deliveries up to New Guinea. After marrying Robin, a Tassie girl, not long before my fall, they had settled in Hobart, out of reach except by mail.

As I had given some design input into the house that he had built for himself and his family, I was curious to see how and if he had included any of my early thoughts. He had done a marvellous job, and I was extremely impressed.

Having thoroughly absorbed the design and atmosphere that Andy had created, I was then introduced to some of his friends nearby who had also designed and built their own home. They had bought a substantial part of the temporary wooden Bailey bridge, erected after the Hobart Bridge collapse, for next to nothing when it had finally been dismantled. After having the wood sand-blasted to remove the asphalt, they had then cut it down as required, using this timber for almost all the woodwork in the house. All the stone had been collected from the site itself, so the material costs had been minimal despite its large size and stylishness.

Andy's house, his friend's house and the not yet completed one belonging to their son were the finest pieces of domestic architecture I could recall seeing. They brought to mind one of my favourite books while a student at Sydney University, *Architecture without Architects*, which dealt with the ingenious design solutions to everyday problems of indigenous peoples worldwide. With no input from professionals, the solutions were nearly always aesthetically pleasing and highly functional.

Having been given the name 'Titchester' by the H5 'Hash' for my single-handed sailing and shirtless running, it was time to heed the ocean's call as my namesake had, and leave. I knew that I'd return, as Hobart in many ways was now the home port of my heart.

Moored off Muir's, Hobart 1986 – before the addition of the bowsprit and Mr M.

Anne, my companion on my return journey, had helped me a great deal with some of the preparatory work, wherever an extra hand was needed, prior to setting out. After hearing of my problems with extreme tiredness on the way down, she had decided to come down and ease the burden. Although she had had no sailing experience whatever, I had worked as a sailing instructor in the past and was sure she could take the helm for at least a few hours now and again, allowing me some rest.

One mid-August morning we set sail, the wind a light north-westerly. It swung into the south-west after we were becalmed off the Iron Pot at the mouth of the Derwent for an hour, then south. Off we set across Storm Bay under full main, Yankee and staysail, out to make progress while we could. Anne practised her steering, with me explaining and forewarning of likely occurrences and how to cope with them if they arose. By Cape Raoul problems did start to arise, as the wind rapidly strengthened and, after some difficulty with reefing in the rough seas, I dropped the mainsail completely. This made the steering much easier for Anne, and we continued under Yankee alone. I had dropped the staysail already to avoid confusion with sheets in the night.

After passing Tasman Island, again in full moonlight, we headed on east to avoid the Hippolyte Rocks, the wind having eased somewhat, then gybed and headed a little east of north, holding this course until morning. It had been extremely cold all night, and two-hour watches were about all we could comfortably take in the night wind. Civilisation must have softened me. I could only marvel at how much more pleasant this was, having a useful and warm friend as co-pilot, co-voyager. This was more like the original 'wing dream'.

Daylight found us in light winds, Schouten Island and Freycinet Peninsula off to the west, with the golden pink light of dawn on the peaks of the distant Hazards. It was very beautiful, but as morning progressed so did the wind's strength; rapidly. By midday we were down to staysail alone, with the wind still strengthening from the north. Here I made a very useful discovery: in very strong winds and rough seas, *Little Wing* looked after herself very well under staysail alone, plugging away a shade off hard on the wind, no tiller lines needed. She steered herself along a steady course through the breakers while we stayed warm and dry down below. At times we were hurled down horizontal when we were caught by a large breaker just at the wrong moment, and Anne was very afraid. I don't blame her. It was rougher than anything I had been through on the way down, with waves breaking completely over the boat and us nearly horizontal on many occasions.

Still, we were making progress right through it, and at a pretty good rate of knots. This helped to explain the roughness of the motion. It had been too rough to get out on deck to check the log for over a day, but when I did I discovered we had been averaging around 5 knots to windward throughout the blow. I had learnt on the way down that all storms must pass, given time, so with me exhorting patience and insisting that there was no need to panic, we waited out the worst until it eased. We waited substantially longer than necessary before setting more sail, but with Anne still terrified by memories of the previous couple of days, we carried sail very conservatively for the rest of the voyage.

The next few days saw some idyllic light-to-moderate weather, sailing over a Bass Strait almost as smooth and free of swells as Pittwater. Moonlit at night, sunny by day, but the wind always from dead ahead, and mostly too light for easy helming. I was forced back into the long hours routine in order to make progress, it being too subtle for Anne with her lack of experience in light windward sailing. One day, however, was perfect – a whole afternoon of windward work in approximately 15 knots of steady wind, with sunny conditions and smooth seas. It made the whole voyage seem worthwhile, the joy of clear skies, clear horizons, no ships, no clutter, just an expanse of blues, sunshine and a little floating armada of clouds prompting thoughts of summertime nor'easters and more tropical seas.

For this return voyage, with its predominance of windward work, I was finding that choosing the right headsail for the conditions in conjunction with the matching number of reefs in the mainsail led to *Little Wing* steering herself perfectly to windward with the tiller left completely free. For any correctly chosen combination of sails she continued to do this quite adequately over considerable changes in wind strength, weaving her own course through the swells almost as well as a good helmsman. It was a most useful discovery, as the cockpit could now be used again without fouling some control line or other.

Landfall at Gabo was exciting. The night was wild with a strong southerly and full moonlight through gaps in low cloud racing overhead. Progressive sail reductions had us down to staysail alone as we surfed our way north. Frequent flashes of lightning, also to the north, made the loom of the lighthouse itself hard to find in the extremely contrasting conditions of light and shade, wind and wave. Luckily, however, we spotted it just before a very heavy rain squall obliterated all visibility for a few hours. Having an accurate bearing, we could at least safely, if blindly, continue our headlong rush up the coast.

Around 9 a.m. it cleared, and there was land, the lovely wooded hills of the south-eastern forests. The first land we had seen for days, and looking a veritable heaven. Some trawlers kept us company at a distance over this stretch, returning to Eden I suppose due to the roughness of conditions outside. We passed several seals, some sunbaking on their backs with flippers aimed heavenward. It was the first time I had seen this behaviour that I was to see much more of on later voyages. How funny they looked on their backs like that, so relaxed and at home.

In lightening winds, the struggle to make ground against the south-running set of the East Australian Current became our next major battle. Keeping as close to shore as I dared, we snuck between Montagu Island and the mainland in the dark. Further up the coast I spotted my ideal rural property. One side bounded by the sea, with a beautiful-looking homestead among the hills and trees, and Mount Dromedary lending a timelessness to the scene it dominated from a distance, almost as Mount Wellington had done in Hobart.

Reaching Jervis Bay, we were trapped by the set and a strong northerly. We tacked in and out between Wreck Bay and the ocean, not making much progress, and waiting for the forecast southerly to take us around. After a few false rolls of cloud from the south, eventually the real thing arrived, and did it ever. Just past Jervis, and with a fetch of 20–30 miles across the Shoalhaven Bight, I glanced up and saw the sea blown white to the west. Down came the main, down came the Yankee. We had only just secured these, when it hit.

Fifty knots or more it blew for the next few hours. The waves were a steep, breaking surf aggravated by the shallow water of the bight. It was hard to believe the staysail could take such punishment without disintegrating. The helming being wild and strenuous in these conditions, I helmed us all the way to Sydney that afternoon and night. It proved to be a very interesting experience, trying to thread a safe course through those breaking crests, but exceptionally tiring mentally – it took 100 per cent concentration at all times for hour after hour . . . That night the old problem of tiredness to the point of hallucination appeared again, but this time in radically different form.

Just on dusk, with the big chimney of the Wollongong Steelworks abeam, I set a course to keep us clear of coastal hazards and we surfed on northwards, still under staysail alone, the wind having moderated to a steady 30–35 knots. Along the distant shore an elongated galaxy of lights stretched from Stanwell Park in the north to Kiama and environs in the south. The South Coast towns, with the lights of the expressway like a string of luminous orange pearls climbing to the edge of the escarpment far above. It was an enchanting sight, but helming still took all my concentration and I was mentally very tired. Several hours later we left the pretty lights of civilisation astern and entered a realm of darkness. This corresponded with the shoreline of the Royal National Park from Stanwell Park in the south to the lights of Cronulla, Capes Baily and Solander – the southern end of Sydney – in the north.

It was here that the strangeness began. At first I saw what appeared to be the masthead light of an approaching ship, but it seemed to approach very slowly. No lower lights became visible to enable me to gauge its course. A most confusing array of various coloured lights then appeared, which made me wonder what strange new offshore construction had been going on in Sydney while I was absent. An oil field? A new offshore port facility? I was confused, but Anne couldn't find the binoculars so I was made no wiser by magnification. Then the canal happened. For over an hour I was convinced we were sailing down a tree-lined canal. I was sure I could see the silhouettes of the trees along the seaward bank as we sailed past, and there appeared to be occasional lights along the other bank. Car headlights then appeared on what seemed to be a beach ahead of us, and my worries really increased. Especially when the silhouette of a large rock breakwater also appeared close by. I called to Anne and asked if she could help me tack. I hoped to turn around before we ran aground and reverse our course, tacking back up the canal and out to sea once it appeared safe.

But I was not at all sure we could turn in time. The car headlights on the beach and the rocks of the 'breakwater' were so close. I thought, what a silly way to lose *Little Wing*, so close to home, and eased her slowly round into the breeze, expecting impact with the bottom at any moment. We made it, and hard on the wind I held an offshore tack until I could see the trees and the canal bank again before tacking once more. I thought,

'Where are these swells coming from if we are in a canal or harbour, or between breakwaters?'

I could not decide, so we sailed offshore for about an hour before the coastal lights of Sydney opened up to the north. Then, with some trepidation, we resumed our northward course with the east showing first signs of light. And with daylight came the dawn of understanding. The 'masthead light' of the 'ship' had been Centrepoint Tower, and the other lights, city and North Sydney office towers. The silhouetted large rocks of the breakwater had been the blank sections of seaside cliff where no suburban lights shone, the absence of light giving the optical illusion of a foreground object – my imaginary breakwater – occluding the lights.

I do not remember ever having approached Sydney by night from a little east of south, so had never noticed these double images before.

How pleasant was the sight of the northern beaches as we sailed slowly past in a light south-westerly. What a delight to see Barrenjoey, the gateway to home, and once around the corner a real surprise lay in store. Sailing a few yards away were a couple of friends from Hobart: *Alias*, on board which I had shared many a happy evening in Constitution Dock, was being sailed by her owners, Rod and Angela, on their way north in search of warmth, having spent most of their lives in Hobart Town. They had left a couple weeks before us and I hadn't expected to see them again unless we met by chance in some distant, exotic clime. To find them once more only 100 yards from 'base camp' and again share music, laughter and good times in their atmospheric aft cabin was a wonderfully happy surprise.

Extreme tiredness had again reared its dangerous head, even with a crew. Once the level of being unable to analyse the unexpected in rational terms has been reached, it is truly time to rest. Sleep must take precedence over all else once the safety of the ship has been taken care of. Obvious, I suppose, in hindsight, but twice more I skirted the limits and beyond, before the lesson was fully absorbed.

Chapter Nine
The Jacques de Roux Memorial Voyage

H ome. A novelty for a while, and great to climb and bushwalk with my friends, exchange stories of our respective Tassie trips and discuss future plans. I realised quickly, though, that I needed work. This time, if I were to ever realise my long-term goals, I needed a steady job, to remain employed for several years. The continual battle to get paid for work done during my self-employed years, the 'too short to be really useful' periods of contract work and the lack of a car or motorbike for transport all suggested it was time for me to find a permanent job as a regular employee. Now that so few expenses were tax deductible for me the elimination of provisional tax was another bonus of regular work.

Recently, Jacques de Roux, a competitor in the second BOC Around the World Challenge Race, had been lost overboard from *Skioern IV* near Gabo Island while comfortably leading his division. It is thought that he hit a large floating object at speed, raced up on deck without a harness to check and was tossed over while looking for damage.

This tragedy, occurring so near in time and place to our own battle to get past Gabo when returning from Hobart, had a profound effect on me. I was so saddened that it began to erode my confidence in being able to single-hand again. I needed to get out there once more, on my own, before my self-confidence seeped away entirely.

I decided to do a 'Jacques de Roux Memorial Voyage' to try and solve the problem. My chosen route was a non-stop return trip to Balls Pyramid, a reconnaissance mission to look at some climbing possibilities for a future ascent by myself and some friends. This would be my first single-handed voyage of over

1000 miles, so a satisfying milestone for me. Balls Pyramid is a sliver of rather rotten and weather-beaten rock rising over 1860 feet from the sea, from a base at sea level only ¾ acre in extent. It lies approximately 15 miles south of Lord Howe Island, about 450 miles from Sydney. This would be my last fling before working indefinitely. There were also a few fresh ideas I wanted to experiment with in sheet-to-tiller steering, as I was still searching for the simplest, most adaptable system.

It was February, and getting close to the latter stages of summer when any tropical cyclones up north tend to move furthest south before weakening and dying. Lord Howe is hit regularly by these southern wanderers, but there was no news or sign of anything cyclonic off Queensland at the time. Feeling all was clear for a dash there and back, I set off.

A gusty 15 knot nor'wester with hot, sunny conditions ahead of a forecast southerly change late in the day gave me a great chance to check my new steering system, this time using a small storm jib set off one of my lower shrouds to windward and set aback as purely a steering sail. It was sheeted back to the tiller, and opposed by a surgical rubber spring as before. It seemed to work wonderfully as long as the wind was of a reasonably steady strength, but as usual its nemesis appeared when things became too gusty or the wind strength increased enough to cause substantial heeling. Maybe the southerly would be steadier in strength once it arrived and settled in – we would soon see.

By sheer bad luck of positioning, my reefing winches on the boom were at just the right distance to foul behind my aft lower shrouds when the boom was squared right off. Less than an inch either way and there would have been no problem. As it was, it had been almost two years since a fouling and I had forgotten. After hurriedly reefing when the southerly arrived, then dropping the main completely, I had trouble centring the boom. Not being able to find the problem, I decided to sheet it home by force, using a primary winch. Bang! Something shiny flew overboard, but I didn't see what. Next morning I found the winch base plate in the leeward scuppers. A reefing winch had been torn off the boom and lost overboard. From now on I would have to do all my reefing from the port side. A damned nuisance, and an expensive start to the trip. I was depressed, and to quote from my log:

> Grey skies, grey seas and constant pounding to windward as the wind has now swung into the east. How lonely it is out here. With the Hobart journey there had been no preconceptions about the future, all possibilities lay open at the other end. A whole new world to explore and become part of, possibly a whole new life lay waiting there. With this trip there is no new world to look forward to at the end, unless one calls getting a regular job and working for years a new experience.

The assumption had to be working for years, as I was still the prisoner of *Little Wing* until we had proved ourselves completely. Then I would be free. This lack of the prospect of new experiences to draw me on was making the trip far harder psychologically than the Hobart one and I was plagued by loneliness, having shared the previous voyage with a friend.

It can be a damned elusive spot to find, Lord Howe, despite the almost 3,000-feet altitudes of Mounts Gower and Lidgbird. On a good day they can be seen for over 60 miles, but good days are not necessarily there when you need them. The tongue of the East Coast Current that bathes Lord Howe in its tropical warmth, making coral growth possible so far south, is variable in strength and direction, casting doubt on dead reckoning. This, along with light and variable winds, numerous sail changes and hand-steering nearly continually, was wearing me out yet again. Another worry was a cyclone on the loose after all. A few days after leaving I heard on the news about a cyclone devastating Vanuatu just 1000 miles away, but they gave no information as to its movements. The anxiety began.

Eventually I decided to work up just close enough to the Pyramid to get an idea of possible routes and their problems, then beat a hasty retreat in case the Vanuatu cyclone came south. At dusk, with the moon rising in the east and the Pyramid still at least 15 more miles to windward, I completed a sketch showing the layout of the main ridges and spurs as seen from the south-west. I already had a good photo taken from the north-east, and the faces were too difficult for me to climb. A strange-feeling wind was freshening from the north as we turned for home, beneath an almost full moon. Until midnight, with my strength rekindled by the wind from astern, we surfed and schussed down the moonlit faces of following seas, the log skipping clear of the water in our night-lit sleigh ride . . . Sunrise came like a molten ball rising from the smoking pits of hell, ringed by impenetrable black rain squalls, and with these came the wind.

Not unbearably strong, averaging around 35 knots, but with the huge swells left over from the cyclone up north forming a cross sea to the new waves, it made the most chaotic, frightening sea I could remember. I was surrounded by a cacophony of sounds from sharply explosive breaks and deep roaring ones. Never knowing when a break would erupt directly beneath us, I wove a course under staysail alone at speed, seeking to avoid the explosions all around. Exciting, and as Eccles would say, '*Gee, dis is livin!*', but terribly wearing after over forty-eight hours at the helm without a break.

Following the mightiest of all line squalls I could no longer take the strain, and having found she would head slowly WSW under staysail alone with the tiller free, I retreated to my bunk. I put on my climbing helmet first to protect my head from some untrimmed bolt-ends overhead in case we were rolled. For a while I had been hallucinating the presence of a companion or companions again, so the warning signs were all there. I rested, at least, being too apprehensive to sleep.

How wonderful and infinitely varied are the faces that nature can put on. After four hours' rest, then another seventy-two hours at the helm without a break, during which time we passed through the line-squall factory for the Southern Hemisphere plus the eyes of two miniature cyclones, we were blessed with a sea so flat and devoid of all trace of swell that we could have been sailing on an infinite

Pittwater, smooth on all sides to the horizon. It was downwind sailing so I had to hand-steer, but with the Drifter/Multi-Purpose Spinnaker set and drawing to perfection in the light breeze, sunshine and a pair of mahi mahi (dolphin fish) each about 6 feet long keeping me company all day, it was sheer pleasure.

What colour! What beauty! Even when about 100 feet astern and around 10 feet below the surface the iridescent, almost luminous leading edges of their pectoral fins blazed forth, making them easily visible. Such electric blue, such turquoise! And the leading edges of their tails a wonderful golden yellow. How could *anyone* be so degenerate as to catch and kill such beauty just for sport? Ever since taking up scuba-diving about sixteen years ago and playing among the fishes in their own element, I have found it impossible to fish, especially when single-handing at sea. Whenever I am by myself in wilderness, the whole living world of nature seems sacred and there to provide food for the mind and imagination, not the stomach.

More rough stuff, more worries concerning position, then eventually the first clear patch of sky in days gave me a position about 10 miles off and 5 miles south of Sydney Heads, after having been unable to leave the helm for a single sunsight on the return journey, doing it all by DR in my head. A final southerly change had us running north for cover under staysail alone, getting back to my mooring around midnight to sleep. Of the last 168 hours of the voyage, I had spent 162 at the helm, 94 out of the final 96! This, I decided, was my limit, and proper self-steering the only solution if I wanted to keep sailing alone.

> . . . Out to sea, the red moon rising
> shook the saline from her hair,
> slashed the thread that bound her downward
> Changed to silver, hovered there . . .
> a reminder sent to banish refuge
> in the swamp, complacency,
> enticing actions always wayward,
> never chained and balanced finely
> Pleasure/Despair.
>
> Raud, 1974 (an excerpt from a longer poem)

Chapter Ten

A Weekend Close to Heaven, Vertical Chess

2 a.m: Quietly leaving my sleeping friend and shouldering two packs, one of climbing, the other of camping gear, I cast a final glance back, remembering our glimpses of heaven, then shut the door of her flat behind me. Reflections of street-lights on rainglisten shine wetly from empty roads and footpaths and the puddles quiver with ripples from wind-driven rain. I stop and don my cape-groundsheet for the mile or two's walk to public transport, the suburb and the city both asleep. Last night the crowds and fireworks, inhabiting the dark with dancing lights. Now morning's burnt-out embers, quiet reflections in the night.

At 5 a.m. Russell picked me up from Ashfield Station and the feeling of everything just slipping into place, of everything being or becoming just right, grew stronger as we drove. Not one red light between Ashfield and Goulburn to slow our headlong flight towards the rock, the wonderful 'faith in friction' granite of Booroomba's soaring slabs. At 9 a.m., at the start of Counterbalance, my weekend's next experiment began. I had never led Counterbalance before, but when I was seconding, reached a point on the second pitch where I would always burst out laughing, overcome by the sheer bliss of the moves, the exposure, the whole situation on high . . . the clouds drifting past overhead, the valley and the whisper of wind in the trees far below, the bush-covered hills opposite. And beyond, in the distance, the plains, the cleared land and Canberra.

Russell, beloved President of the Sydney Rockies, and many other climbing friends, led two lives. During the week they worked as responsible professionals in a variety of fields; at weekends they worked at the more anarchic disciplines of climbing/vertical chess. Russell's memory for climbs was prodigious. It seemed he could remember every piece of 'pro' he had placed, and its position, on virtually every climb he had done. A veritable climbing encyclopedia.

The first pitch, a steep little slab, then corner above, was wet, slippery and very hard to get off the ground – I slipped back 15 feet or so to the bottom twice before getting past the wet. An earlier party had given up on the first pitch and rejoined the climb at the walk-in ledge at the start of the second, but this was my first go at it and the full climb was my goal. I persevered. The corner above went without too much trouble, with the usual uncertainty of left-hand jams making the lead more interesting – a climber's euphemism for frightening – for me. Soon we were both at the belay 'ledge' at the start of the second pitch, but a 'ledge' at Booroomba is no bigger than a foothold at most places.

Slab-climbing with its long run-outs and sparse protection is helped a lot by confidence and today I was in love so all the holds were there; the crystals for the fingernails, the friction for the feet. The moves just flowed together, hardly needing thought; I floated up, I laughed, it was so good, so very good . . . .

Feeling fine that evening back at camp – tired but happy, listening to the dreams, tomorrow's schemes. The scenes mingled with thoughts of mine – 'Yes, now's the time . . . while its flowing, now's the time.' With Counterbalance led, and climbed with ease, there waited Equilibrium. Why not? A climb whose long third pitch has two in-situ bolts as the only protection, and with approximately 80 feet between them, the most likely fall would be in the order of 150–180 feet. Phil had never even seen it, but was keen. It was, after all, the classic of its grade; we teamed.

The first pitch, steepish, but a long and sloping crack, was easy to protect. The second, thin in places. We were there. The third pitch traverses the slab a while before heading directly up past the first bolt, once found. The upper bolt was not visible from this first, but the minimality of holds, the climbing itself, would lead the way. Gorgeous. Delightful. Challenging. But not that hard today. I cruised it, high on happiness, on love. Again, the holds, the moves, the sequences fell into place, a pattern plain to see . . . comfortably, with feet sticking like glue, sticking with a confidence that grew. At first Phil, used to sandstone, found no holds at all. I called down, 'Trust your feet, the friction, just keep moving up and through' and he found it, tried it and, enjoyed it too.

On the long drive back to Sydney that night it occurred to me for the first time the similarity between the type of climbs I particularly liked, the style of ocean sailing I did and the style of my long solitary bushwalks. In each case I was really putting myself out there on my own with no protection other than my own abilities and mind. I was still exploring limits as to what I could and couldn't do in my post-fall mode. Still testing this modified me for flaws.

Daily life tasks did not always reveal these flaws. Mostly they were revealed in unusual, often demanding, situations that had not been anticipated. A good example was the discovery that I could not operate the J-valve lever on my scuba tank with my left hand, as is normal. This occurred when I ran out of air at a depth of over 90 feet while diving off Palm Beach. I could neither pull the lever for reserve air nor adequately indicate the problem I was having to my dive buddy. It was a close thing before my message got through. After analysing the problem later, we solved it very simply by rigging my tank back to front in the backpack to enable me to reach it with my right. Almost all tasks are like this, with me having to evolve my own system to bypass the hand problem.

* * * *

Arapiles for the first time . . . slowly and with wonder approaching this huge archipelago of rock. Glowing with the golden pink of dawn, while still in shade the level fields around stretched far away . . . to an almost sea horizon, flat and pure, broken only by another island group of hills, the distant Grampians. The architecture of the rock so complex, varied, new . . . an infinity of routes from which to choose. First, back to the campsite for an early mug of tea. It was time to find a climbing partner, work out this day's moves.

Tiger Wall – Syrinx wanders up to and through the overhangs just right of centre.

Brolga – straight up the waterstreak – 100 vertical metres of Arapiles 'slab'.

The 'Watchtower' face – 'Arachnus' climbs the outside face of the tower.

*From high on Tiger Wall – the lone and level plains stretch far away
– to an almost sea horizon.*

First day, a kind of smorgasbord, a varied sampler, seconding, to become familiar with the rock. Jon, an old hand at the Piles, became our leader/guide. While climbing the Arapiles version of a slab – ultra smooth, 'thin' and steep – following up a waterstreak, I spied a climber above and to our left, moving silhouetted up the vertical last 100 feet of another climb. Moving up on jugs and hanging out so comfortably, checking out the moves . . . looking so relaxed. What a perfect situation, climbing towards the evening sky. I had to find and lead that climb, just had to have a try. Heather knew the climb (Arachnus) and had done it long ago. She didn't mind seconding me – I wanted to lead the entire climb if possible – if I then seconded her on a climb she wanted to lead, Hot Flap. We teamed on what was to be the first of our 'Oh damn it, it's gone dark . . . Well, keep climbing' days together on the rock.

Arachnus, after the bottom bulge was overcome, was sheer delight. A lovely bit of wall and overhang before the eyrie belay cave, and then that upper 100–200 feet of juggy wall. With holds large enough for me to use with either hand – I can't use my left on small holds due to the lack of feeling and fine control – the verticality was therefore not worrisome. I could just bask in the wonderful buzz from the exposure up on high. It was a satisfying lead for me, relatively easy climbing, but wonderful situations, wonderful memories.

Hot Flap was next, the central slabby section being Heather's goal. To lead as practice for leading Brolga, the slab climb from which I had seen Arachnus. The first pitch I led, then Heather leading through took on her slab – in places more a wall in steepness, and with a very thin and tricky bit causing some delay. We alternated leads and ran pitches together to save time, as the end of the day drew near. After sunset, approaching the top, the guide book was rather vague. I found and led a truly inspiring unmentioned pitch, long, very exposed and sustained, and just the perfect way to end our climbing day. Returning down the track to where we'd left our surplus gear we met our friends looking for us! It having been dark for some time, they had become worried.

The next day I climbed with Jon and his wife Penny, on Dunes, leading all of its six or seven pitches except for a part of the third where I lost the route. Jon, knowing it, led through. On this climb I first encountered rope drag so ferocious that I was totally unable to move against it. This was from not using a long sling on one key runner, the rope becoming jammed as it pulled around and not past the overhang above. Still learning. Next day, after hours spent walking, exploring and photographing the Arapiles archipelago, I got back to the campsite just on sunset; Heather was there also, with nothing to do. 'Conifer Crack?' . . . 'Reckon we could do it before dark?' . . . 'Oh yeah, if we hurry.' Another of our nocturnal climbing sorties had begun.

As with most climbs, I found the climbing more enjoyable the higher we got. This climb started up the front of an almost vertical rock rib, one of the Organ Pipes. The second pitch moved back and around to the side following an absolutely vertical line up one or the other of a pair of cracks. Very, very enjoyable climbing, even in the gathering gloom. The forbidding wall facing the upper pair of cracks across a narrow cleft was where Heather had earlier been doing a much harder climb. Although the area was vaguely familiar to her, the descent route from our climb was a mystery to both of us, especially in the dark. With the aid of head torches we avoided plummeting over the surrounding vertical drops, looking for a way out without long abseils in the dark to unknown places. This was becoming a real adventure. Down a slot in the ground, then on down through a cave system of huge fallen rocks to another opening. Damn . . . another vertical drop. We tried a side passage, roped up. I carefully edged down more chimneys and slots, all of which I thought I could reverse-climb out, and called Heather on down. A steep but almost certainly down-climbable slab fell away before us into the darkness . . . as did my headtorch, which chose this moment to come loose and disintegrate somewhere below. We pondered this in darkness, then a light seemed to approach from below. Adrian had come to search, knowing from his daytime climb how complex the route back down could be. Back at camp, 10.30, and much too late for tea!

This Arapiles trip was the first time Heather had seconded me up a variety of climbs and I think my good placements of 'pro' surprised her somewhat as I had a reputation for not placing much protection at all. Ah, but all the times seconding Adrian, my climbing friend over from Britain, had taught me well. Struggling until exhaustion to remove his exquisitely precise runner placements had evidently taught me to place mine too.

My preference for long multi-pitch climbs was known by now amongst my friends. But their preference for short routes could have made for trouble the next day. Phil was keen again, though, and Syrinx, an all-day wander up myriad varied pitches, was our aim. Alternating leads to speed things up and also since we were both keen on leading something every day. The first pitch, a chimney and corner, Phil led. I found it desperate with a day-pack as cargo, the space being too confined. What a struggle, what a terrible start, but often first pitches are the worst. One pitch up and I'm really enjoying it and moving freely as a rule. Heather had suggested running the next two pitches together and I did. Lovely wall moves here . . . Steep and sustained, with small holds and far enough above the deck to be getting that delicious buzz from exposure. It was the most delicate and technical climbing of the route, a very satisfying 100-foot lead.

When my turn came again it proved to be another long and enjoyable lead – a rising traverse along the junction of red and grey rock. Long run-outs between 'pro' to save rope drag, but always a comfortable jug or foothold for reassurance. And by now very exposed, some 400 feet almost vertically above our start. Phil triumphed over the crux overhang, leaving another one for me, and we were off . . . almost! I had to reverse-climb the last pitch and its exposed traverse to find my guide book, dropped at an earlier belay. Terrible rope drag almost caused me to do the traverse unroped but commonsense prevailed, and with Phil's help to clear the drag problem I eventually rejoined him above, having led that final pitch three times – forwards, backwards and finally forwards without runners to get out.

On the last morning I led the climb that I had seconded with Jon on our first day. With Heather, just to compare. How easy it was now, after five days' climbing in a row. It confirmed my belief that climbing was the best physiotherapy my hand could get. A few weeks at Arapiles would be ideal, but my 'long voyage' still had precedence. After that?

Chapter Eleven
The Pyramid, Second Take

T he working days stretched into weeks, the weeks to months, now years. It was a pleasure to be working where I was, with John my employer, another architect, Bill, and myself. The three of us shared John's office space at Manly, near the sea. Each lunchtime I would sit on a favourite rock at the very edge of the ocean and in my mind be out there . . . swells rolling by and breaking at close range, the seagulls in the sky, mermaids on the beach. I was watching my savings grow, able to plan a future once again and able to repay Anne for expenses in Hobart and money she borrowed to fly there. With summertime approaching the sea called strongly from its distant, dark-stained rim . . . come over, and beyond . . . the wind is free . . .

Time may not heal all wounds, but time certainly puts pain in perspective. It was time to put ourselves to the test again, the *Wing* and I. During the summer holidays I would have just enough time to squeeze in another non-stop photographic reconnaissance of the Pyramid, object of my Jacques de Roux Memorial Voyage and return. I was no longer satisfied with the results of the previous voyage and wanted to photograph all sides of the rock and at far closer range. I also wanted to try a final set of sheet-to-tiller experiments before moving on to more adaptable but more complex and expensive self-steering. I had designed and built the rudder for fitting a semi-balanced trim-tab to be used with a wind vane as the next simplest method, and I would have to build this if these experiments failed.

This time we started in conditions made to suit, a south-easter swinging east before I tired. To windward, just right for the sheet-to-tiller gear. On the starboard tack with the Yankee alone doing the work we ploughed steadily on, for day . . . after day . . . after day. It was a good thing the wind held so steady, because the compass light had died and I did not fancy hand-steering night-long stretches without its pink glow, a companion in itself. After checking that there was nothing wrong with the fuses, or wiring breaks elsewhere, I finally located a break in the compass's own internal wiring. Doing delicate soldered connections while bashing to windward would be difficult enough even with two good hands. For me the aligning of wires, heating the soldering iron and keeping the various parts in precise contact while being hurled about underway or rolled about if stopped, was impossible. By sacrificing one of the two bulbs through a redesign of the wiring, then twisting the wires together to hold until soldered, I managed to get one bulb working again. Success.

In all my thousands of miles single-handed, this had revealed for the first time the problems I would face with my left hand and its lack of dexterity during the 'long voyage' to come. The reasons were simple in hindsight. Firstly, due to having no truly functional self-steering for all points of sail, I had been hand-steering in the cockpit for most of the duration of every voyage so far – or hove-to, resting. I had thus avoided normal daily tasks where fine two-handed control became necessary, and was yet to cook a hot meal or make a hot drink at sea! And nothing had been used enough yet to break down or require repair. Secondly, apart from the Tassie trip which was nearly all hand-steered, thus needing mainly gross hand control, all sailing aboard *Little Wing* had been done in quite warm air and sea temperatures. Cold had a devastating effect in reducing control and mobility, and my hand hadn't yet discovered this at sea, only on rock – I'd forgotten.

One problem solved, another appeared. The port-side primary winch refused to work in its more powerful gear ratio. This was obviously a stuck pawl or broken pawl spring, but dismantling the winches safely at sea without losing parts overboard – a negative attribute of the very large deck camber, would be impossible. I used my smaller, secondary winch on that tack, luffing to depower and sheet in harder when necessary. Each problem brings its own gift, and while pondering the winch question a purely aesthetic gift was given to me – the wondrously beautiful turquoise of the back-lit wave tops as they peaked just to windward before splashing aboard – a shot of colour amongst the grey seas, grey sky and the overall greyness of the day . . . A few minutes only of strong light, and the mood of the day transformed. With this consistency of wind and the self-steering working well, I felt extremely lazy in comparison with past voyages, lying in my bunk reading for hour after hour, musing on the past, thinking of the future. Sleeping even! Four hundred and thirty miles on one tack, a record for us. In a lightening breeze at about the latitude of Elizabeth Reef, to the north of Lord Howe, I tacked south-east to approach the Pyramid from the north – for a new experience both visually and navigationally, with the current helping for a change.

Early one morning, in a light north-easterly breeze, the island appeared dead ahead, but still about 50 miles away. We were sailing under full main and Drifter/ MPS. We had no more sail to set and I doubted we could get there before dark. The wind remained light and headed us until hard on the wind. I didn't much like the mackerel sky overhead by afternoon, nor the obvious ring around the moon, both indicators of wind to come, but I pressed on, hopeful of our being away by then.

It would be hard to imagine more idyllic sailing than approaching Phillip Point, Mount Eliza, and the Admiralty Group, before the high cloud thickened. We sailed under an almost full moon over long, low swells, the water rippled, but not made choppy by the 5–8 knot breeze. We were sailing under full main and Genoa, the impressive silhouettes of Mounts Gower and Lidgbird having been our target since afternoon. There was no noise through the water, no unevenness in our motion. A heavenly approach to this tropic paradise. Off Neds Beach I sailed in close to watch some people barbecuing near the palms. Memories of earlier visits flooded back and I hove-to, sorely tempted to launch the dinghy and row in for a quick visit, but sanity prevailed. What if a breeze had sprung up while I was gone? I stayed aboard and watched awhile, then slept.

My camera had been giving trouble of late, not winding on properly. It was an underwater camera, so this was an automatic function with no manual override. I thought I had deduced a way to solve the problem, however, so at 5 a.m. and a mere 15 miles from our destination, decided to fix it. And 'fix' it I did! accidentally stopping it from working at all. No photos, no point in going further. With time starting to be a worry, I headed home, Defeated again . . . and so close. Adding insult to injury, we were becalmed within sight of the island for two more days.

The return gave pictures for my memory alone, now that they could not otherwise be recorded. The ripples from a very slow-moving hull passing through smooth grey water . . . the ruffled surface patterns on a calm sea and swells with only 0–1 knot wind ripples on them . . . the moonrise, full moon pink-orange in the mauve of evening, reflecting across a smooth sea towards me. And later, looking towards the sun low in the early morning, rough seas all light and shadow . . . The sun just before sunset, bright but hazy, with the sparkle of light on the wave tops and the Yankee back-lit a very deep maroon – almost a black silhouette, but glowing.

After the overly quiet start to the return journey, conditions once again demanded long hours of hand-steering, with numerous sail changes, until a fairly peaceful afternoon's sailing should have given me the perfect landfall, spotting Barrenjoey light ahead as first landmark seen. I saw the coast first, a long way off, and there, on the correct bearing was a group four flashing light – it had to be it, but I had always found my silent counting of seconds to be accurate in the past and this light, to my overly tired eyes flashed four every ten, not every twenty, seconds. It would have taken very little effort to go below and bring up a watch and a torch to check it properly, but I was so sure.

I pass within sight of Barrenjoey lighthouse every night on my nightly run, and had been doing so for years. I should have given that familiar-looking flash another chance – even an idiot would have done a simple check. Not I! Instead I searched my charts from Gabo in the south to Fraser Island in the north, and there was no other four flashing light – surely this should have prompted another check?? But no, I saw the loom of another distant light, convinced myself I was lost north of Newcastle, became amazed at the sudden compass error that could have caused this, and worried, puzzled, muddled.

Rather rapidly I had to forget all this as a distant electrical storm I had been watching materialised above. With wind coming in at around 70 knots and nearly continuous lightning, it was a truly spectacular scene. Surrounded by breaking waves, spray and rain flying horizontally past, I managed a very rapid sail drop and furling session and soon had us down to bare poles. I figured that the compass error couldn't be so bad that a course due east, away from land, would get me in trouble, so after the initial onslaught was over I hoisted my mainsail to the third reef and headed slowly eastwards in the fading breeze. On a safe course now, I retreated below to sleep.

It was amazing, next morning, how many things faintly visible on the distant shore could have been in either the Newcastle/Stockton Bight, or the Pittwater vicinities – at least from so far offshore and to someone who had never studied the Newcastle region from the sea. I headed south once a light north-easterly came in. Eventually, as I continued south, the large number of aeroplanes taking off and landing convinced me I was off Mascot, south of Sydney, so I headed back north towards Pittwater. It had been Barrenjoey!

This incident really sealed the matter of self-steering and tiredness at sea for me. I have been a regular meditator for years and the mental rest afforded by even a few minutes' uninterrupted meditation at the helm had enabled me to continue for the extraordinarily long periods there during the last few voyages. But this only worked so long as conditions and events remained more or less predictable. Now it had finally been proven to me that this was not sufficient rest; ultimately sleep was needed as well if I was to cope with the unexpected. To comprehend it and act on it rationally, with common sense intact. In this dangerous, devoid-of-rest manner, I regarded sea trials as over.

It may seem strange to have done two trips out to the island of my youthful dreams without even attempting to call in, to stop a while and soak it in anew. These trips were, however, mainly sea trials, experiments toward the real voyage ahead. And engineless, the risks of calling in outweighed possible gains, as on both occasions I was pressed for time, because of cyclones moving erratically not far to the north, and the need to get back to work on time. They would not have been relaxed stop-overs and my sacred island deserved better than that.

Chapter Twelve

The Essence of Romance

In his day, almost every voyage undertaken had been a romantic adventure. As we read the accounts of them they distil for us the essence of romance – the light-hearted pursuit of a perilous quest. In more humdrum times, by following in the track of John Davis, we had sought and at times slightly savoured this elusive essence.'

H.W. Tilman, *Mischief in Greenland*

The essence of 'single-handed sailing' – what was, what is that essence? An analogy may be drawn here between doing a climb in original style, that is, using only the forms of protection and climbing equipment available to the first ascensionists, and repeating the same climb with all the advantages provided by more modern gear. Whereas it required a fantastic steadiness of nerve and daring to launch oneself out on to the long protectionless run-outs required to 'put up' some routes, with modern equipment these climbs can be repeated very safely. New forms of protection and stronger, more sophisticated ropes having removed most of the original dangers.

Largely due to the primitive short-strand natural-fibre ropes used on early climbs and their inability to withstand the impact loading of even a moderate fall, an ethic built up in climbing circles that the leader should *never fall*. A longish fall would almost certainly prove fatal, not only to the leader, but to the others on the climb who might be unable to advance or retreat without a rope. This notion led to a procedure of learning whereby people gradually increased their skills, attempting harder and harder climbs but with a similar degree of safety as their abilities advanced. This was akin to the sailing philosophies of the wooden-boat seamen whose childhood influence I acknowledged earlier. As one's skills on the water advanced one could take on more and more challenging voyages, neither expecting nor depending on outside assistance in case of trouble. The belief being, as with the early climbers, that you should be voyaging or climbing only at levels where you could get yourself out of trouble, using only your own skills and equipment.

By today's gadget-ridden standards these earlier seamen were very ill-equipped. But since most things electronic tend to break down at sea, with the only truly reliable instruments proving to be your own brain, skills and knowledge, they were not so ill-equipped as they might at first appear. As with climbing, in tending all the time towards following the path of maximum safety and the elimination of risk, the essence of the original experience of single-handing has been lost. Most modern claimants to single-handing are mere hyped-up parodies of the originals considering their dependency on some or all of the following:

(1) Forms of satellite navigation to fix position precisely with no input of either effort or skill from the operator. A sailor using satellite navigation devices cannot honestly claim to have rounded any 'Great Capes' at all, having removed the navigational problems that earned such capes their reputation. All he/she has done is pass another latitude and longitude, no more, no less.

(2) Radios capable of transmitting long-distance in order to:
 (a) be able to call for help if necessary;
 (b) be able to keep in touch with friends, peers and loved ones, thus being able to receive a morale boost in times of trouble as well as
 (c) receive advice on carrying out repairs from others more skilled, or
 (d) receive advice and warnings regarding approaching weather, and be given courses either to avoid or take advantage of such.

(3) Alarms to wake-up or warn, in case of anything from getting off course, wind strength and direction changes, obstacles becoming visible on the radar screen, etc., etc., etc.

(4) Radar to act as a never-resting eye to watch out for land or sea dangers and warn through alarm systems.

(5) Weather-facsimile machines to keep one up-to-date with developing weather situations. Courses can then be laid with confidence without skill in interpreting natural phenomena.

(6) Argos transmitters to keep the position of the vessel pinpointed at all times via satellite in case of emergency or if rescue is required.

(7) An auxiliary engine just in case it is needed to get out of trouble, eliminating the need for greater forethought and tactical thought if sailing without one.

And neither last nor least – *sponsorship dollars* to pay the cost of the 'adventure'. The list goes on and on . . .

Is someone equipped with all these things single-handing in the original sense of the word? In any sense of the word? Or are they merely hyped-up frauds as they parade before the media? When a boat has the names of twenty or more manufacturers of products to be found on board plastered around the hull to advertise their wares, can her skipper truthfully claim to be unassisted? Modern media-enslaved 'single-handing' has become a sham, concealing its true nature through hype.

This hype devalues and is an insult to all past endeavours where the 'essence' was strong, with persistent effort required, in contrast to the instant modern 'adventures' of PR puppets where 'gift of the gab' and the ability to spend money are the main ingredients of a successful result. The 'wilderness experience' is as much a victim as the 'single-handed experience' of these media puppets. Even a journey cross-country inside the cabin of a four-wheel-drive vehicle is regarded as a 'wilderness adventure' by most city dwellers and the media-enslaved.

I would place in a separate category those sponsored sailors who made use of their sponsorship to explore and extend the limits of both the art of yacht design and human performance in single-handed sailing: Eric Tabarly, Phillipe Jeantot, Titouan Lamazou and a few others. By sailing to the limit and beyond for such extended periods as in the Vendée Globe Challenge, they too in a pioneering way sought out the 'essence'. In these cases the sponsorship dollars extended the frontiers of design and ultra performance over extended periods of time well into virgin territory. In this category also could be placed those in any field of endeavour whose use of sponsorship was to push back the frontiers of their field, pure scientific research being a more valid branch of exploration than almost any other if we are to understand the workings of our planet before irreversibly destroying her capacity to support life.

The great Bernard Moitessier's circumnavigation-and-a-half during 1968/69 remained the only genuinely single-handed circumnavigation south of all the Great Capes in original style at the time I set out – a circumnavigation south of Cape Agulhas, Cape Leeuwin, South-East Cape (Tasmania), South-West Cape (Stewart Island) and Cape Horn, without radar, radio communication, engine or other 'necessities' for 'safety' as defined by the modern world. But even Moitessier did not design his own vessel, so was not single-handedly responsible for creating his own safe passage. I had been an admirer of his ever since he came to my attention with his 1965/66 voyage non-stop from Tahiti to Alicante via Cape Horn with his wife Françoise, so his influence on me was more than subconscious.

For several years it had been growing increasingly apparent to me that I needed to complete the 'long voyage' in a vessel of my own creation and also in my own style. For my continuing evolution as a human being I felt it necessary as part of the renascence after the fall. Since it would become the most important task in my recreation of self – in terms of instigating new directions and strengthening those I desired to keep – I determined to start completely from scratch, sticking to my principles as far as humanly possible, and choosing to be solely responsible for my creation: *Little Wing*, and the entire 'wing dream'.

Hence the taking up of a formal course in yacht design, so that I could see the whole task through from drawing the first line on paper through all the necessary calculations, the process of building/construction, the design and fabrication of fittings where no suitable standards were available, to deciding on the inventory of equipment, tools, spares, clothing, food and drink required for my voyage. And the stowage of these by myself alone so I could find things in a hurry. In keeping with the principles previously discussed it was necessary to finance this whole exercise from my own work efforts. This in itself necessitated a recovery far beyond that thought possible by the so-called medical experts who had showered me with negatives back in hospital days.

I would sail, single-handed, without radar, long-range radio transmitter, satellite navigation systems, weatherfax, engine or life-raft, with no way of communicating with the outside world beyond line of sight and no means of abandoning ship except swimming – no superfluous cargo! This was to be a true test of *my* abilities and judgement, with no one but myself to blame for any failings. As close as I could get, it was to be a voyage embracing the 'essence of romance'.

Chapter Thirteen
Respite on Rock

Booroomba: the frozen work of countless winters with their frosts and thaws. Breaking close-knit bonds of crystals, cracking, splitting, seeking flaws until one day, there lay created a climb skirting the fringes of folly . . . in the grandest, most joyful way.

The Ivory Coast: an alternative top pitch to some other climbs, steps up and around a blind corner, the only clue to its start being a tiny slit (for a finger jam) through the rock edge – so small that the young Swedish climber seconding me didn't even see it and so missed the pitch, continuing up the orthodox finish. This little slit, on turning the corner, develops into the edge of a huge ultra-thin flake of granite roughly the shape of Africa (hence the name) like a huge potato crisp just landed on the body of the slab. It is less than ½ inch thick at the edge, flexes and booms alarmingly, and moves the whole time you are very gently climbing around its perimeter, wishing for weightlessness at times. About 100 feet before a runner can be placed, once off the flake, for the next belay. The flake itself flexes open and closed too much as you climb it to make putting in runners along the way worthwhile. This whole experience is situated about 400 feet above the deck so the exposure is inspiring, the moves as refined and gentle as you can create – the thought of riding the flake all the way back down to the bottom of the cliff makes sure of that, as there can't be much area of contact holding it there . . . Absolute joy, a total delight.

That night, sitting beside the campfire with a glass of wine in hand, inspired by the day and working on tomorrow's plans, the idea was heard and then considered . . . lead Bird of Prey tomorrow?

Yes, yes, my mind was saying, but seconded by whom? Very few people had made it down to Booroomba that weekend and fewer still who knew Bird of Prey wished to second a certain death-fall climb if anything went wrong on the upper pitch. However, Pa, the young Swedish exchange student who had seconded me on Denethor with the Ivory Coast finish, was willing to climb with me again, so in the morning . . .

A slightly larger crystal here, good for a fingernail. The tiny edge of an incipient flake to aid foot friction there . . . subtle rugosities of surface between the smooth and waterworn . . . all signposts of a way. . . . A way to move up over 100 feet of virtually holdless, unprotected rock between a not-too-good belay and a place for a possible runner. Second pitch Bird of Prey. Slab climbing at its best, very committing, very thoughtful, very delicate moves, and sustained throughout the pitch. Watching above me, one of its namesakes rises and falls, hovers and stalls, searching, swooping, sweeping curvelines through the blue. A morning spent in very heaven, it couldn't be improved.

*   *   *   *

There was the usual trouble in finding the place to branch off from the tourist track, but here we are, ultimately, at the foot of the West Wall (Three Sisters, Katoomba). Heather has not climbed it in years, and I, having led only the easier pitches before, am out to lead the whole climb, bottom to top using none of the bolts placed along the route or even the modern camming devices called 'friends'. Just good old hexes, for runners, belays, the lot – sort of approaching original style for my first lead of the entire route.

The second pitch, one of two crux pitches, brings out the old hand problem again although I find it no harder to lead – possibly easier due to no exhausting of my good arm in removing runners – than to second. It does force a rather 'no latitude for error' decision halfway up, though. Since I cannot place runners with my left hand and need my right to hold me in to the corner, at this point I have to weigh up: is it more dangerous to go for the top without any runners in the upper half of the pitch, risking a serious groundfall if I tire too soon, or is it more likely to cause an immediate fall if I try to stop and place a runner in that upper half? I opt to go for it and make it with strength to spare . . . great!

The next pitch, which I had also never led before, produced a similar decision time. Again I opted to keep moving, having confidence in my ability to climb through to safety before tiring. Now we were up in the sun, and warm, and what a wonderful place to be . . . High above the valley below, my solitary bushwalking territory stretching as far as the eye could see to Mittagong, beyond the Wollondilly far to the south. How I love these multi-pitch climbs, just being up there on high.

The second crux pitch was far longer and steeper than I remembered, but very satisfying for me to lead; then the upper chimney was as uncomfortable as ever. Chris, of the Chris and Heather duo, met us on top, and at sunset they pointed out a climb on distant Sublime Point that was just 'made' for me. In parts like the almost runnerless slab climbs that I liked. Sweet Dreams was its name, and a dream it would remain . . . until the future, after the sea.

Chapter Fourteen

Recon-naissance and Retreat, the First Attempts

A Sydney Harbour evening, summer. The setting sun, the city silhouetted across the water to the west. Centrepoint and the surrounding office towers forming a jagged spine towards the iron lace of the Harbour Bridge arch. The whole framed by the deep green foliage of the Botanic Gardens, spreading its soothing foreground to the harbour's edge. The north-easterly breeze, quite strong earlier as we sailed down to Watson's Bay for my departure the following morning, faded with the evening light to the gentlest of zephyrs. Soothing my mind in its contemplation of the challenges ahead.

My parents had sailed down to Sydney to see me off, so we hung alongside the *Wraith* for the night in order to have a final meal together and to save unstowing my anchor gear, very securely stowed in preparation for rough weather ahead. This was a mistake, as the wakes of passing ferries, water taxis and other Sydney Harbour motor-boat traffic caused us to slam very heavily against our fenders intermittently all night, making deep rest all but impossible as I worried about damage to both vessels.

Eventually dawn displaced the darkness, and with a final frenzy of effort a dozen small unfinished tasks were completed, Customs formalities carried out and I was cleared to leave. Marion, who had sailed down with me the day before, and Frank, who had arrived in the morning to help with the last-minute frenzy, both moved aboard the *Wraith* with my parents to sail back to Pittwater. I, on my own for the foreseeable future, hoisted sail and worked out towards the open sea, crossing tacks close astern as we cleared South Head so they could take a few final photos. I was on my way. The date was 18 January 1990.

The previous day's sail down to Sydney had been my only chance to try *Little Wing* with her newly installed self-steering system. Although supposedly the best of its type available – a Monitor servo-pendulum unit bought second-hand – I expected it would take me a while to discover how best to use it. As with my sheet-to-tiller experiments, different sail combinations would prove far superior to others for different points of sail in different conditions. The advantages I had now were in firstly, having covered so much experimental ground in sheet-to-tiller days concerning viable combinations, they would be easier to work out; and secondly, having a system inherently more capable of coping with changing conditions, the frequent steering and sail adjustments that had been required to hold a steady course with wind from astern would no longer be necessary.

In relatively mild conditions for the first few days I was able to experiment and learn a lot. Particularly satisfying was the discovery that with the addition of the bowsprit and new outer forestay, the shift forward of my centre of effort in the sail plan enabled me to make far better use of mainsail area, without reefing as much, precisely as planned. However, the main reason for the outer forestay was for self-steering with sheet-to-tiller under storm jib alone in case the Monitor broke down.

All looked well. Every modification I had made for the journey to make life a little easier at sea seemed to be working according to plan. Then it came time to change film in my new camera. For doing so much photography at sea, often in rough conditions, I needed an underwater type camera to take the spray-bursts and rain without damage. This unfortunately means automatic wind and rewind on all but the most expensive model available. Now the film wouldn't rewind. I couldn't load a new film without destroying the previous one but never mind, I would use my trusty old spare camera (repaired and working again after the Balls Pyramid problems) instead of the new . . .

You wouldn't believe it, but when its time came, it also refused to rewind. For the first time in its life! What to do? Only 400 or so miles out, over 600 dollars worth of film unusable, and a brand new camera under warranty refusing to work after its first film. I couldn't stand the thought of circumnavigating without a single photo to remember the journey by, so decided to set up a dull light and try to salvage the film from my old camera prior to attempting a repair. The new camera was too complex for me to try fixing. With one camera working, hopefully we would continue on our way.

It had been years since I did the electrical wiring, and some things had been bought pre-wired. In trying to adapt a pre-wired socket to light a tiny compass light bulb, I unfortunately shorted something and no fuses blew. Whether this was due to clumsiness with my bad hand or an error in wiring I shall never know, but we had quite an electrical fire, with all the insulation burning off tens of feet of double 4 mm electrical cable in seconds. I was near the battery and fortunately managed to disconnect one terminal, stopping the trouble, but oh! the stink of burnt rubber and plastic. The boat was almost unlivable and this sealed the fate of our first attempt. I would return to Sydney, have the cameras fixed, re-do the electrics and set off again as soon as possible. The lateness of the season would now be quite a worry if I were to avoid cold problems down south . . . I would have to hurry.

The return voyage to Sydney involved the most pleasant single-handed sailing I had yet done – with a self-steering system that worked on all points of sail enabling me to be well rested. Beautiful mild conditions and dolphins by the dozen at sunset on a couple of evenings to cheer me with their frolics . . . But nothing could make up for the terrible sense of failure in having to return so soon for such an apparently trivial reason. All my modifications and improvements had worked marvellously well down to the last detail, yet something so minor had brought about my demise! But I needed a photographic record, for a book, for an exhibition with my paintings, for my future . . . Return was the only viable decision, but how hard it was.

Attempt number two would be more thoroughly self-contained. I decided to make whatever farewells at home and consider myself as starting the voyage from the moment I left my mooring. I would anchor in Watson's Bay for Customs clearance, then restow the anchor gear in the harbour prior to the open sea. As fate would have it, my friend Marion had to get to Sydney that evening for a meeting, so we decided to sail down together once more. She would hitch a ride ashore from the Customs launch, leaving me to set off on my own once cleared.

Initially strong headwinds and rough seas, then finally very light breezes had us not making it to Watson's Bay until 8 p.m. Just as I had my anchor down, the Customs launch appeared to clear me. Five minutes earlier would have saved us anchoring at all! Luckily they allowed me to remain anchored overnight as I was too exhausted to set off again immediately. A quick hug and Marion was gone. I felt on my way already, there being no other person I would see until my return.

A windless and rain-sodden dawn greeted me on awakening, which suited me for restowing the anchor gear at a leisurely pace, but the wind was subtly on the increase and one gust put us within little over a boat length of going aground in Watson's Bay itself while I was below lashing the anchor securely. Fortunately I reached the deck in time and quickly put the helm hard over, praying that there were no hidden rocks between us and the visible ones as we ever so slowly came around towards deep water. Wow! What an embarrassing start/end to a voyage that would have been! Not even making it to the ocean itself.

By the time we passed through Sydney Heads it was blowing 15–20 knots from the south-east, where we wanted to go, so we (*Little Wing*, my mascot Young Mist and I) held the offshore tack for several miles before tacking and heading south. Young Mist is a baby harp seal toy, all white and fluffy, with her dark eyes always aware. She had been given to me by Marion, and we had named her the night before I set off on my first attempt.

Parallel to the coast only a few miles offshore and so near Sydney, my radar detector allowed little rest. We were in converging shipping lanes and it was also triggered by aeroplane ground radar as they approached and took off from

Mr M at rest with windvane removed and servo paddle hinged up – note the glassed timber rudder that I built to replace the hollow steel and steps for climbing back aboard if necessary.

Sydney Airport. Hard on the wind on port tack, our course took us gradually away from the shore, but many a yacht has been lost through a slight windshift while her crew was asleep, causing her vane steering to sail her blindly into danger. It was a sleepless night. Every time the radar detector woke me I would check our course, look around, and adjust the sheets and self-steering before returning to my bunk. At 5 a.m., during one of these checks, I sighted the distant loom of Point Perpendicular lighthouse, right on the limit of its visible range. This was my last sight of Australia.

Grey seas, grey skies, grey thoughts still tinged by fears and apprehension . . . We drove our way almost due south with a little east, hard on the wind all the way. My aim was to get directly down to latitude 40 degrees south or more before making our easting across the Tasman. This was to try and avoid having to work our way around the bottom of New Zealand and Stewart Island into the teeth of a southerly or south-westerly gale. I aimed to be at a latitude to clear the dangers there well before reaching them.

An afternoon of east-north-easterly wind gave us some respite from the windward bash and enabled me to work at re-organizing my halyards, all of which are external so I can keep a close eye on them for wear and replace them more easily than internal ones. The aim was to eliminate chafe problems, but the new running backstays were making things difficult. Taking heed of the cautionary tales of other sailors of the Southern Ocean, I had finally got around to fitting these from my upper spreaders/inner forestay level to help support the mast in extreme conditions when at risk of being rolled. Although I had chosen oversized mast and boom sections when designing her rig, and had allowed for a huge reserve of rigging strength to cover all eventualities, I had finally been persuaded and so added the extra stays. I had fitted tangs especially for them when putting the mast and rigging together years before, but they were proving to be a terrible nuisance in ordinary sailing conditions. The added chafe problems to sails, sheets and halyards created by the two wires had me trying solution after solution in an effort to eliminate their menace, but to no avail. I had attached them so securely to the mast tangs that they were impossible for me to remove at sea.

A few hundred miles south of Sydney the first albatross of the journey paid us a visit. Slip-sliding, gliding, wheeling, whirling, circling silhouetted into night. A big fellow, too, with a wingspan of 8–10 feet, performing its silent aerial ballet against the backdrop of the evening glow above the wine-dark seas. A couple of days later a brief rain squall right on dawn woke me in time to get a bearing on the sun to check the easterly compass error and catch sight of our albatross friend again. Silhouetted between us and the rising sun this time, in its never-ending circling, searching flight.

To the north-west, simultaneously, the stubby bottom ends of two rainbows manifested themselves, reminders of the two pots of mental gold I hoped to achieve through this voyage, namely, inner contentment and total inner acceptance of myself. These would free me to relate more easily to all others whose paths met mine in future.

Squalls had me reduce sail to being almost hove-to under triple-reefed mainsail alone while the weather sorted itself out to a definite wind strength and direction. An hour or two later I had decided staysail plus triple-reefed main would be the best combination for the conditions, so after yet another halyard rearrangement, up went the staysail and forward motion resumed. As if to echo this new life in *Little Wing*, a squadron of fast-leaping dolphins hurtled past in a similar direction, leaving me behind almost immediately as they pursued their urgent errand.

All day we plugged southward, hard on the wind in largish breaking seas, a clear sky overhead making the scene more dramatic with sharp contrasts of shadow and sunsparkle. I had noticed it becoming noticeably cooler over the last day or two, and my sunsights today gave me the reason. We were now at latitude 41 degrees 15 minutes south; we were definitely getting into the Southern Ocean and it was time to try and make easting once the weather allowed.

A parcel of many little presents and thoughts from Marion was opened in the afternoon, it being her birthday, and I was overwhelmed by the kindness and strength-giving nature of this gesture. I resolved to open a new package only every 1500 miles covered, so that the happy little surprises would last for the whole voyage.

Next morning, I put to use every bit of this renewed inspiration in a risky combination of rock-climbing moves, primary-school exhibition gymnastics and sheer nerve, to retrieve a halyard lost in the night and seemingly inextricably tangled aloft amongst my twin backstays, the radar reflectors strapped to these near the masthead, and the boom topping lift wire. A locking-pin shackle had unlocked, let go of the Yankee that it had been attached to and, after swinging around had tangled all these items, ending up precariously hooked to a backstay about 15 feet above the outboard end of the boom.

For some reason, probably laziness combined with a dash of early morning stupidity, it didn't occur to me to extricate the bosun's chair from its stowed position beneath my sail bags forward, hoist myself up clipped to the backstay that had captured the halyard, and retrieve it in safety and comfort. Instead, while continuing to bash our way to windward I opted to climb up on to the outboard end of the boom, which overhung the water by several feet. And with only ocean below me I endeavoured to ride the end of the boom, standing on it in balance, minimally aided by my left hand pushing or pulling against the thin topping lift wire as my sole aid to stability . . . While riding thus I tried with my good hand to snare the temporarily captured shackle with a boat hook, unwind it a myriad of times from around the backstays and topping lift until I could pull it down, slip a spliced eye at the end of a rope tail into it, close the shackle (all this with one hand only), then retreat to the deck without either falling into the sea, dropping the boat hook or losing the rope tail.

Once back on deck, I continued the unravelling process via the newly attached tail and refastened the halyard in its proper position, the head of the Yankee. This piece of climbing/gymnastics so exhausted me mentally that I decided to have my first cup of coffee of the voyage. While drinking this I listened to the ABC news from Hobart and discovered that we were no longer alone out here. Guy Bernadin, the skipper of *Biscuits Lu* in the last BOC Single-Handed Around the World Race, was just leaving Hobart that morning, having been forced to put in there to have a tooth abscess treated before continuing his own circumnavigation in the Vendee Globe Challenge.

With the wind easing overnight, but remaining from the east and keeping us hard on the wind on port tack, I decided to modify the Yankee halyard so that I would no longer have to climb on to the pulpit and balance precariously whenever I connected or disconnected to or from the head of the sail. This was asking for trouble when conditions were anything but mild. Ultimately, either I or the halyard would be lost during these unnecessary performances of gymnastics in motion. Inspired by my success in solving this problem I spent the rest of the day catching up on other sailorising tasks – cutting and whipping tack pendants for my storm jibs, setting up my running backstay blocks and handy billies, cutting and whipping spare headsail sheets, polishing the brass and so on. Sunsights put us at latitude 42 degrees 30 minutes south, longitude 152 degrees 30 minutes east, so we were still making more southing.than easting, but with the prevailing conditions it seemed the best option.

The large albatross which had been keeping us company was still wheeling and gliding over its endless domain. In the two to three days it had been with us I had not seen a single flap of wings, just endless pure gliding making use of air motion invisible to us mortals.

That night was probably the most silent and peaceful I have ever known at sea. So peaceful it was almost as if we were floating through space. The breeze was a mere 1–2 knots and with the swell having almost vanished this was enough to steady us against any rolling. No sound of blocks rattling, halyards shaking or sails whispering. Pure silence from the boat herself and the wind, being so light, moved us through the water at only 1–1½ knots, so there was also no sound of passage through the water. There must have been a bright moon above the cloud layer, but no sign of it was visible from below, just an all-pervasive silver glow as if the air itself were faintly luminous. The off-white decks, cockpit area and cabin glowed silver-white, the surrounding sea a smooth silvery grey with the only sign of motion through this ocean of light being the thin, dark line of a ripple peeling off each side of the boat in the region of the lower shrouds. The jewel that gave all this monochromity such magic in the absolute stillness was the pink glow of the compass light glowing from the centre of the cockpit. A warm presence, like a friend, as we slowly traversed the void.

This relative windlessness, magical for a brief spell, had become a pain by the next morning, with an increasing swell causing the sails to slat around ferociously as we rolled. I was discovering that windlessness created far greater chafe problems with my sails and sheets than any excess of wind – largely due to those damned running backstays. Maybe they would yet prove to be of some worth, but so far they were only a source of problems. I spent considerable time fitting lengths of hose over the Yankee sheets at points of wear against the rigging, but eventually the torture of needless chafe became unbearable and I dropped it completely until there was enough wind to keep it steady and filled.

The inconsistency of positions obtained from sunsights began to worry me at about this time. I ascertained that a calculator I had bought to help me wasn't performing as it should in averaging out sight times, and some other aspects of its performance seemed unreliable. I decided from now on to do all my navigational calculations and plotting the traditional long-hand way, so out came all my old navigation course notes from eighteen years earlier and the next few days were spent primarily as a serious student of navigation. I needed to refresh my memory and regain confidence in my sight-taking before the unlit rocks and islands to the south of New Zealand loomed too close.

At this point I was becoming a little despairing. Life at sea so far had seemed an endless succession of problems to be solved; most of them had been unforeseen, and it was a little unnerving having only troubles appear so early in the voyage. As the great Bill Tilman pointed out; it is rarely a single disastrous event that causes the loss of a vessel at sea; rather a whole chain of little events, none of them disastrous on their own, but gradually building up to a situation where there is no longer an option open, either to explore or make use of as an escape. I had bought many new books to read and had looked forward to much stimulating reading, thinking, writing and drawing time. But the reality was proving to be concentration only on survival. I was by no means defeated yet, just anxious and growing a little more so.

In the previous ten days we had been either hard on the wind or virtually becalmed for all but 3–4 hours. This lack of progress was a key factor in my feeling depressed. One evening, though, a little magic appeared and I felt restored. We were still beating to windward, averaging about 5 knots in a fresh north-easterly of all things, and I was reading about sequences of warm and cold fronts in *Meteorology for Mariners* yet again when I noticed it had become quite dark. It was only mid-afternoon, so this surprised me a bit. When I took a look outside the reason was immediately apparent. We were sailing through thick fog, with visibility only extending a couple of boat lengths at most in any direction. This was a new experience, as I has never come across thick fog at sea before, and rather a worrying one at first. Obviously there would be no time to avert a collision with another ship if I were dependent on eyesight alone. It was time to trust the radar detector absolutely, in giving both fair warning and a reasonable bearing on any sources of danger. Later, sitting on my bunk listening to music by the light of a candle, it seemed I was in a cosy little cocoon forging our way through the invisible dangers of the external night. I had to go on deck to put another reef in the mainsail at around midnight, and from out there this feeling was reinforced, looking in through the cabin windows at the warm glow of security below while fog swirled around and dripped off the sail as I reefed. Visibility on deck was now only 10–20 feet. Returning below I had the strong impression that all my friends who had wished me well were with me and I fell asleep in the glow of their friendship, feeling absolutely safe.

The next day I noticed that the poor visibility seemed to have lost us our albatross, but the Wilson's storm petrels were still about me, flitting like moths and washing their feet as they flew a hair's breadth above the surface no matter how rough the sea. Absolutely amazing me by their being here at all so far from shelter. How well adapted to their environment are all these dwellers in the world of nature, and how pathetic they make man seem in comparison, with his inability to harmonise with any environment, be it of his own making or Mother Nature's.

Australia finally faded from the dial as a source of radio time signals. This *did* make me feel as if we were making progress, albeit slowly. I would continue to pick up Radio Australia intermittently, but until my return there would be none of the familiar ABC programmes for my ears.

After the fog barrier was pierced, a marked change in conditions arrived. For the first time we started to 'run our easting down', or more accurately 'reach our easting', but at least we were not hard on the wind for once. The breeze had swung into the north-west, a precursor of the cold front to follow, which would clear the poor visibility we were continuing to have. It was almost impossible to pick the true horizon for navigation purposes. I only hoped that when the front arrived, it would cause no new problems.

The barometer continued to drop as the front approached, and before dark I reefed down to triple-reefed main and dropped the Yankee, setting the smaller staysail in its stead. With my dependency on sight to feel with my hand, I found sail changes at night extremely difficult, even with a head torch to aid me. In situations where deterioration in the weather seemed imminent I developed the habit of reducing sail before dark in an effort to minimise situations both unneccessarily stressful and potentially damaging to gear. I didn't really regard the voyage as having started in earnest until I had rounded the first corner and got beyond New Zealand, so didn't want to risk damage to gear at such an early stage.

Needless to say, the front did come through in the night, at about 4 a.m. and the 'little rig' that I had set up didn't prove small enough. In driving spray and almost horizontal rain, I dropped the mainsail completely, leaving us to hurtle east just off a square run under staysail alone. There was little point in staying on deck to get wetter and colder as rain, wind-driven spray and breaking waves washed over us. Once I was satisfied we were holding a steady course I retreated below for some rest, hoping this initial squall would ease up in a couple of hours and enable me to get good sights, with a clear sky and horizon.

Ha! sights in that maelstrom? Just after sunrise I decided I could risk the staysail no longer, so I dropped it and for the first time in her life *Little Wing* was running before a real gale under bare poles. As occasional overtaking waves broke directly into the cockpit and against the aft end of the cabin and entry hatch, a serious and totally unexpected problem emerged. Each time this happened, squirts of water would jet in from around the perimeter seal of the hatch, not only making my bunk sodden and barely habitable, but deluging the burners of the stove and threatening them with serious corrosion damage.

This problem would have to be solved at the first opportunity. In almost 10,000 sea miles this problem had never appeared before and I lacked the materials with which to solve it. I decided to tear off the existing rubber seal all the way around until I reached a level base. This meant ripping off about ½–¾ of built-up rubber sections. Then I would build up a new seal with layer after layer of silicone – one that would form itself accurately to the imperfections in the stainless steel perimeter ring it sealed against. All I needed was a gale-free day to get started. At around this time it also became apparent that my supposedly repaired new camera, the main cause of my retreat from the first attempt, was in fact still a dud. Never mind, my trusty old spare was still working fine, so there was no cause for alarm this time.

Rain squall followed rain squall, and front after front came through over the next two days until I lost count of how many we had weathered, still running before, still under bare poles. The barometer hadn't risen a shade with the passage of any of these fronts, making me rather apprehensive of what things would be like out there when the real one arrived. Massive breaking seas surrounded us, the occasional one breaking completely over us and this occurring with greater regularity as the seas continued to build. It was too rough to get out of the hatch and on deck to fix anything without risking a flood coming in as I got out. All I could hope was that the self-steering continued to cope and that ultimately these conditions would ease to a more manageable state. As if to make an absolute mockery of my concerns, there, just outside my cabin windows, the tiny storm petrels continued their flutter and dance, somehow avoiding being buried in the foam as they continued their search for food. Some birdies!

By next evening the elements had calmed somewhat and I was joined by a family of six to ten New Zealand fur seals, some leaping and jumping around me as they matched pace with the boat, others lying on their backs with their flippers in the air 'sunbaking' and being left astern in our wake, only to rejoin the troop a few minutes later. The sight of seals torpedoing through the air alongside the boat was entirely novel and rather amazing. I was used to dolphins and fish leaping out of the water, but one knows they have fins to propel them so there is little surprise. These seals as they flew past me, airborne, were so sleek and streamlined they appeared to have no means of propulsion at all. Even more amazing than storm petrels!

At this point we should have been getting within range of the first of two radio direction finder beacons shown on my New Zealand charts. These would prove of great use if the weather continued such that reliable sunsights were impossible as we made our run around the corner. My charts were new, my RDF unit had worked at last try, but no Puysegur Point beacon appeared. I mainly wanted it as a warning that I was closing the coast, if necessary, but it looked as if I would be rounding entirely on DR unless conditions changed for the better.

Water continued to squirt in the hatch as each breaker boarded us, causing me deep concern and making me desperate for just one calm day. A rope lashing one of my self-steering control-line blocks chafed through next morning. Out in the cockpit working on a new lashing, I was unaware of one approaching breaker until all of a sudden I was underwater. After several seconds of deluge I was free to breathe again and thought little of it as I had shut the hatch behind me and dogged it down. Then I returned below.

My bunk and galley region was one sodden mess with something like one to two buckets of water having apparently gained entry through the closed hatch. From just one relatively innocuous wave! I was in deep despair. Clothes, bedding and mattress all drenched. No sun or warmth to dry them, and seemingly no way of curing the problem.

I was almost ready to concede defeat, but could not stand the thought of another failure so soon after the first. If I gave up now I would not be able to leave again until the following summer at the earliest and something might come up to prevent me from making another attempt at all. I had always felt so secure aboard *Little Wing* before, in all weathers. She never leaked. I never had to pump the bilge. I always felt absolutely safe once down below, the weather shut out and me ensconced and dry. Now, in our first real Southern Ocean gale, the Southern Ocean had found a way to breach our defences and shatter my confidence completely. It was not a good day

The next morning, dodging around among wet sheets, bedding and clothing draped over hastily rigged internal clothes-lines, I hunted frenziedly for a variety of tools and silicone sealant. Morning at least had dawned relatively calm, with a following breeze of only 20–25 knots, so this was the time to get into action. Rrrrip . . . rrrrrip and the rubber came off where I had decided. I was now committed to finishing the job before the next storm or we would literally drown! On went layer after layer of silicone all day. As one layer hardened, another was overlaid, with the hatch pushed shut a few times, gently, to get the seal to conform to the irregularities in the steel band it would mate with. Luckily, the night also remained calmish, and I left the hatch wide open, both to try and dry a bit more of my 'washing' hung up below, and to allow the silicone to cure unmolested. I almost froze. The wind chill from even that little wind while lying on a wet bunk in wet clothes and bedding was torture, but I had to give the hatch every chance to become waterproof. I shivered on.

Blessed dawn, sunshine and warmth, and time to test the hatch. Cccrack! One of two hooks that I used to dog down the hatch tightly from inside tore its teak mounting block in half. Now there was *no way* of shutting the hatch from inside at all! Another frenzy amongst tools and spare fittings quickly located items that could be used to improvise a new and improved system to replace both hooks. If one had broken, the other also could at any time. I went to work and by

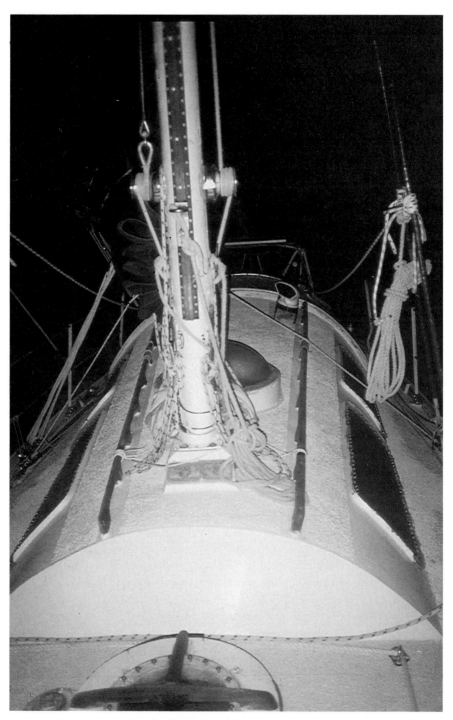

Ahead of her time when designed in 1975
– cabin window strength through curvature, through design.

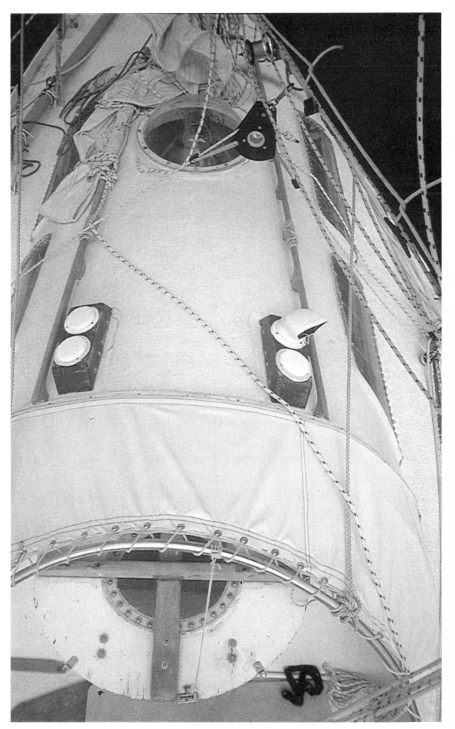

Life support capsule. (Cabin from aloft.)

afternoon we were once again more or less watertight. I felt on top of the world. If I could improvise my way out of those problems so rapidly, there was nothing to stop me now. We sailed on, hatch wide open, the washing drying below, storm jib set ready to fly, hatch ready to repel invading water . . . Barometer dropping.

It hit us early next morning in the gloom of first light. Rain, along with wind I'd rarely experienced – a steady force 10–11, gusting more. While dropping all sail I noticed over the stern not only my log rotor and weight spending almost all their time in mid-air, being blown clean out of the water by the wind, but more seriously, my self-steering lines to the servo rudder shredded and virtually chafed through on one side. After a couple of hours working almost continually underwater in heavy surf, right out beyond the stern of the boat, I succeeded in shortening the line on that side back to a section of undamaged rope. Able to try steering a safe course again, I set about securing my dropped sails more securely. On looking astern again while doing this – no vane! The plywood wind vane controlling my self-steering ('never known one to break,' according to the manufacturers) had snapped at the clamp. Believing the manufacturers' claim, as this make was considered the best you could buy, I had only two spare vanes of normal-use type, and two specifically light-weather ones.

I could not risk breaking another vane so early in the voyage. After a couple more hours of desperate struggle in that strength of wind and an air temperature of only 2 degrees centigrade on deck, I succeeded in setting the trisail for the first time, very afraid of losing the halyard aloft as it was also used for the mainsail. The trisail would hopefully keep us heading very slowly to windward, almost hove-to, not losing ground and not needing to risk another wind vane. In fact it was too small to do that, and only held us beam on to the wind and seas, moving slowly forward. Life down below in the cabin became like an extended journey over Niagara Falls in a transparent barrel, with the large cabin windows totally underwater every time a breaking swell swept over us. The 10 mm thick polycarbonate, in conjunction with two large transparent acrylic backing beams at third points along their length, gave heaps of strength, so I didn't have to worry about them breaking – in theory. It was satisfying to see this was also true in practice, there being no replacement possible out here.

Without curtains to hide the scene of chaos outside it became mentally very wearing. Whenever I opened my eyes I was reminded in full of the reality we were in. The wind whistled and whined in the rigging, waves hit us sometimes like the pounding of a 100-ton sledge-hammer and hurled us bodily sideways in their breaking crests. It was not restful sailing. It was also not totally devoid of beauty. The transparent turquoise of the wave crests, especially as they broke back-lit by a spell of late afternoon sunlight, was a sight of supreme loveliness. In fact, once I realised we were appearing to cope and would most likely survive, I could enjoy the sheer majesty of it all for extended periods.

It was too rough to risk getting out the hatch to work on deck, so I set about choosing a piece of plywood flooring I could sacrifice, without causing heavy objects stowed underneath to go flying, to make a small replacement vane for heavy and ultra-heavy weather. There was only one piece of flooring I could sacrifice in this way without a major reorganisation of securely stowed items. I removed it and started sawing, our wild motion notwithstanding.

Since the flooring was far thicker than the original vane material, I had to estimate how much smaller to make it such that the existing counterweight would still function and maintain a good degree of sensitivity. I hadn't counted on this problem, and had no secure way of modifying the existing weight. All that day and all the next it blew without let up and navigation became a worry. It was hard to estimate our drift in these conditions and it had been days since I had managed a reliable sight. The thought of all the unlit rocks and islets in our vicinity, the Traps, Snares and further to the south the Auckland Island Group – all notorious wreckers of ships in the sailing ship days – was a worry. Being en route from Australia to Cape Horn via the Roaring Forties they claimed many a victim when thick weather like this prevented accurate navigation. A modern sat-nav system would have eliminated this uncertainty as to position, but I regarded that as contrary to the spirit of single-handing. One of the spare vanes, apart from my new 'survival' vane, I had made smaller for very heavy weather, and in a brief lull I fitted this to try and get us heading more to windward. I was very worried about hitting the Auckland Islands in particular, being so far south. It didn't last long: a breaking wave snapped it shortly after in the next rain squall, so I resolved to wait until morning and try my 'ultimate' one.

At 6 a.m. things looking quieter, wonderful. Time to drop the trisail and try her under triple-reefed main and storm jib. But first I had to untangle the mess of reefing lines and halyard tails from around the base of the mast, which had become thoroughly entwined by days of being tumbled underwater. An hour or so later the mess was cleared, mainsail set at third reef, trisail safely lashed and storm jib flying, but we appeared overcanvassed. I decided to drop the storm jib, see how we took it under triple-reefed main alone, and see if the self-steering would cope under this previously untried rig.

Alas, the self-steering didn't appear to work at all with the new vane. Probably too heavy, I decided, but there was no time for change. I had just removed it for modification when Wham! In it came again, and with a vengeance. Gusting 70, maybe 80 knots, with rain. My hands were too cold to drop the mainsail without damage or loss of halyard – I had no feeling at all in either by this stage. I just waited for the mainsail to explode, sadly, but there was nothing more I could do. Heeled over with our spreaders touching the water at times I could only try and pick a gap between waves to escape below and await the inevitable.

This I did, and to my growing amazement everything held! We even steered a perfect course to windward with no damaging sail flapping or flutter at all! Very slowly, mind you, and probably our course made good being almost sideways like a crab due to our extraordinary angle of heel. But everything held. I was stunned that she could take such treatment in her stride, and could only hope things hung on intact a little longer until it eased.

For almost three days the only level piece of 'floor' I could stand on was the oven door of the stove, normally vertical. Standing on this I could lean back against my bunk, rather as one would lean against a wall on land, and 'rest'. The temperature in the cabin hardly ever reached above 5 degrees centigrade and fell to almost zero at night. At this time I noticed something very wrong with my left hand.

Searing stabbing pains shot up my arm from the fingertips, making sleep impossible and forcing me to take di-gesic painkillers for three days, only the second time I had taken a painkiller in my life. The pain eased after this time, so I thought no more of it until some Elastoplast dressing over the tops of those two fingers came off. They were almost black, a deep blood-blister colour, and then the realisation dawned. The fingers had become frostbitten down to the second joint while I was working on deck for long hours exposed to water and wind chill – and with it being my left hand, the air temperature/body temperature compromise they managed this time wasn't above freezing. I checked with alpine climbing books I had aboard, and yes, the symptoms were all there. A totally unexpected development so relatively far north – approximately 51 degrees south, and with winter not fully set in.

With all the clawing to windward of recent days, the aft hatch had been fairly well protected by the cabin itself and the dodger over it, but occasional waves had given us a good swipe from abeam. It was evident that though much improved, we were far from being satisfactorily waterproof for extended downwind sailing in very rough weather. I had already designed the solution to the problem in my head, but there was nothing more I could do out there. It was time for a serious rethink.

With (i) a leaking hatch continually causing drenching of bedding, clothing and self without a chance to dry out due to the cold;

(ii) frostbitten fingers with winter not yet truly underway;

(iii) self-steering that would no longer work in the most common conditions to be met with, necessitating long periods at the helm in colder conditions to come;

(iv) my total dependency on sight in using my left hand, yet nights of around twenty hours of darkness looming before long; and

(v) the continuing chafe and damage problems from the running backstays, it seemed to make most sense to regard this as the reconnaissance trip for my real voyage, and retreat while basically intact and undamaged. I could then remedy the problems and set off again later in the year, at the start of the southern summer. The remedies themselves would cost me very little financially yet make things easier out of all proportion in overcoming problems from the hand. By living on my perishables during the year, I figured I could just afford to hang on until late November/early December, fix the problems, reprovision what I'd eaten and be off again.

Easier said than done. We still had to get ourselves out of that gale-torn region without hitting any of the obstacles previously worried about. Due to the conditions I had still not been able to get a sight to find out where we really were. The wind eased, and being more to the south-west at last enabled us to reach up north-westward back into the Tasman, and away from obstacles, namely land. I still had no self-steering working, so had to use another sail combination whereby she would reach with tiller free and maintain a steady course. This she would do under staysail alone in that strong wind, so with mainsail dropped completely off we set, still on the port tack. We seemed to be doing a circumnavigation of the Tasman on the port tack in lieu of a circumnavigation of the world! From my estimates of drift and the previous lack of a westerly current, this course should have taken us straight up and across towards Sydney, a long, long way from any land.

It was rough enough still for waves to be breaking over the cabin and down the other side, but I was so used to this by now that it just seemed a normal day's sailing. What was a problem, though, was the staysail sheet chafing against the running backstay and lifeline to leeward. Although I kept replacing anti-chafe hose and rags wrapped around the worrying spots, they kept being torn off by the force of the waves. One night I was sure that unless conditions eased the sheet would chafe through far enough to break. Being under great strain in that wind it wouldn't need to chafe much more.

Sure enough, at midnight the frenzied flapping of a sail out of control woke me, and after donning my wet-weather gear out I went to do battle. The flailing of sheets out of control can almost knock your head off if you are in the wrong place at the wrong time, and in the dark it is rather hard to judge where to be. I was afraid of another serious head injury from just such a knock, so dreaded headsail changing at night in very rough weather. This time I dropped the staysail and decided to continue under bare poles for the rest of the night, sorting out the problems fully at first light. Back I went to try and get some sleep, secure in knowing that nothing more could go wrong that night . . .

It didn't, but on rising at first light to fix things, what did I see dead ahead of us and not very far away? A lee shore! Land where no land should be for over 100 miles! Once I had hastily reset the staysail with a new sheet and set the mainsail at the third reef to give us the power to clear the headland and off-lying islands, I had time to savour this unique experience.

This was how the early explorers must have felt when land appeared ahead of them as they traversed uncharted seas. There were two prominent peaks visible and it could only be South-West Cape of Stewart Island, my first corner, viewed from rerounding it east to west – after already having rounded unknowingly, swept by current, wind and leeway. Unfortunately there were no views of South-West Cape in the *New Zealand Pilot Book*, an indication of the death of the old sailing-ship routes if ever there was one. In a different book, however, I found reference to those peaks, and if Solander Island appeared shortly that would confirm my position. It also demonstrated that my supposedly updated chart was wrong in showing RDF beacons at Puysegur Point and Dog Island. I would have been in unobstructed range of both later that day, and close, but neither was operating. If they had been, I would have known where I was all along, from bearings. Sure enough, in a clear spell between squalls Solander Island did appear where it should have done. I was no longer lost, just an ocean away from base camp/home.

This sudden appearance of land, and interesting-looking land at that – with altitude and steepness and aesthetically pleasing – had me rather entranced, and I was looking forward to tacking back around the corner relatively close to the shore to get a good look at the Fiordland region and its alpine hinterland. In the middle of the night, with Point Puysegar light very visible ahead, I lost my nerve in trying to sneak around without having to tack, tacking offshore to get a little sleep while on a safe course.

Safe from the shore and land, yes, but this corner of New Zealand wasn't through with me yet. By 6 a.m. it was howling from the north-west again at approximately 40–50 knots, with very steep, breaking seas so relatively close to land. Down to staysail alone, and after wearing ship to get about – the waves stopped us dead when trying to tack – she managed to hold an approximately northerly course (compass). I hoped this was enough just to clear the corner, as the coastline then fell away a bit to the east and we would be clear. With the magnetic variation being approximately 23 degrees east in this region, and us making considerable leeway, this wasn't good enough. With land appearing ahead again between rain squalls, we headed back out to sea.

The land that had been such an almost-pleasant surprise had now become a dangerous lee shore and we were tacking, tacking, tacking, just to keep clear of it and stay alive. So much for the anticipated pleasure of viewing spectacular new scenery at close range. Such is life! After the north-west gale came a calm; but with so little wind and such a big swell still coming from the south-west it was not possible to sail on the offshore tack. The swells shook all wind out of the sails on that tack, so I was condemned to a collision course with land, hoping for another gale at least to give us steerage way in a safe direction.

For nearly three more days the mouths of various sounds were visible up to a very low cloud layer – not enough to identify them positively without the higher ground as a clue, nor to gauge our distance off accurately. Ultimately relief came in the form of a crisp south-south-westerly breeze with a real Blue Mountains autumn feel to it, and we were finally safely away.

In this finer weather, I decided to retrieve another halyard lost aloft in southern gales, but this time by bosun's chair, in safety, unlike the boom-walking episode. To my amazement, having cleared the backstay part of the tangle, I discovered that it had been also blown right up above my upper spreaders and back down the wrong side, necessitating another journey to sort this out before I could use it again. Back aloft I went, taking a camera this time for photos, and was soon back on deck very pleased at having used this calm patch to such advantage.

Even the albatrosses were on strike that day. From aloft I could see about half a dozen resting on the ocean, waiting for enough wind to make it worthwhile getting airborne again. Even in that calm, work aloft would hardly have been possible one-handed had it not been for an assortment of rock-climbing gear I had brought with me. By using a combination of slings and karabiners, I clipped myself to various bits of surrounding rigging and limited my swing sufficiently not to need two good hands to get the jobs done. This was a useful revelation for future work aloft, but as it turned out, apart from a calm spot one day out of Sydney, this was the only day when such work was possible.

With the barometer rapidly dropping, we were obviously in for more rough weather. But before it arrived, an interesting sea condition occurred. In relative windlessness the sea all of a sudden developed such a confused and chaotic joggle that we could have been in the famous joggle off Sydney Heads – in shallow water and getting reflected waves back from the cliffs along the coast. But here, we were supposedly in thousands of fathoms of water, with no land for hundreds of miles. Having noticed confused seas and currents in the proximity of sea-mounts between Lord Howe Island and the mainland, I wondered if we were not in the proximity of another, not yet marked on the charts.

Reflections on underwater topography were soon brought to a close by the arrival of a strong southerly change. Once more into grey seas, grey skies, large breaking waves and minimal sail. I quickly reduced sail to staysail alone, but even this seemed too much after a while, during which I hand-steered using the whipstaff for steering from inside the cabin. Just on dark I went down to bare poles, hoping to run slowly before it overnight while I got some sleep. By noting our lack of progress in logged miles the next morning, it was evident that the self-steering with its floorboard vane hadn't kept us on course. A breaking wave had probably knocked us beam on to the wind shortly after I retreated to my bunk and we had lain a hull most or all of the night. I didn't notice a thing, being very worn out both mentally and physically and remaining blissfully asleep until first light.

At dawn I reset the staysail and by doing so made an important discovery, namely that she steered far better with her small vane given some sail area, and that the greater speed seemed to help the steering dominate and not be dominated by rough conditions. Up to a point. This hadn't worked further south in the really rough stuff. From here on to Sydney, though, I did manage to get her to self-steer fairly well with the small vane. As long as I set a sail combination that was well balanced enough almost to steer us on its own. I still wouldn't risk the last standard vane – I wanted it intact for templating when I got around to designing new improved vanes for the next attempt.

At around 11 p.m. that night while up on deck fixing an accidental gybe, I saw the first visible moon of the voyage, after over 2200 miles of sailing. And the next day dawned clear enough to get a bearing on the rising sun to check compass error, the first dawn clear enough to do this also. A great start to the day indeed. A crisp autumn westerly blowing, so reminiscent of the Blue Mountains that I could almost smell the camp fire for an early morning cuppa. Sailing under triple-reefed main and Yankee, to windward, and of course still on port tack. So far we had spent less than 100 miles on starboard tack in the entire voyage!

Around midday, though, my happiness was diminished somewhat by the discovery that my solar panel had suddenly died for no apparent reason. We would have no more battery charging until I could wire up the spare panel, if and when the weather calmed enough before Sydney. In the meantime I would try to use kerosene lanterns at night in lieu of navigation lights, with the aim of saving what battery power remained for my navigation lights when nearing Sydney – a place where shipping would definitely be around.

Even this fool-proof plan had its setbacks later that night. My damned hand, unable to feel the lantern handle due to its small size, proceeded accidentally to let it go while I was setting it up. With one bounce it vanished over the side in the darkness and sank. Two lanterns remaining, and one of these proved useless, being blown out by the wind even in mild conditions. In effect, we were down to one. This one worked splendidly, but how nervous I was each night when balancing precariously, trying to set it up. The old adage of 'one hand for yourself, one for the ship' was totally useless in my case – it was one for the ship at all times, and the self learnt to manage by balance alone, helped by the occasional steadying push or pull at best.

The following night the Yankee somehow unshackled itself from its halyard

while set – an unbelievable occurrence, I would have thought, but it lowered itself deftly into the sea nonetheless. So, only one good headsail halyard remained also. This was becoming a race to get back while it was still possible!

In my fascination with peculiar weather around sea-mounts I decided to sail virtually over Gascoyne sea-mount, which was not far ahead. With water of around 15,000 feet deep rising to only a little over 200, there could be some dramatic effects. I had often wondered also if seagoing fishing boats from the coast ever came out the few hundred miles necessary to fish for exotic species there.

That night, right on cue, I came across a set of stationary navigation lights indicating a ship at anchor. Exactly where the shallows over the sea-mount should be. Was it a boat fishing the mount, I wondered? I passed by at a good distance in case it had nets out, which I didn't want to foul in the dark. But as for weather peculiarities, there seemed to be none this time. There had been a large swell running all day and I was concerned a little that they might even peak enough to be breaking over the mount, but I noticed no difference. I missed the shallowest part, which would have been where the ship was anchored, but I thought there would have been some effect in our vicinity. There was no noticeable difference, either, in wind strength or direction, so my theories took a bit of a beating this time.

Becalmed between 100 and 200 miles out of Sydney there was little point in doing the jobs that I had waited for a calm day to carry out. Very soon we would

Aloft in the Tasman, clearing the mess from below New Zealand.

These two almost matching photos give a good view of the deck layout.

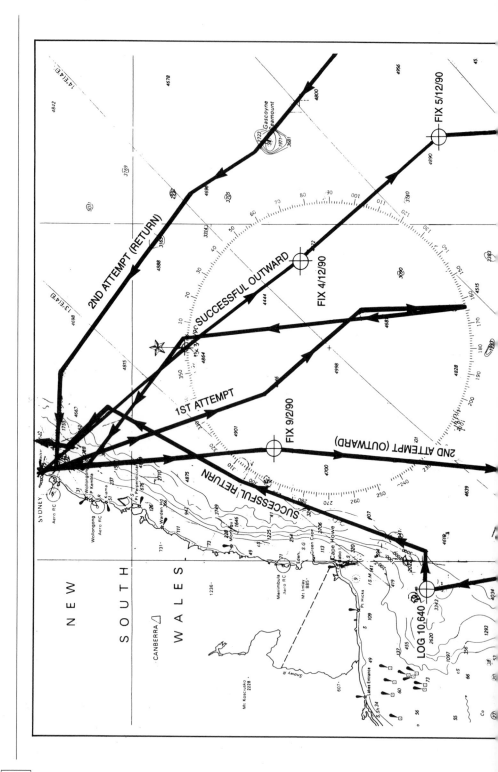

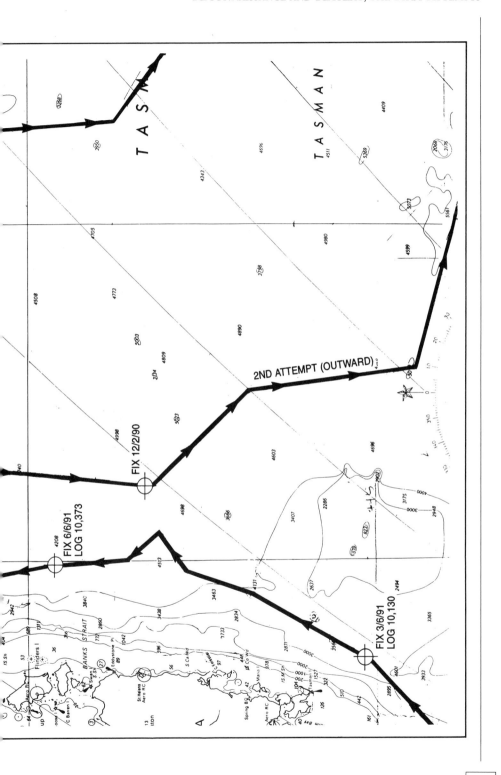

not only be in completely smooth water, but would have more complete equipment for testing and finding the location of the solar panel problem. And we could surely make it now on our remaining headsail halyard. I basked in the sun, waiting for a southerly change due that evening. By midday it was so hot that I was missing the region of storms just left behind, and the lack of progress so near to home was beginning to annoy me. We drifted slowly through a region thick with very young specimens of what become huge purplish jellyfish with long, deadly-looking stingers trailing in profusion, and another region thick with tiny suspended particles which I took to be plankton.

At dusk we still had over 100 miles to go, but the signs were growing for a change. With triple-reefed main and Yankee I hoped to weather the initial squalls by hand-steering, then maybe the self-steering could handle it for the rest of the night with me surfacing regularly to check for shipping, the loom of Sydney in the distance or the loom of lighthouses if we were closer than expected.

It didn't hit with a bang, this one, but strengthened gradually. At midnight I dropped the mainsail completely, and decided to hand-steer the rest of the night instead of reducing sail further. The wind was from the right direction really to make a run for it. I figured we could cope with the compass light, at least, since it drew so little power, but I had no nav lights, only a kerosene lantern burning in the cabin, hopefully visible through the cabin windows. Another reason for hand-steering as we crossed shipping lanes.

In the cockpit it was the most enjoyable night's sailing of the voyage. Not too cold at this more northerly latitude, we hurtled through the night under Yankee alone at an average of between 8 and 9 knots for fourteen hours straight. A moon, intermittently visible between flying scud, once more bathed the cabin, decks and cockpit in silvery light. A warm golden glow from the kerosene lantern down below was visible through the cabin windows, steering-dome hole and trans-parent centre to the aft hatch. The compass light glowed warmly pink in its silvery white cockpit and the foam rushing astern as we surfed through the night glistened whitely against the darkness of shadowed troughs. It was wonderful. Every half-hour or so I would decide that it really *was* too much wind for carrying the Yankee and that I should drop it and travel more sedately under staysail, but each time I would resist as we took off on yet another wonderful ride. The waves were not big at all in comparison with the south, but enough for plenty of fun!

No lighthouses were visible, but there was a loom ahead that could be Sydney. A quick RDF check put Sydney Airport dead ahead, and after the most spectacular sunrise of the voyage to cap the most enjoyable night ride of the voyage, the entrance to Botany Bay appeared soon after. I gybed to head north and by 4 p.m. we were at anchor in Watson's Bay, awaiting re-entry formalities. How wonderful Sydney looked, all that civilisation close at hand, but I knew I would have to try again. I was only elated at our return, not fulfilled.

Chapter Fifteen

Sweet Dreams and Deathbed Confessions

Fifteen to twenty feet above the ground and no runners yet to break a fall. . . . The only left-hand hold for me, a flake, had just snapped off. I would hit the ground too hard. Steadying myself, I searched for anywhere I could place some pro . . . A bolt to my left was all, but it would have to be an entirely left-handed clipping, and at the limit of my reach.

I had practised these moves left-handed, off and on, with a bolt I set into the wall beside me at work. Doing them while in total security, however, was rather different to getting my hand to work in a situation where there was no second chance. I placed a 'friend' in a greasy flaring crack as a purely psychological runner, told myself that my feet were on great holds – a lie – and tried again, all the while skirting the very edge of being in balance. Victory, bracket on . . . now for the krab and rope . . . Voila! I sighed with relief, the sun shone again on the trees in the valley below, the sound of morning birdsong was again audible. Life continued. I climbed on, relaxed in knowing that from here on I at least wouldn't hit the deck.

Chris was working that day as an instructor with the local climbing school, so Heather and I once again teamed for what was this time hopefully not to be a night-time special. All of us had to be at Mount Victoria by 8 p.m. for the Sydney Rockies' Annual Dinner. I climbed on, the second half of the first pitch being reminiscent of the first pitch of the West Wall. No worries. We swapped leads to save time, Heather leading the second pitch which proved to be far steeper than it looked from below at my belay. It involved getting through several miniature overhangs and one very dense and inconveniently route-blocking bush/tree before reaching the end of the pitch.

My turn. On my right lay the slab region that Chris and Heather had thought I would so enjoy . . . but slab? It looked very steep to me, more a wall, and somewhat intimidating as it rose approximately another 150 feet in height and about the same in width with very little visible in the way of cracks to place runners. Maybe we would have to resort to using the bolts that supposedly peppered this rising traverse, ruining its character.

I spied an old rusty peg (piton) in a crack where the roof of the cave we were in

Looking diagonally up the Sweet Dreams slab towards the next belay about 200 feet away in the corner.

met the grey slab. That must have been where the original route lay, so up under the overhang I went, clipping the peg at its lip. It looked quite sound, better than a mere psychological runner. Off I set, remembering my broken handhold of the first pitch and hoping the rock here was more sound. I was 80 feet out from that rusty peg before I could place another runner, and that a very marginal 'friend', but I spotted another rusting old peg well camouflaged against the dark grey rock a little further on. I must still be on the original line. It looked in usable condition when I reached it, so I clipped that one also as another runner and continued on, searching for either a 'nest' of bolts for a belay position, or any place at all that offered secure enough runner placements to act as a belay. Nothing in sight. I ran out a full rope length, moving in several directions and keeping my eyes peeled, but not a bolt was visible. Twenty feet lower was a rather solid flake with a crack behind that would take two 'friends', one good and one more marginal. I linked these and called Heather up to join me.

It could have been worrying, those endless run-outs without protection, over – despite its appearance – suspect rock. But my heart sang with the beauty of the day itself. Hardly a cloud in the sky, the ridges and valleys below us receding into an equally sunlit distance beyond the Kowmung River, Byrnes Gap, the Wollondilly River, Nattai Tableland and on toward the Mittagong/Bowral district. Memories of my long solo bushwalks across those seemingly endless miles flooded back as Heather picked her own line up towards me, seeing no sign of bolts on her variant of the route either. Swapping leads again, Heather led off across the remainder of the slab traverse, cautiously moving over suspect plates of rock until she found a bolt to clip 30 feet or so further on. After this a 'friend' could be placed at a similar distance, then a 'nut', then another bolt. A very exposed step up and across a void the full height climbed so far led to a good tree belay. We thought we had almost done it, all the crux pitches being below us. *But*, the sun was sinking fast, and already near the skyline.

It being very near the shortest day of the year, we couldn't afford the time to sit around admiring our position. Donning my rack once more I took over the lead for supposedly the final climbing pitch. A long steep corner, overhanging at the top and with a grey wall with some bolts on it to the left. The grey wall looked far too thin for me to climb, the holds sparse and very small, too small for my left hand to use. I returned to the corner. Twilight settled in about half way up this corner and I called to Heather to read out the route description, as all ways up and out from here seemed rather chancy. I think I confused left and right, which I sometimes do since my fall. Either that, or the way out to the right seemed too left-hand dependent for me to risk. I decided to continue up the corner until I could find a way across to a bolt visible on the grey wall near the top.

Not having climbed for so long, I was not sure just how far I could stretch across on my left to reach new holds for hands and feet or how large they had to be to use them securely. I could see a way across, but I couldn't judge the distance to the holds very well, and the exposure up here was really something. The whole cliffline fell away vertically below me.

We decided that if I could find a spot to place a good runner or two I would bring Heather up while there was still a bit of light to see, and she would try to reach the bolt by branching off onto the wall. The moon set as the thinnest of crescents behind Katoomba, silhouetted in the late evening glow. The streetlights of Katoomba came on, looking very pretty and a reminder of the warmth and friendliness of the dinner to come at Mount Victoria. If we could get off this climb!

With considerable trepidation (I had warned her of my marginal belay) Heather stretched up to the limit of her reach and the edge of remaining in balance, slipped a bolt-bracket over the bolt; then, ever so gently, a krab into the bracket and finally, the climbing rope through the krab. . . . Shades of my starting pitch to the climb, but a fall here would probably have taken both of us to the next world.

In darkness now, it was time for me to make my move across – via the line I had seen and baulked at in daylight because I couldn't judge the distance! One advantage of darkness is that you can no longer see the exposure, so in a sense the move was less of a worry. Heather had a secure belay, and although I would have swung off into space over the void below if I came off, I was confident I could get back to the rock somehow and find a way back up. I had tried to memorise, before total dark, where the holds were to link our lines. I aimed my foot across the darkness until out of balance, stepping across to where a little knob should be. Simultaneously I moved my left hand across as I 'fell', to where a lip of rock should be to arrest my 'fall'. They were both there. With a sigh of relief, the remaining left-hand-only traverse moves seemed easy, and soon I joined Heather at her stance and continued on, still roped up and hoping to find a direct way up and off.

Vague silhouettes above us in the gloom indicated that we weren't through with climbing pitches yet. Half a rope length further on it seemed as if we could find a walking/scrambling way up, so we unroped, only to find another band of cliffs. There had to be a gully up through this final band, so we set off skirting the bottom until we found one. A while later a miniature canyon led up into the dark, looking climbable unroped. Up I went, but damn . . . overhangs above. I brought Heather up to where I was (we had roped up again) and with a tiny pen-light torch we searched out a route. It appeared straightforward once I bridged my way over the initial overhang, so off I went, torch in my teeth, and soon reached a track above. After I attached the torch to our rope Heather pulled it back down for herself to use and soon we were back at the car.

Chris, of course, was rather worried at our lateness by this time and I didn't even bother washing before we set off again for the dinner – just changing into my good clothes to honour the occasion. As a new feature of the dinner, awards were given for various categories and I was awarded a most useful daypack as

'Globetrotter of the Year' for my voyage attempts. With members having climbed in Russia, Britain, France, the Americas and New Zealand during the year, this was a total surprise.

*　　*　　*　　*

Deathbed Confessions. What a wonderful name for a climb; but the story behind it is a sad one. A climber had fallen to his death from another climb nearby, landing only a few feet away from where this new climb was being put up.

It was Carol's first visit to the Wolgan Valley and as we drove towards the old ghost town of Newnes, near which we were going to climb, the sun splashed the east-facing walls of the valley with fire. Mile after convoluted mile of sandstone glowed above the darkness of the bush below, like a giant seam of opal hundreds of feet high, ringing our world with colour. I had hoped for sunshine when we crested that last rise and the valley opened suddenly ahead. It would bring the valley to life, and, for her first trip, would be good.

Excitedly, we drove the remaining 10–15 miles further into the valley to where we would leave the car and continue on foot to the base of our climb. It had been a while since I had climbed here, and although I would recognise the climb once I was near it, I was no longer sure of the easiest way to get to that part of the cliffs.

Luckily, another climbing friend, Ian, and his climbing partner had just arrived, so we joined them for the walk up and I borrowed more quick-draws, knowing ours to be a climb protected only by bolts. Even so, I brought a minimal rack with me, since I might be able to find places for natural 'pro' and there could be enough time for other climbs if the weather stayed good.

A shallow horizontal break, petering out as it went, led out from the hill, gaining height as the ground fell steeply away. This allowed a foot traverse across to the left where, near the arete and out of reach overhead, was the first bolt for pro. Until this was clipped a fall of over 20 feet was on the cards.

None of my hexes in the rack I had brought would fit in the few likely-looking pockets along the traverse and I cursed not having brought a few 'friends', ideal for these parallel-sided slots. Wishing wouldn't help me out, though, so with a purely psychological runner in place I worked my way carefully up until I was within reach and with my feet secure, so I could use my right hand to fit a bracket and clip.

The next 50–60 feet of the climb was almost vertical, involving some very delicate wall climbing. Above this the pitch continued for another 80 feet or so, but laid back about 10 degrees off the vertical. It was a very pleasant change, as I no longer needed to hold myself into the wall with my questionable left.

Between the first and second bolts it was unprotectable with the rack I had with me, still very steep and with few secure holds. Also, the bolts had been placed such a distance apart that if the second bolt was not reached and clipped prior to falling, a nasty if not fatal ground fall was inevitable. There were a couple of ideal placements for 'friends' between, but nothing of use to me. It was an interesting section indeed! And with the name of the climb and its story clearly etched in my mind, 'interesting' was some understatement at times.

Above the second bolt I felt free to enjoy. As long as that bolt held I was safe from a groundfall and the next bolt was not so far away – about 15 feet – whereas the last run-out had been around 30 feet, making a possible groundfall of 50–60 feet. Although very thin in parts and steep and sustained, the climbing was wonderful, even relaxed once it laid back a bit. I was in heaven. It had been the highest graded climb on sandstone that I had attempted to lead and it was proving to be such fun. Carol also enjoyed the climb muchly, finding the lower part steep and hard also. By this time heavy clouds were rolling in and it was time to evacuate, leaving the second shorter and easier pitch for some other time. Ian and his friend had finished their climb almost directly above our belay position, so we combined ropes for one long abseil to the ground and hurried back to get Ian's car across the river before the deluge hit. We made it, also managing to set up our tents while it was still dry.

With everything safe and secure, we spent the evening having the last few drinks ever in the original Newnes Hotel, which I had helped relocate in a frenzied volunteers' effort some months before. The hotel had almost been swept into the river during the last big flood when the river bank under it had collapsed. Half suspended in mid-air, it had been shut down as unsafe. A huge group of volunteers demolished it in large pieces, moved them a couple of hundred yards to where they'd built new footings to match, and re-erected it just as before in the new, safer, position. All in one frantic weekend work effort to try and prevent its licence from being revoked. To no avail. The newly strengthened Theatres and Public Halls Act, which had been proving such a headache to us over the last couple of years in our architectural work, was once again being applied with no reference to common sense, and so claimed another victim. This time being so inflexibly enforced that it was snuffing out the last living relic, the last surviving spark of the ghost town's colourful history. Bureaucrats! Bureaucrats and fools – can't the bastards ever think without recourse to the 'rules'?

A warm glow of happiness enveloped us beside the fire as we talked to Ian of climbing, and the publican of his last option – closing down. Outside the night had cleared and frost crackled underfoot as we made our way back to our tents. The sky ablaze with stars, the moonlight bathing the paddocks with silver, and apart from the murmur of the river, not a sound.

Chapter Sixteen

Prepara-tions (Two)

Unfortunately, the solidity and security of rock were not available for me to play on during the months that followed Sweet Dreams. A list of twenty-four tasks (see appendix) awaited me. These were relatively minor alterations and refinements thought out while returning from south of New Zealand, but none quite so simple as first impressions had led me to believe. Each involved many tasks within tasks and thus a far greater outlay of time and effort than expected. Almost all were refinements to make life in the Southern Ocean more workable for a uni-handster – a term of mine derived from a Peter Cook and Dudley Moore sketch in which a one-legged applicant for a film role as Tarzan is referred to as a uni-legster.

Despite the quantity of work to be done, and I knew that only I could do it, our departure date remained 'the beginning of summer' – suitably vague, and with the winter westerlies still rattling the windows at night ashore or whistling in the rigging while aboard, seemingly a long time off. I didn't hurry. The prospect of not being alive in a few months also occupied some space in my head, so I developed a tendency to be sidetracked along a number of paths seeming to lead to fulfilment. These diversions were generally aimed at convincing myself that there really was a lot worth staying alive for – many good reasons for returning intact. In this regard they worked, but six months to departure was suddenly only six weeks and the frenzy had to begin.

From my earliest years at university, when I nearly always arrived at the most satisfying solution to design problems after all-night sessions at the drawing board, I have found these binges of total commitment the only way to achieve real progress. My preparations for the voyage were no exception.

These final six weeks saw my list of twenty-four tasks increase to well over forty, all of which were done while I was also busy on the usual necessities such as making food lists and shopping for them; making, preparing and packing clothing; checking medical supplies; checking and making sure of general ship's supplies; putting together sailmaking, electrical and plumbing repair kits, stove and kerosene lamp spares and repair kit; checking all sails and running rigging and repairing where necessary; servicing all winches and buying spare parts; cleaning and refilling all water containers; checking the compass for errors and making up a deviation table; completing unfinished joinery – the lists were endless. Then, of course, all the food and supplies had to be moved across to the boat and stored securely enough to take a 360-degree roll in any direction without causing havoc by flying loose around the cabin.

It was a busy time, and I looked forward to being at sea more and more – for the sheer peace of it after the rush, and the utter simplicity of existence once underway. It would then be too late to worry about tasks not done. From the moment of departure I would just have to improvise my way out of all troubles with what was at hand. I was confident this time that I couldn't have prepared either *Little Wing* or myself better. If we could not complete the circle south of all the capes at this attempt, I would have to admit it was beyond me – and that was not a thought I could return and live with happily. Not after approximately sixteen years of creating *Little Wing* and just over eighteen in recreating myself after the fall.

As time passes, one gradually learns that the shades of grey are too numerous for counting. Looked at more closely, black and white often turn out to be the fringes, the outer edges of grey and not what they at first appear. And grey is not colourless. Often it reflects the colour and mood of its surroundings, a subdued mirror reflecting hints and memories of the full intensity. Awakening early to complete my packing, I found that night had not quite parted from the day. The world was grey. Today my voyage would begin not from when I cleared Customs in Sydney Harbour, but from when I sailed from my mooring, Sydney-bound. From that moment I would truly be on my own.

A pre-dawn mug of coffee had the mists of doubt disperse and the last few jobs were underway as morning broke, just a normal summer's day. My mooring, lying as it does only a couple of boat lengths from the rocks and surrounded by other moored craft, has its tricks in leaving or returning engineless as I do. Today looked to be no exception, with the north-easterly I would be leaving with putting me in the windless lee of the hill behind. A southerly change was due late in the day, but I hoped to get to Sydney ahead of it, and get alongside the Customs wharf before dark.

Little squirts of wind trickle down a nearby gully in a north-easter, some of them fanning out far enough to reach the *Wing*. The trick is not to let the mooring go until I judge either by intuition or experience that an approaching squirt – terminology from my days of racing Skates when a 'squirt' of breeze would jump us up on to a plane – has enough wind in it either to get us moving sufficiently for steerage way or, preferably, get us clear of moored craft and shoreline hazards completely. Likewise, when returning, I must successfully pick up my mooring at the first attempt or we could easily end up on the rocks.

These confined quarters engineless sailing skills would be needed on arrival in Sydney, as Customs had moved to a new onshore facility in a very narrow and confined bay, and I would have to judge it just right if I were to tie up alongside successfully alone. Daylight would make things easier, and with the weather looking good for a fast trip in a freshening nor'easter, there seemed no need to rush.

Those last few jobs . . . even they doubled in number within the final hour, and thoughts of a leisurely departure went flying. A couple of surprise telephone calls from friends brightened my mood, then finally the time had come to go. A farewell glass of wine with my parents and a quick little tour of inspection since they hadn't seen any of my recent woodwork or preparations down below, and I was ready.

Although we didn't have much to say to each other for a little period of twenty years or so from the late Sixties, there remained an underlying respect for each other, at least from my side. I think from theirs also in recent years. Few people would have been able to give a more knowledgeable second opinion, when requested, than my father. One of the few whose learning in matters nautical came first-hand from the men and the era of working sail. There would no longer be many more competent in matters pertaining to the sailmaking and rigging arts – now mostly lost in the modern era of synthetic cloth and lines and almost no handwork. In sailmaking, as elsewhere, the machine and brute force have taken over as mankind becomes more and more enslaved by its obsession with 'saving' time.

Love of the ocean and wilderness runs strongly in my mother. She had shared bushwalking and ocean-sailing adventures with my father since long before I was born. Having brought up two children aboard the *Wraith* and sailed countless thousands of sea miles aboard her as watch captain, crew, co-skipper, bosun and cook, her advice and help in provisioning, clothing and other practical matters was also welcome when requested. The two of them, sailing the *Wraith* with no extra crew, had almost made it around the Horn a few years previously, but the rudder had been torn completely off in a gale just a few hundred miles short. They spent over fifty days steering by sail trim alone to reach Valparaiso and thence Quintero, where they built a new rudder and returned non-stop across the southern Pacific, the season being too late for another attempt at the Horn.

This was a magnificent piece of seamanship, handling a vessel of her size alone and at their age, without working self-steering, nor, in the end, even a rudder. And all the while threatened by probably the most dangerous lee shore in the world. This would rate very highly indeed in the eyes of anyone experienced in those waters.

My parents therefore knew what the Southern Ocean was like. They knew at least some of the problems I have with my hand, and I am sure they were worried. I had found their opinion valuable when I asked for it during my preparations, and resolved to get a message through to them to ease their worries once I had rounded 'the corner'. At least two recent single-handers had lost parents while they were at sea and I thought that both my parents and I could die happier if they knew I had made it 'around' – should either they or I not last the full distance!

The north-easterly that had promised a fast and comfortable ride to Sydney ahead of the approaching southerly was no longer in evidence now that all was ready. I hoisted sail and waved my farewells, but it was over half an hour before a faint zephyr with maybe enough in it to get us under way chanced by. Scarcely moving, we edged our way out through the obstacles and found clear water at last. I hoisted the Yankee and waved again. We were on our way. Ominously dark clouds, the bases of thunderstorms, were massing over and beyond the western shore as we headed out. About three-quarters of a mile in from Barrenjoey Headland, at the entrance to Pittwater, the wind deserted us completely and in an oily grey calm we waited, whistling for wind. It came ultimately, nearly an hour later, from the west. This was a sure sign that the southerly was not far behind, but at sea it swung back to the north. We headed south.

Capricious as a flight of fancy, the wind boxed the compass twice in the mere 16-mile straight-line distance between Barrenjoey and the entrance to Sydney Harbour. It also varied in strength from zero to over 30 knots when the southerly arrived as we were working toward the harbour from several miles off. If the weather's intention was to give me sail-changing and reefing practise before I left Sydney behind, it was perfect. But the last things I needed, mentally exhausted as I was from the preparations, were added complications. In driving rain and greatly reduced visibility I tacked up harbour in the dark for the first time, without a chart, looking for a tiny bay I had never entered before. I was not sure I would even recognise it, having never seen it from the water, even in daylight. I reefed right down, taking it very slowly so that the southerly could ease a bit before it was time for tricky night-time manoeuvring to come alongside the wharf. Probably I was too cautious, and edged my way up harbour too slowly. Twice I fell asleep at the helm, once waking up when we were already among moored craft and heading for the rocks! This second time frightened me enough to keep awake for the rest of the journey. A moored submarine at the naval base opposite Customs was a fail-safe clue to it being the correct bay once I was close enough to make out its silhouette. After a trial circle to gauge distances, I came in quietly alongside the Customs launch tied up at the jetty, and with all peaceful and secure, retreated below for a few hours' sleep. It was 3 a.m.

The marine traffic on Sydney Harbour started at first light. By 6 a.m. I was up again to adjust fenders and mooring lines, as the wakes from distant workboats caused us to ride hard at times against the launch I was tied to. It didn't improve. Until the Customs men started work and moved their launch elsewhere to work on her, I was constantly adjusting and readjusting to keep us apart. I had noticed on the trip down several things either not set up yet, or set up slightly wrongly. In between fending off either the launch or the wharf, I set about working my way down this new list of tasks. Also there were the Customs formalities themselves to go through, but these were almost relaxation after the rest.

A nondescript day it started out, not really sunny, not deeply grey, a nothing sort of day with very little wind to move us smartly on our way. A sort of 'office day'. The hum of commuter traffic soon drowned out the harbour sounds, and for all those thousands upon thousands, routine held them in its sway.

The wind being so light, I joked with the Customs people about needing to bounce off the submarine moored opposite in order to go about, not being sure of our ability to get up steerage way in time. And how nearly true, the bay was that narrow. I made it about all right, but when only just clear decided to get the Yankee ready to set, to give us more power and speed. I had forgotten the self-steering was lashed and couldn't move, so we luffed, then went back about. I raced aft to correct, but too late. With no speed to tack again I tried to run off, gybe and work our way out of the bay once more. If there was enough room to turn. There wasn't. Plan two: try and get up speed by turning downwind as long as I could, and then, with the little extra speed, hopefully make it up and about before ramming the navy wharf or submarine head on!

It was very close. Navy personnel came running from all directions to fend off the impending collision, but with a little push against a wharf pylon to help us gain an ounce more speed, I had us about again on my own and clear. Just a few yards later I had the Yankee set and drawing. Phew! Off at last . . . As if to reward our efforts the sun appeared as we cleared the bay and there followed a glorious sail up harbour towards the sea. A couple of tacks to get us past Fort Denison and over near the eastern shore, then a very pleasant close reach towards the sea, my mind flooded with memories as we sailed past various harbourside suburbs that had figured strongly in my past. A fire tug was out, spouting water towards the sky; a square rigger I had helped with work on motored by; all those memories, bathed in sunshine. Unnoticed, we sailed on by.

Chapter Seventeen
"Old Ground to New.."

I've got to follow that dream
Wherever that dream may lead
I've got to follow that dream
And find the love I need.

(Keep a moovin', move along
Keep a moovin', move along)

When your heart gets restless,
Time to move along.
When your heart gets weary,
Time to sing a song.
But when a dream is calling you
There's just one thing that you can do –

You've got to follow that dream
Wherever that dream may lead
You've got to follow that dream
And find the love you need.

As 'The King' sang, all those years ago – when a dream is calling you, there's only one thing you can do – follow the dream on through.

The initial idea, the process of self-education and preparation – all that accumulated experience had led us to here. But it is probable, as Moitessier suggested, that no one at the start of such a long journey entirely alone has the ability to carry it out. The capacity to cope with all the situations met along the way grows gradually, as the miles fall astern. For those with easy two-way contact with a shore base or others external to their vessel via radio or other means – for advice, weather information and general assistance this capacity cannot develop fully because they are really *not* sailing single-handed.

It was not possible, therefore, on clearing Sydney Heads, to plan the voyage in its entirety. I could only aim to get past successive milestones along the way. With one successfully left astern a new one would be aimed for, and so on around the course.

The first was merely to get beyond my previous point of return south of New Zealand – to make it successfully around South-West Cape of Stewart Island and on into the wide blue yonder of the Pacific. This was my point of no return. Once Stewart Island had been left behind there was going to be no coming back except by completing the circle eastabout to Sydney. I lengthened this first stage to include getting past the Chatham Islands, since they too are a part of New Zealand, and also because this would take me further east than I had ever been.

From here, the next stage would be the traditional running the easting down between latitudes 42 and 47 degrees south approximately, depending on weather, to a longitude of about 100 degrees west, when the next crux would appear. This would traditionally be the most difficult part of the voyage. The descent on the 'Big Dipper' down to approximately 57–58 degrees south around Cape Horn and back up and away through iceberg alley, hopefully intact.

At Cape Horn, weather permitting, I would try and make contact with the lighthouse via my hand-held VHF to relay a message back to my parents. They had made friends with an engineer at the Cape Horn lighthouse during their enforced stop in Chile for repairs. With him forewarned by letter of the possibility of my rounding, this seemed a viable if somewhat complicated method of getting a message through. Failing this I would send a telegram from the Falkland Islands just around the corner. This would be more certain, but I was not sure if I could do this via the hand-held VHF or if I would have to call in and send it personally. I would worry about this when the time arose – there were many thousands of miles and no doubt a fair sprinkling of gales to be put astern of us first. There seemed no point in looking further ahead than this.

The lights of Sydney strung out along the coastline astern, a thunderstorm and lightning over the sea to the north, and the sound of the city (a background hum quite noticeable from the sea) fading as we edged slowly towards the south-east. These were to be my final impressions of Sydney until our return.

Like floating jewels the fragile blue transparency of Portuguese men o'war dotted the gently heaving surface of a sunset-tinged sea. An oily grey sea with a featureless grey sky, broken by the rising of a pinkish-red sunball as the pre-dawn greys dissolved before the day. Two long-finned pilot whales blowing softly as they swam languidly past, introducing life . . . Many deadly-looking jelly fish, purplish and formless almost, except for the long trails of stingers underneath, yet each apparently a home for many little fish darting in and out from under their deadly array. I wondered in these miniature worlds who was living on whom; or were they both living on unsuspecting others passing by?

As if to delay our descent to higher latitudes, we seemed to have been caught in the centre of a very slow-moving region of high pressure. For the first few days there was hardly ever sufficient wind to make progress. I wasn't prepared to risk setting my Drifter/Multi-Purpose Spinnaker yet, so early in the voyage, and for much of every day I had the log pulled in, helm lashed and headsail dropped to ease the chafe problems caused by windless slatting. The mainsail I kept set to try and ease our rolling in the windlessness. After three days of constant effort we had made but 70 miles. So much for a rapid start to keep my enthusiasm intact!

I could, however, complete storing things away in a more weatherproof manner, and catch up on many other tasks to help ready us for when we hit real weather. I also decided to introduce a daily exercise routine early, while the easy weather lasted, evolving a system of exercises that I should be able to keep up in most weather. Immediately I began these I noticed I started to sleep and dream much better. On land also I have always slept far better while sticking to my regular exercise routine, but how regularly I could keep to it in rough weather at sea only time would tell. We drifted on. A full moon rising orange through the purple haze of evening, a path of liquid silver later, lighting the wine-dark sea . . .

Motion! On the morning of our fourth day at sea a light east-north-easterly breeze came in, strengthening to the point where I was considering taking in a reef, unused as I was to heeling after so much calm. It was time to get used to these new noises again, so I carried on instead, listening once more to the sounds of motion . . . The pounding and crashing of waves against the bow, the splash of the lee rail dipping as we rolled down to a passing wave, the thrum of the headsail sheets vibrating to the wind. We were sailing almost hard on the wind, but in the right direction and how beautifully she moved. I stood near the mast at sunset, watching her bow move over and through the waves, entranced after so much calm.

Our first albatross of the voyage put in an appearance that evening, somewhat further north than I had expected. A Cape pigeon appeared at around the same time. Both birds I had previously associated with more southern latitudes. No doubt they just whizzed up to remind me that colder and more windy regions were not far away.

The following day proved another perfect summer day and a great one for maintenance, boat tasks and 'sailorising' preparations. I set up anti-chafe gear on my headsail sheets, treated some incipient rust to try and keep it under control until my return, sanded and varnished some severely weathered parts of my tiller as a preventative to further damage, added extra silicone sealant around the perimeters of all cabin windows, steering dome, aft hatch window and forward anchor rope exit/inspection port. This made me think that if she wasn't waterproof now, she never would be. A dangerous thought!

On her mooring – the sun shade cloths protect the hexan windows from ultraviolet degradation when not at sea.

Mount Arapiles from the campsite at sunrise (the 'Dunes' face is at the top of the hill, 'Tiger Wall' and the Watchtower etc. around Bard Buttress on the right).

Approaching Lord Howe from the south-west (Mount Gower [foreground] and Mount Lidgebird with their heads in the clouds).

Tasman cloudscape.

Southern Ocean, fine – looking ahead.

Southern Ocean, fine – dancing with waves.

Pencil in hand, plotting position nearing the Horn – my emergency inside steering whipstaff (the original tiller extension cut down) in the foreground at right.

Myself at the tiller during early trials – with the tiller extension in its original place and state.

Birth of the Wing
(Note original hollow steel rudder replaced by the one illustrated in Chapter 14).

Interior, looking forward.

Interior, looking aft.

A few hours after Kamirez, wind and wave rising (crests half to three-quarters of a mile apart).

My beloved Southern swells – marching past forever.

Easting at evening – deep south Pacific.

Off northern Tasmania, headed home.

Stepping out east-south-east – on the wind.

Lat 50°S below NZ – blowing.

Waiting for wind – deep south Pacific.

Southern Peace.

South, down the Dipper.

Night Driving – racing, winter
whenever there was wind.

Winter Evening – Blue Motion.

Summer's Blue Tasman.

Cirrus swirls – my 'weather fax'.

Young Mist – *my Southern Ocean crew and confidante.*

Slipped after my return – and ready for more.

My 'engine' – outward bound at around 48°S (the 40's not roaring).

Sunny day south of New Zealand.

Tasman sunrise.

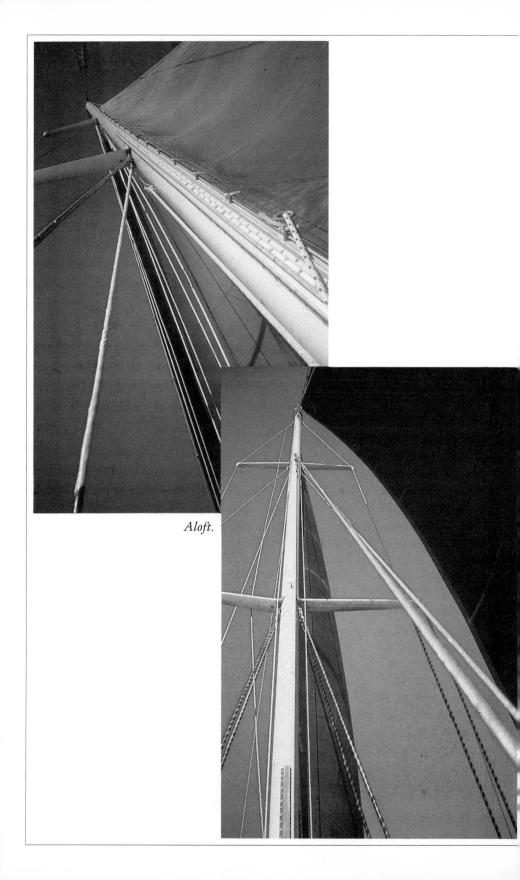

Aloft.

Low pressure to the south approaching from the west.

Warm front weather.

Into lengthening night.

Ahead, and Astern – views on the way down 'the Dipper'.

Brancusi's 'Bird' – Yankee down, and waiting.

I was still thrilled by the way she moved over and through the water the previous evening, and it seemed to confirm an idea I had developed during the winter. I was down at the auction of the *Svanen*, a square rigger I had helped with some work on. Looking forward along her endless bowsprit at the sunglisten on the wind-ruffled water below, I was reminded of the long swells of the Southern Ocean on a good day and the thought hit like the proverbial ton of bricks. Namely that *Little Wing wanted* to complete her southern circuit, and that for her sake alone I really must try again. She *wanted* to prove herself in the conditions for which she had been designed. Nothing else would do.

Watching her move so nicely had reminded me of this. She seemed to be alive, leaping and bounding towards the future with great joy and purpose. I also experimented with setting up my rain-catcher and around midnight returned on deck, spending several hours taking my first flashlight photographs at sea and watching her surging through the swells in moonlight . . . Soaking it in, soaking it all in.

The next day demonstrated that it doesn't have to be in the Forties in order to roar. In the morning I had good reefing practice, going from full main plus Yankee to Yankee with mainsail at first reef, to mainsail at second reef, to dropping the mainsail completely and trying under Yankee alone, then dropping Yankee and sailing under staysail alone! Still heading south-east, in a strengthening north-north-west wind, sunshine, many large breakers with exquisite turquoise tops as they broke, and large areas of white foam all around. This was more like Southern Ocean weather.

From time to time breakers would come clean over the cabin and down the other side, washing the leeward windows for me, but this was normal for these parts. As with last summer, but sunnier this time and not worrying. I put in some sight-taking practice in rough seas for the first time this trip and it appeared to work out well. Altogether quite a pleasant day of action in bright sunshine and not disquieting at all when the wind was not too far above 30 knots. There was still little need to wear much clothing for warmth, despite the water temperature having gone down to 16–17 degrees centigrade. It had peaked at 23 degrees a few days ago when we were becalmed in the East Coast Current off Sydney.

This had been Southern Ocean doing its fine weather act. The next day dawned more usual, with grey seas, grey skies and wind moaning in the rigging as we continued to run south-east before a strong nor'westerly backing slowly to the west. I gybed and reset the Yankee, as the wind eased with the onset of light rain. Soon after, the wind went around to the south, but we maintained the same course, now hard on the wind into the drizzle and grey. We were almost on to the New Zealand half of the chart. Once I decided to switch to the new half, the East Coast of Australia would not appear again until my circumnavigation was almost complete – too far ahead even to imagine from here.

We were genuinely into the Forties latitudes by now and although the weather was becoming very changeable and rather unpredictable, I was finding the journey really enjoyable. I was far more sure of both myself and *Little Wing* than I had been at the start of our previous attempts. This feeling of security allowed a great feeling of warmth inside, and I was very content in my little cocoon. We were still plagued by windlessness to a far greater extent than anticipated, and it seemed as if virtually every day, for at least part of the day, I would lash the helm and self-steering, haul in the log line and drop sail until wind reappeared.

All these precautions were to save unnecessary wear and chafe. The misty lack of visibility and all pervading wetness of the greys surrounding us was a bit downing, as it usually coincided with very little or no wind and therefore no progress. Ultimately, however, the cold front following would arrive, and progress would begin again. In the meantime I was trying to catch up on reading all the books I had bought over the past two years and had been saving for the voyage. With such frequent trips on deck, to try and keep us sailing, not much reading was possible.

Before taking in or letting out a reef or changing headsails, I was in the habit of staying out in the cockpit for a while in order to get a good feel for the weather and how it was changing. I tried to take in all the little subtleties not apparent from down below, insulated from the wind and the wet – despite the large cabin windows that made it seem like sailing an open boat. Particularly in very rough weather when the only escape was to keep my eyes closed!

After the greys, the fine and windy days of westerlies, white foam, turquoise tops and rigging's moan. The barograph and barometer were elevated to the status of gods, consulted often, oracles of rise and fall. The sunshine on this day brought me worries, though, as, glancing at the ammeter, I noticed it read no charge. The solar panel would normally be putting out 3 amps on a day like this, so here was cause for concern. Without electric power I would have no navigation lights, no compass light and very importantly, no easy-on interior light to switch on at night when rapidly getting into wet-weather gear for deck work or searching for necessities. With my hand being virtually useless in the dark for most tasks, lack of light was a great fear for me at sea, rendering me a cripple.

I didn't think we had had enough sun to charge the batteries to the point where the regulator in the circuit would automatically cut out. The weather was too rough on deck to check the various points along the circuit outside to try and locate the problem area. Instead, I set about disembowelling my storage areas under the floor to locate all the necessary or even remotely likely tools I would need to fix things once the weather eased. Having amassed this pile of tools I created yet another electrical repair kit in a separate bag to my two electrical repair bags already in existence and the next day set about locating the source of trouble. My electrical panel is not the easiest to get at, being behind some cabin panelling, but soon it was removed and testing began. My first test indicated that power was coming from the panel to the regulator, so either the regulator was at fault or it had reached cut-out point after all. Hopefully the latter, as my spare was of an earlier, antiquated design quite different from the present one and I no longer remembered the correct terminals for the input and output leads.

The quickness of this test was not time wasted. It had been years since I had done all the electrical work and I had entirely forgotten the layout of the circuitry behind the panel. This refamiliarization, therefore, was a useful exercise.

Surprise, Surprise! On returning below after getting sunsights later in the day, there was my ammeter reading a decent 1.5–2 amps again, smugly laughing at my worries and doubts. What a relief this was. I just could not face another failure due to minor causes. I had decided to continue anyway, even if I was to have no electrical power. I would just have to sail a slower, more conservative 'race'. I had no financial resources in reserve for another attempt and probably too few mental resources if I allowed myself to be defeated so easily, so early on.

In fact, I regarded this episode as the rounding of my first and probably most important Cape. The Cape of Real Commitment. If the problem had proved to be the regulator and the spare proved unusable also, I had decided I could wire the previous panel, now repaired, directly to the batteries and put it out in the cockpit whenever conditions allowed. This would generate enough for running the compass light when necessary, if nothing else. The ammeter had taken to periods of fluttering near zero as if it couldn't decide whether to work or not, but I had brought along a spare in case of problems there. I now felt quite ready for further electrical surprises, and quietly confident of my ability to rectify them.

I had been reading *The Mists of Avalon* not long before leaving, and now it was the turn of reality to imitate fiction. Mists befell us in earnest. I say mists because they were not like previous mist and fog we had been through. They had been all-pervasive, like another form of air. These were wisps of mist, strands of different density streaming around us, and arriving in conjunction with legions of new cross swells with no apparent source and from several different directions. These caused a very confused and heaping sea, and there was now hardly enough wind to keep the sails filled. It gave the impression of sailing through a weird and ever-changing landscape, along valleys with hills on both sides, suddenly cut off by the appearance of a mountain dead ahead. A side valley would open, and on we went, cautiously. Cautiously, because I had been unable to get good sights for a couple of days and the west coast of New Zealand's South Island was lurking out there somewhere. The sight of a gannet flying past fuelled these fears, as they are usually coastal, not mid-oceanic birds. All the while a strange new noise, a low humming like the sound of distant engines, provided background 'music' to the scene and I was at a loss to locate its source. I was almost ready to believe the bottom of the South Island was my 'Avalon', and these were the mists there to hide it and its mysteries from me.

The barometer continued to fall and at midnight, while I was busy with my usual course and sail adjustments, the wind arrived. I had thought earlier that merely by dropping the Yankee and continuing slowly under double-reefed main, I would get a good night's rest. Not now. Lit only by phosphorescence from

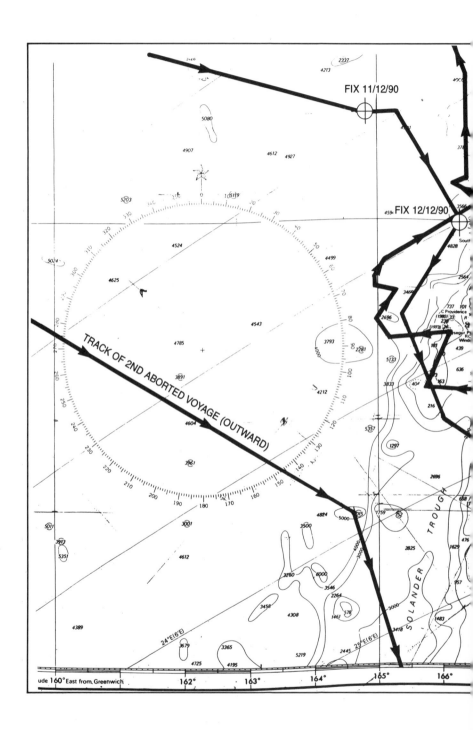

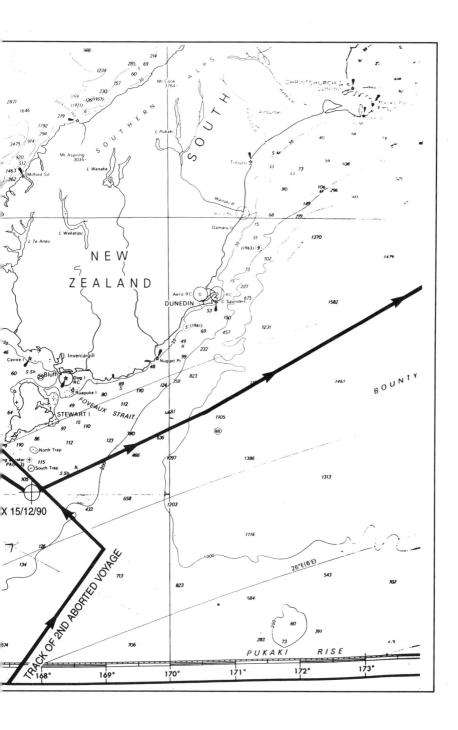

surrounding breakers, I dropped the mainsail completely, continuing under bare poles at 3–4 knots, and returned to my bunk for a couple of hours before rising at dawn to check that there was no land around. At sunrise I decided to set the staysail to help our progress, and a few hours later managed to grab a few quick sights which confirmed my fears about nearby land. They positioned us perfectly for a landfall at Point Puysegur that evening, however. A sighting of the lighthouse there would be a great confirmation of our position before aiming just south of Stewart Island to miss the Traps, the Snares and other hazards.

It all sounded so simple, but it was not to be. I did spot a piece of the Fiordland shore lurking in the distance between rain squalls and low cloud, but not nearly enough for a confirmation of where we might be. But the day was young, maybe things would clear. They did, but not in the visual sense. We were nearly blown clear out of the water instead! The wind went into the south, blowing steadily around force 11, and gusting more. This was too much to risk damaging gear so early in the voyage, so I again dropped all sail and lay-a-hull, drifting slowly down onto the lee shore I had seen just an hour earlier. How far we were off I could only guess, the scale of the landscape being unfamiliar and too little of it glimpsed for clues. I could only hope that we were far enough off for the wind to ease before we drifted within sight again and I had to sail clear. So near to having been safely and relatively easily around, and now . . . skirting the edge of disaster instead.

In the afternoon, the wind swung more towards south-west to west, so I reset the staysail and aimed southward again on a course to clear the remaining land. I had glimpsed more while busy with sail changes, and had by now given up all thoughts of keeping in relatively close to catch sight of Puysegur light. Survival itself, which meant staying well clear of the shore, had taken priority.

Nothing hitting that rocky shore in those seas would live to tell the tale. Water temperature was down to 8 degrees centigrade and the air similar, but with the wind-chill effect quickly rendering ungloved hands totally useless for any work. I sensed it easing a little on evening, so reset the mainsail at the third reef to try and hasten our clearing of this gale-torn realm. Ha! The wind was playing tricks. Just after dark it came back at around force 10–11 from the south to south-south-west. The lee shore problem once again. Under triple-reefed main alone I was not sure if we could hold our own in the attempt to claw further offshore, but there was too much wind to try anything else.

I was up every few minutes peering into the night for signs of land, and at one stage thought I saw some lights. But it was too rough, the swells too large to gauge whether it was a flashing lighthouse light, distant car headlights or what. The barometer, which had bottomed at 980 mb earlier in the day, stayed down, worrying me more. For days I hadn't removed a rubber glove from my left hand in an effort to keep it warm, but it was completely numb with cold and useless; my right hand was much the same.

I began to have doubts of my ability to complete the trip after all if conditions remained like this. Having a sat-nav or radar on board would of course have defused all worries by giving an accurate position fix despite conditions outside. I may even have been able to heave to, relax and let it blow over before sailing again, but this would have been outside assistance, and would have rendered any claims to a single-handed circumnavigation farcical.

The punishment went on . . . bash, crash, smash, bash, as we fought our way away from the coast. I could hardly bear the battering *Little Wing* was taking, could hardly believe she would hold together, that anything could hold together under such treatment.

The next day dawned with more of the same but laced with heavy rain, so no visibility at all. The suspense about whether we would hit the shore, the Traps, the Snares, Solander Island, Stewart Island or maybe sail clear of them all was almost unbearable. I kept choosing the safer course option in my continuing DR navigation, but with unknown currents, leeway and drift in these conditions, my DR was riddled with uncertainty. Nor was it helped by my log being blown airborne for much of the time. I resolved to give Cape Horn a wide berth if we survived this corner, having no wish to tangle with any more potential lee shores in regions where accurate navigation would most likely be impossible.

It was almost a classic rock-climbing predicament. If I hung on where I was, I would be safe for the moment, but exhaustion would ultimately cause me to fall. If I committed myself to the next move and for some reason couldn't complete it, I would also fall. If I committed myself to the move and made it, one more crux would be behind me and I would be at peace – thousands of miles of ocean ahead with no land to cause trouble.

I reviewed our DR position and it was apparent that if we took advantage of a new wind shift to head east we would either safely round the corner that night, or end this voyage and this life in the dark amongst the Traps or Snares. I could also head further south, but was worried about the possibility of hitting the Auckland Islands if a strong current had been running south during our recent struggle. I chose east. Under staysail alone we reached off through the murk, hoping it would clear before dark. It didn't, but nor did we hear the sounds of ocean fighting rock. We sailed on . . .

Almost imperceptibly, as if infinitely to prolong this game of chance, morning stained the edges of night with light. We hadn't hoped for more. We were clear . . . Fly on, *Little Wing*, fly on. If you will excuse the borrowing, we really did round this corner on a wing and a prayer – a *Little Wing* and a large prayer! The wind remained the usual 30–40 knots, but with sunshine, a new ocean before us, and a new course of north-east, up to a more tropical latitude around 45 degrees south.

I managed to get some good sights and back-plotted our DR course of the last few days. It was satisfying that after all those gales and unknowns of the past few days, my sights put us within one mile(!!) of my assumed DR position. On looking at our course, we really had cut it fine, however – no wonder I had been so apprehensive. For the second time in under a year we had threaded the eye of the needle between Traps and Snares in total darkness and with severely limited course options available. The sun sparkled from the now benign-looking seas. The turquoises, the whites, the deeper blues and blue greens. Fur seals reappeared to play around us, and in the air Cape petrels and Antarctic prions flecked the sky. In the evening some wanderers, black-browed and white-capped albatrosses came out to wheel and glide, continuing their endless searching, sliding, soaring into night. I could probably have set more sail, but occasional squalls still came blasting up from the south we were leaving behind. I remained under staysail alone, averaging 5 knots anyway, trying for a peaceful night.

A milder 15–25 knots of breeze on the following day allowed me to catch up with more sailorising tasks – pre-whipping the self-steering lines at new lengths to bypass the chafed parts, setting up the new 'bullet-proof' storm jib in conditions that allowed for proper adjustment and fine tuning of sheet lead positions. I had noticed the solar panel no longer showing any current the previous day and had ascertained that this time it was not the regulator, that in fact no current was getting that far. It was still too wet on deck to dismantle exposed parts of the panel and wiring to pinpoint the problem, but if I minimised power use this could wait.

I was continuing to have very vivid and colourful dreams. These had commenced from the first nights at sea and were a very enjoyable nightly show. I was also full of happy memories of my departure time, and the days preceding it. The visit by John Grant, the architect I had worked for, along with his wife, sons Matthew and Mark, Matthew's wife Debbie and their children, James and Hannah. There was a dinner locally with a surprise new friend, and a great 'Last Supper' with my climbing friends in town. I was really feeling good. I was also eating well this trip with a cooked dinner every night, a different concoction nearly every time for variety, as well as dried fruit and nuts during the day and my own muesli mix for breakfast.

I hadn't set more than about 100 square feet of sail for about a week now, but we were making reasonable progress. I was happy and enjoying it, not feeling pressured or rushed. It was, after all, going to prove more a war of attrition, this voyage, than a contest where one or two brief battles would bring success. I had to be prepared in all ways for a long haul and it looked good. We even sailed through a perfect semi-circular rainbow between squalls and I took it as a good omen, following this colourful path toward the future.

Chapter Eighteen
Open Spaces

*L*ittle *Wing* has always been more than just a yacht to me. With virtually every decision relating to her design, construction, fitting out, rigging and provisioning having ultimately been made by me, most of the construction having been carried out by me and the costs of creating her having been borne by me, she truly is my child. I felt badly over the terrible hammering handed out to her getting around the bottom of New Zealand, feeling she deserved more considerate treatment in future. I was happier not driving her into the ground for the sake of a few miles – she always has given miles when they were needed, and with style . . . playing with the waves, seeking horizons, going beyond. She would carry us far.

The south had not yet heard of summer, and with water and air temperatures below 10 degrees C, I felt grateful for the marvellous job my Monitor self-steering gear, which I called Mr Monitor or Mr M, was doing for me in reliably steering us through squalls that would have frozen me to an ice-block in no time. Even relatively rapid sail changes had both hands frozen to incapability of fine control. If I had had to hand-steer for long periods, hypothermia would have destroyed me.

I had often wondered what albatrosses and other seabirds did when they were seated on the water and were struck by a large breaker they had not seen to avoid. It seemed a rare enough sight to see them seated even in windlessness, let alone at that exact place and time. This morning revealed all . . . a large black-browed albatross was happily sitting in the sun, quietly contemplating whatever, when it was suddenly engulfed by a large breaking top, totally disappearing beneath the break. After the foam had passed, it shook its beak twice, maybe blinked once or twice, and remained seated, quietly meditating and apparently believing in the theory that lightning never strikes the same spot twice!

Royals were now becoming the most common of the albatross family as we approached the latitude of Dunedin. This was where the creation of *Little Wing* began as the first tentative lines on paper in combination with a name that spoke in harmony with the Dream. There was a breeding colony of royals on Taioroa Head at the entrance to Port Chalmers and Dunedin Harbour and I was almost tempted to call in and visit Dunedin friends from 1975.

Even under staysail alone we rattled off 166 miles in the day we crossed latitude 45 degrees, but the barometer was getting high and the wind seeming to fade. The water temperature had now climbed back to 10 degrees, almost tropical! I still slept in tracksuit, bini, socks, Marion's sleeveless warmie and jumper under a sheet and doona of sorts, but was never hot. I decided to try and cross the Pacific in latitudes where the water temperature stayed around 10 degrees, and maybe summer would catch us before the Horn. An uninsulated tin can is not a very warm place at sea. In an easing wind I reset the Yankee, which maintained a good speed and eased the rolling with the doubling of sail area up high. The sun still shone, but by evening clouds were approaching from the south. I hoped for a peaceful night.

We were blessed. Conditions held overnight and although the following day dawned grey and cloudy with a substantially stronger breeze covering the surrounding ocean with whitecaps, it had started to clear by early afternoon. Back up went the mainsail at second reef, and we sailed through the afternoon and into evening in a bubble of easy sailing weather. Sunny but cool, over a sea that could only be described as calm. A bit too calm, in fact, and by the time darkness fell I had once again dropped the Yankee to ease chafe problems, lashed the tiller and self-steering, and hauled in the log. Becalmed again!

The wisps of cirrus in the sky towards evening, the only clouds in a perfect blue dome, had not been merely decoration. In the dark of pre-dawn I was woken by the sounds of wind in the rigging, a strong wind at that, so rapidly put back the third reef in the mainsail, lashed the Yankee down more securely to the pulpit forward, and reset the staysail in its stead. I had raced up on deck still half dreaming, half asleep, and found it very dangerous on deck with the unexpectedly lively motion. Later in the morning with the wind continuing to strengthen, I decided to drop the mainsail completely, almost creating a serious problem.

As I dropped the mainsail and was about to start lashing it down, the captive pin shackle securing the halyard to the head of sail was somehow flicked open and the shackle itself went flying towards a watery grave. Purely instinctively my good hand shot out and caught the end of the halyard before it too was irretrievably lost. Phew! With the halyard lost to the masthead I would have difficulties in setting the mainsail again until the weather was calm enough for a trip aloft to retrieve it. It would need to be very calm, as to get to the masthead proper I would have to construct steps in the upper rigging beyond where the bosun's chair could reach and this had only ever been possible in the calm of protected water. It would have been possible to use one of the headsail halyards in an emergency, but then my use of headsails would be limited, so it was a lucky grab. I decided to replace the lost shackle with one that I could wire permanently closed. That way, the halyard and sail would not part company until I really wanted them apart.

The barometer continued to fall, the world outside all greys. Wind whining mournfully in the rigging punctuated by the crack and smash of waves breaking over the cabin, and now the patter of falling rain on the deck overhead. It was time to remain in my bunk and read. Let the elements fight outside. The wind eased a bit towards evening, so I wired the new shackle and reset the main, triple reefed. The barometer had not yet bottomed, and would not until the cold front came through behind the warm. But the wind had eased enough for our motion to be atrocious in the new cross swells and confusion. We needed more sail to steady us.

All day I had been noticing a strange new sound along with the usual wind in the rigging and ocean music. It was a choir singing! I couldn't quite tell, because of its remoteness, if it was a choir of South Sea Islanders, a large Welsh choir or a church-type choir, but it oh so closely resembled the sound of massed human voices. I enjoyed the performance as I lay in my bunk and tried to think out the cause, but secretly I suspect I wanted the mystery and the magic to remain. The weather had not yet been calm enough to risk dismantling the solar panel wiring outside to locate the cause of death, so I couldn't waste power listening to cassettes. This heavenly choir, free of charge so far, was welcome to entertain me in their place!

The performance was unfortunately interrupted at about 1 a.m. when the cold front finally arrived. I hastily dropped the mainsail completely and remained on deck awhile until I was sure she had settled down to the new conditions and was maintaining the correct course. Working on deck next morning I found my left hand usable inside a washing-up glove, but my right was frozen into immobility very rapidly. The water temperature was back to 8 degrees and inside the cabin it was only 7 degrees at the day's hottest. No wonder I felt cold. Dangerous cross-sea combinations would explode from time to time as the large swells from the south-west intersected those of the recent days' northerlies, but I decided we would make good miles if I dared keep staysail up and nothing broke. Some breakers hit our stern so explosively that I was amazed to see Mr Monitor and his vane still there – every time. The reinforcing I had done had certainly improved matters since the last attempt and I so far hadn't needed to use my new super-strong aircraft ply vanes. (This was just the last of the normals reinforced with Kevlar as an experiment.)

The following day I ascertained that we had finally crossed the International Dateline, almost bringing this first stage of the voyage to a close – only the

Chathams to go. Unfortunately, I also discovered that my solar panel problem definitely lay in the external region and was not due to problems with the wiring between deck and electrical panel. I had previously worked out that no power was reaching the ammeter below, but thought the rough weather might just have loosened a connection en route. This was not so. As I had earlier frozen both hands despite wearing rubber gloves in trying to set up the rain catcher, it was obviously too cold for fine electrical work outside – and too wet. Well, tomorrow is another day.

And it was – in a way. In fact it was our second crack at the same day due to crossing the Dateline. Conditions were somewhat milder, so it was time for some early Christmas presents for *Little Wing* and myself. Firstly, I discovered that one of the self-steering lines had almost chafed through near water level due to a whipping not holding and allowing too much slack in the system. I knotted it off at a new length and rewhipped, sewing through both parts of the line this time to ensure no slippage. Suitably inspired, I checked the connections within the connection box of the solar panel itself. Power! Thank heavens for multimeters. I exposed the next set of connections joining the external to the internal wiring; one had broken. I crimped the wires together again and looked down below. All the dials smiled back at me, working again. Bliss.

Minor successes that these were, for me to work both beyond the deck edge and directly over it for a period of several hours with a variety of tools without losing a single thing overboard was a major triumph. Continuing to sail at full pace all the while. As soon as something placed in my left hand reaches near body temperature I can no longer feel its presence there at all, so I am inclined to drop things inadvertently. Alternatively, they will stay in my clenched hand for hours while I search everywhere for the lost item, only to discover it has been in my hand all along! To cap a really confidence-boosting day my sunsights gave a position exactly on the RDF bearing of the Chatham Islands – a good day.

'Daybreak makes all earth and sea, from shadow brings forth form.' Never had the dawn been so welcome to me in its arrival each day as here in the Southern Ocean. Squalls may come and squalls may go and problems with gear ditto, but being almost totally sight dependent whenever a two-handed effort was called for made daytime comparatively heaven. Night-times were tense times, and seemed long even in the southern summer. I tended to ease this mental burden by sailing undercanvassed through most nights unless the indications were towards good.

Periodic rain squalls, wind from the south-west at around 25 knots, moving comfortably under Yankee alone and the solar panel putting out 3–4 amps at times; 170 miles in a day and hardly trying – looking good. The calm spell following was also useful under Drifter/Multi-Purpose Spinnaker. I dropped the mainsail to replace some broken slide lashings, varnished the tiller again over the first temporary coats, tightened up all my shrouds after the stretching given by the rough weather down south, polished the brass and caught up on washing, too. It was interesting to watch an albatross cruising nearby in conditions so windless as barely to fill my Drifter at all, yet not needing a single flap of wings to help its endless glide. It must have been using the faint updraughts on the faces of approaching swells. What subtle skill. We were forced to drop all sail as for us there was no motive power there at all.

Cirrus wisps in the evening spoke of wind to come. I dropped the Drifter and reset the Yankee with full mainsail. A very light northerly had sprung up to give us progress. It was Christmas Eve and I felt warm inside, feeling the presence with me of all my friends. It felt so good this time with no long gap between farewells and departure, no false starts to fracture the rhythm of the sea.

Christmas Day saw me up at 4 a.m. to reset the Drifter and get us moving again, but heading almost south-east, back towards the cold. It was the start of an almost perfect day. The wind came in with greater gusto later, necessitating an unscheduled fancy water drop of the Drifter and a reset of my favourite, my windward-slicing Yankee blade. It was now blowing almost a typical Sydney summer nor'easter, even the sunsparkle on the water was the same. Sailing under single-reefed main plus Yankee, lee rail just dipping under at times, truly a windward wizard's heaven. And the motion – how smooth it felt sailing steadily to windward over a relatively calm sea in comparison with the manic rolling of running before in large breaking seas and an excess of wind.

A damper on the day was the discovery of water in the bilge, necessitating over 100 pumps. This may not sound much by normal standards but in thirteen years the bilge had never needed pumping at sea, so this sudden influx was a cause for concern. I hadn't noticed any leaks from the many holding-down bolts through the deck for deck fittings, but it was too late in the day to search properly. I decided to continue the search next day. Now was time for my first celebratory champagne. Not really for Christmas, but for having succeeded in leaving my previous turnback point well astern – and likewise our first cape.

With a temperature of 12 degrees the ocean was my ice-bucket, and with evening settling over an entirely non-threatening summer Sydney sea, contentment coursed through my veins. Any similarity with a Sydney summer nor'easter faded with sunset. Sipping champagne in the cockpit became too cold for comfort. I retreated below to the psychological warmth of the cabin, sitting by the hatch opening and looking astern, thoughts wandering freely.

The air is cold – the albatross wheeling – the sun is down, horizon glows, warm orange is the feeling . . . It is like heading up the second pitch of Bird of Prey, out here – no protection, no stopping, no turning back – what a glorious evening . . . The wind outside is ice, the dark enfolds, the albatross now circles, wheels unseen through night.

Morning found the wind a little further to the north and up to around 15 knots. The beautiful blade of a Yankee slicing us to windward to perfection, hard on the wind. This was the point of sailing where I had always made greatest gains when racing years before. It felt just as good now. A strengthening wind saw us go down to triple-reefed main plus Yankee, then down again to triple-reefed main and staysail. With an easing wind later, up went the Yankee again. This was fun.

The search for leaks did not go as well. Down below I succeeded in unearthing the equipment breakdown that would cause more sheer mental agony over the next couple of weeks in trying to rectify it, then, after conceding defeat, more daily stress than any other single aspect of the voyage. I discovered a small leak from the perimeter of the toilet pump.

The entry hatch to the cabin and the foredeck hatch I had designed like submarine hatches, with one thing paramount – keeping water out. Sacrificed to some extent in achieving this was ease of entry and exit. The problems in propping the hatch open with one hand and delicately manoeuvring a fully loaded toilet bucket outside without spills in rough weather, while at the same time exiting myself then rapidly closing the hatch behind me, had, I confess, not been considered at all.

The toilet pump had been set up to be usable as a bilge pump as well; thus if I could make no adequate repair I would have no spare bilge pump either. It has often been said that a bucket in the hands of a frightened man leaves all other bilge pumps for dead in terms of efficiency. But it is not much use in getting water out below floor level, and even at this level boat motion sloshing the water around would make life virtually impossible in the cabin, ruining or rendering useless all electrical equipment and nearly everything else stored aboard.

I wasn't convinced that I had found the main source of our leak and the weather was now too rough for a thorough search. Having dropped the Yankee, set the staysail and put two reefs in the main, it was time for a third. While putting in the third reef I noticed one halyard winch almost off the mast, and the leeward one at that. I quickly tacked to put it on the windward side, where gravity could help hold it until I returned with tools. The screw holding the drum and the internal workings of the winch together had almost undone. A bit of juggling to centre it, a brief burst with an Allen key to tighten it, and that was done.

Almost hove-to under triple-reefed main alone, it seemed a good time to deal with the toilet pump problem – I'll fix it almost as fast, thinks I. Even hove-to, the motion forward where my toilet is situated is not conducive to jobs requiring dexterity and fineness of touch. With *two* good hands. It was sheer hell, working for hours without a break, in a situation where nothing could be allowed to drop into the bilge below. If it did, it would be lost forever in a chaos of anchor rope and stores. At first, a tightening of the perimeter bolts along with a thick application of Vaseline between the halves of the pump casing was all I thought necessary. Even this took the whole day. And the leak remained.

OK! Next time a total dissembling of the pump and replacement of the diaphragm, inlet and exit valves and cover seal with a spare parts kit I had bought for such a time. Meanwhile, we were still bashing slowly to windward under triple-reefed mainsail and staysail, heading inexorably south back below latitude 45 degrees south, the barometer dropping. The wind remained steady the following day and after ten hours the replacements were done. I slept as one totally exhausted, mentally drained right out.

For a change, I next took on more pleasant tasks, catching enough rainwater to refill my main galley tank and the two-litre fruit juice containers drunk so far. Also, hand-sewed the staysail where stitching had chafed and rewhipped the ends of some halyards and sheets. Again we were beset by windlessness and my despair was deep. Hour after hour of slap, bang, chatter, rrrrasp, twang, whooosh, crack, thwack, clatter, rrrasp, as we rolled and pitched in totally confused swells. Showing no progress for all my efforts. I wrote in my log that I 'dips me lid' to the old clipper captains trying to gain easting in similar conditions, in vessels with no windward ability to speak of.

And the pump still leaked! The plastic lugs on the back of the pump to lock the tightening nuts weren't locking properly, it appeared, so again I removed the pump entirely from its hoses and replaced all the bolts with ones that could be tightened down hard, and it still leaked . . . I couldn't decide if a seal over the hole where water now came from had been sucked into the pump body or whether that hole was meant to be there as an air intake. Whatever, it leaked from there, so I again removed the pump, tapped a thread in the plastic of the pump body and sealed the hole with a stubby machine screw, but I didn't dare test it just yet.

Instead, I went crawling aft to where the transom plate, hull bottom plate and skeg plating met. With a torch I searched carefully along the seams. I had had a skeg plating weld open up minutely in the rough weather south of New Zealand during my previous attempt. This had been repaired, and had been very minor since the problem only opened up the hollow of the skeg, which I had filled with sump oil, to outside water. It could not leak water into the boat. But now? I had suspicions.

The noise and motion aft as the counter stern was slammed by wave after wave, the noise of the rudder and self-steering rudders resisting being forced from side to side, and everything even slightly loose rolling and clunking made it an almost unbearable excursion. Combined with the fact that it was well nigh impossible to move up there, hemmed in by four cockpit drain tubes, stored ropes, spare solar panel and more. It is not a part of the boat I have ever visited for pleasure.

With a head torch, a spare torch and eyes as my only tools I reached the stern. Squirt, trickle . . . squirt, trickle . . . every time our stern slammed down on to a wave a little squirt and trickle of water came in from, presumably, tears in the welds joining transom plate to hull plate to skeg side plates. On both sides of the hull/skeg/transom joints. The top of the skeg is in effect the base of a cantilever, thus where the stresses would be greatest when thrown about in rough seas. The stresses from the rudder, that is – hence my reason for looking there. I set about drying the area as best I could (impossible) and laid down a thick bed of silicone over the whole area, hoping with many coats ultimately to get enough to stick and dam the leak.

What if this were only the start of a process that would tear the skeg substantially off? I thought very hard and long at this point . . . It seemed that a year that had started with failure was heading to end the same way. No, no, I would never get the chance again. I must continue . . . I had been spoilt up to now with a non-leaking boat, I rationalised. Most yachts leak a little continually through stern glands that I had avoided having, so I must learn to live with a leak for this trip and just hope it didn't increase or my bilge pump break down too! These were not really the thoughts I wished to be having to consider so early in the voyage, but there they were and they weren't going to go away until the voyage was over one way or another! At least they were a very successful distraction from the still unresolved toilet pump/spare bilge pump problem! Ah, c'est la vie. Tomorrow was not another day this time. It was another year, and I was determined to make it a year of successes. This year concluded with only 5 miles of progress to show for over twelve hours of unremitting struggle against confused seas in misty windless conditions. It could not get worse.

Flashes of sunsparkle on water to the north, to windward as the first zephyrs of incoming nor'easter ruffled the otherwise glassy calm of a Pittwater morning. Summer holidays, schooldays and soon I would be around at the sailing club rigging, then setting off alone, while conditions were still mild enough for single-handing the VJ with spinnaker practice in mind. By late morning or early afternoon when conditions were generally too windy for single-handing the 'Jay' for someone as small and light as I was, I would return to the clubhouse. It being holiday time, there was almost always someone around whom I knew, so I would then borrow a Manly Junior and continue my solo explorations of wind and wave into the peak wind period of mid to late afternoon.

On race days, if the wind was light early, I would again single-hand until race time; if not, me and my forward hand would spend the time blasting around at speed with spinnaker set on screaming reaches between practice gybes, sets and stows. We worked well together as a team and the other points of sail needed little practice since we sailed together so frequently.

They were happy days, and the memory of them most welcome as I worked below in the stern region, laying down layer after layer of silicone in an effort to stem the leaks. Outside, in the world of the present, conditions remained wet, windless and grey, with large swells from the south-west, south-east and north-west heaping irregularly in a triumph of confusion. I winced each time they slammed under the stern, imagining the way each thump and squirt of water was rendering my repairs useless with no drying time to form a bond. I pumped the toilet to run salt water through it as a test. The first few tentative pumps were fine and then the fatal sound again – a hiss of air, a leak somewhere, somewhere a faulty seal.

My left eye had been extremely bloodshot and painful for days now and no eyedrops in my medical kit had any effect. It was time for stronger medicine. By deduction I arrived at the most suitable antibiotic in my kit, Erithromycin, and took some. Not having taken any antibiotics for years, it should fix the problem fast. A rain squall during the afternoon gave us the longest distance sailed in one stretch for the past three days – 5 miles!

Day after day.

An extract from the log for that day reflects my extreme despair at this time, the conditions being *impossible* for progress. Or anything. Even reading in my bunk was impossible due to the violently random motion:

Tues 1/1/91, 6 p.m. (WILL IT EVER END?): The tops of the waves are exploding into breaks all around us as the swells from different directions try and rush through each other, heaping into pyramids and disintegrating upwards as bits of each swell-train keep going and overtake the momentarily heaped mass below, or get left behind as the swell below penetrates the one from the opposite or side direction. All grey, not enough wind for self-steering, hand-steering in the cold until I drop sail and lash tiller etc. again for the night.

9 p.m. after just finishing yet another attempt at fixing my toilet pump, in the dark by torch light, I discovered that rain had really started to come down. The wind shifted and died yet again, heading us back where we came from for the second time today. Tried to tack but on the other tack can hold only north-west or worse, so gybed back around and am now heading due south. I have given up for the night. If any wind comes I will try and get her to steer a course again, otherwise to hell with it – the leaking boat, the voyage, the god-damned impossible weather. Damn the whole bloody lot of them.

I noted the next day that I had been able to sail only one full day without dropping sail, lashing tiller, etc., due to windlessness since 24 December. I also crawled aft to discover water still forcing its way in under my silicone. Without being able to dry the area or degrease it perfectly, there was no more I could do. I had used almost three full tubes of silicone and adding more would obviously not help. I would just have to count the number of bilge pumps required each day from now on and hope they remained steady and that the dud welds would tear no further. I also noted in the log that for the past eight days I had yet to make good even 10 miles in any one day!

So much for my hopes of a speedy crossing to the Horn and getting back out of the Southern Ocean before winter set in. I had been reading Robin Knox-Johnston's book of his circumnavigation in Suhaili in 1968. His despair at the 'unscheduled' easterlies around here prompted me to compose this little ditty while at the helm:

> I've got the Knoxy-Johnston blues today
> the Knoxy-Johnston blues I say –
> these easterlies are in my way
> and bloody calms where should be gales,
> the Knoxy-Johnston blues today . . .

On the good news front, I had an aesthetic victory for a sailor in completely removing the bubble in my cabin table compass. Filled with happiness over this, as it is usually very hard to remove a compass bubble entirely, I spent the late afternoon on deck and was rewarded with a visit from about a dozen dolphins who hung around for nearly half an hour despite us not having enough speed for them to play.

Just before dark a stiff south-easterly arrived, and we roared off north-east under triple-reefed main and Yankee, covering 80 miles overnight, and in comfort too! At midnight I had a wonderful spell on deck, watching some strange light effects through the cloud cover, and thought that I might be watching the first aurora of the voyage. Shortly after, the disc of an almost full moon appeared through a thinner patch in the clouds and I was forced to conclude that the optical tricks were all due to it. Including a brightness near the horizon that had me thinking of 'ice-blink', despite our latitude.

The wind eased next morning to a day of beautiful light weather summer sailing, and I was tempted to dry and clean and silicone one more time. This would definitely be the last attempt at leak repairs for that stern region. Hopefully I would be finding no more. It was calm enough to attempt some anti-rust treatment in places on deck, and do some washing, drying and airing as well. A happy, relaxing day.

On the following day I recorded that it had now become my longest single-handed (or any-handed) voyage so far, with 2,880 miles covered. I also noted that attempting to fix the toilet pump, due to the intricate left-hand usage continually required and the threat of losing irreplaceable parts, had become the equally most stress-producing event of the voyage – along with rounding the bottom of New Zealand in continual bad weather and uncertainty as to position. On the lighter side I noted that working all day on the toilet pump was good for one thing, reducing one's appetite. Apart from a few light snacks I ate virtually nothing during these attempts at repair.

Standing outside the hatch that evening, braced against the dodger frame, I marvelled at the smoothness and the power of *Little Wing*'s drive, close reaching at speed into the night. The swells now long and even, hills and dales that we could sail up one side and down the other without pause or bumps. Choosing to ignore the falling barometer was easy – this was sailing – people would kill for this!

At midnight I could ignore the fall no more. It was time to reef the main, but having done this it was not enough. I dropped the Yankee, set the staysail, and all seeming fine, returned below. Not for long. In rapidly increasing wind I dropped the mainsail completely and under staysail alone drove on through a rough and windy night.

Morning revealed not only a barometer still dropping, but a wild grey scene of breakers and rain squalls surrounding us. In a gesture of defiance to the conditions outside I worked forward all morning on another idea to repair the pump, until I could ignore the conditions no longer. For the first time down came the staysail and up went the little bulletproof jib, my ultimate storm weapon, in the conditions for which I had designed it. How pleasant and easy the motion became as we slowly ran before. With no more sail reductions to worry about it was time for sleep.

Refreshed in the morning it was time for another inspired idea. Alas, it leaked as badly as ever. And not only that, in trying to shift the Y-valve which switches it from toilet-pump use to bilge-pump use, the Y-valve broke half open so it would not work as either. I tried to remove the entire valve and replace it with a spare, but when my climbing friends had helped me put the plumbing together long before, we had so thoroughly heat-softened and fitted the hoses to the valve that they were immovable in this cold. So. A couple of desperate hours later the valve was dismantled enough for me to force it fully open again, then reassembled and the decision made: from here on I would use a bucket and concentrate on the sailing – I could do no more at sea.

Once again, the mists of the Pacific enshrouded us in their moist and almost windless hold. Through a grey entombment of mist and drizzle with the sun a mere silvery glow, we reached eastward, making slow miles through the atmospheric gloom. With the Genoa set we would be making much better progress, but I would only have to get caught with it up once in a sudden squall and that would be its end. I could not afford such wastage for the sake of a few miles, a few days, even weeks.

These periods of mist and drizzle in conjunction with light winds from the northern quadrants were associated with warm fronts coming through in advance of the cold. But whereas they seemed to last forever, the clear weather and wind following the passage of the cold seemed to vanish almost at once. These windless drizzling mists seemed the dominant feature of sailing in the mid-Forties latitudes this summer, making progress a continual struggle. I was trying to keep at around latitude 44 degrees south where the water was around 12.5 degrees and the weather generally a bit warmer and a bit more bearable. I had been unable to pick up the time signal stations WWV or WWVH at all across the Pacific so far, but did succeed in catching Radio Australia a couple of times, even listening to the end of the day's play in a cricket test on one occasion while chasing a time signal.

My hand was giving me problems in the cold, with chilblains appearing to be hell-bent on completely eating through a couple of fingers as they refused all attempts at healing. The frequent wetting they received from the fresh water of rain during work on deck effectively prevented any scar tissue forming, as did the wearing of rubber gloves, as they 'sweated' inside. I noted in my log at this stage that the main contributor to moments of hell was the unpredictability of my hand. Never knowing when it was going to cause the next disaster by dropping, losing or spilling things of great value. It imparted a continuous 'background noise' of uncertainty and unease, not to mention fear at times on deck. But we were making progress, even if slowly and were now on to the last chart of the voyage (apart from a plotting sheet to help span a void between charts) on which no land at all appeared. This at least indicated easting being made. I began to spend quite a bit of time poring over my large-scale charts of the Tierra del Fuego/Patagonian Channels/Cape Horn and Beagle Channel regions. These were the areas that had first fired my enthusiasm as a child, and how they still fascinated. I was already feeling like returning to explore them, but not alone. I hoped that I would still feel the same about them in another month or so, after Cape Horn.

The drizzle patch we were in this time was proving wonderfully consistent. For five days straight we sailed just a shade off hard on the wind, single-reefed main and Yankee, requiring only minor course adjustments and changes in sail trim, not changes in area. Whereas my previous attempt at this voyage had ended up a circumnavigation of the Tasman on the port tack, this trip was seemingly becoming a circumnavigation of the globe on the port tack! Apart from a couple of short tacks away from shore to clear southern New Zealand, I couldn't recall sailing on starboard in nearly 4000 miles. The motion was steady and candle-lit dinners every night were the norm. It was cold, yes, but comfortable.

Unfortunately, things that stay up must also come down, including barometers, and its turn was now. By sunset the wind died almost completely away, reviving the almost forgotten frustrated feeling of slatting around in windlessness. A mixed residue of swells kept whatever wind there was from filling the sails and we moved nowhere. Despite the lack of wind, I took in a second reef before it was completely dark, being sure that more was to come. At midnight, sensing a change in our motion, I went on deck to discover the wind now from the south-west but no increase in strength. Back to my bunk after self-steering adjustments only.

At 4 a.m. there was definitely more wind, so up on deck again to take in the third reef, and after staying awhile to see if all was well and that conditions were remaining stable, back to my bunk again. But I still wasn't happy. Up I went again and dropped the mainsail completely, so that next morning found us doing that old rolling, reeling, rumbling, rhythmic, Yankee-only ride, and moving miles, all smiles. 'Where, oh where is some bloody steady wind?' Noon found us becalmed again, dinner calm and candle-lit, barometer dropping. Still.

Midnight: up for my usual course check, look around and adjustments; all was well. The wind maybe a little stronger, but that could have been just darkness distorting the scene. Barometer steady. 2 a.m.: wind definitely stronger, but not enough to worry us under Yankee and triple-reefed main. Barometer steady. 3 a.m.: wind definitely increasing but I go back to bed hoping to hold on another forty-five minutes until daylight, since I find it very nerve-wracking dropping a big sail like the Yankee in the dark. 4 a.m.: wind from the north and still strengthening at first light, so I dropped Yankee and put up staysail. Feeling uneasy with the barometer falling rapidly again, I dropped the mainsail also and continued under staysail alone. Barometer plummeting, rain pouring, spray flying, me worrying.

Forward motion at a reasonable speed helped the self-steering a lot. Also, it gave more course options, so instead of running off before this impending gale under bare poles, I went back on deck, dropped the staysail and set the bulletproof jib, adjusting our course to a broad reach taking the waves from astern at an angle of 20–30 degrees.

By 7 a.m. the wind had swung to the north-west, with fleeting appearances by the sun adding stark contrasts and highlights to the truly magnificent spectacle of undiluted wilderness on the rampage. We seemed to be coping, so I retreated below to try and get some rest.

At 9.30 a.m. I had to go on deck again to sheet the bulletproof in a dash harder. Never had I seen an ocean so rough. Although the bulletproof jib is approximately one-eighth the area of my Genoa, it was blowing so hard that even using my most powerful, oversized winches, I could barely tighten it in at all. Deck was not a place to stay. Solid water was everywhere – hurtled through the air by wind, cascading down wave fronts, toppling from above. It was frightening, it was chaotic, and inevitably we were rolled. Not a 360-degree roll, just a roll down, with the mast about 30 degrees below horizontal, but enough for a fright. My ventilators and Dorade boxes on top of the cabin were completely underwater for the first time, water gushing into the cabin as down became up and their operation reversed.

The clatter of falling objects normally so securely stowed was the only sound I could recall. It was very quiet and peaceful for a moment. No wind whistling in the rigging, no crash of waves, and the turquoise out of the cabin windows quite breathtakingly beautiful. I regretted not having a camera at the ready, it was so good! These were impressions of an instant, we were not down for long.

For nearly thirty hours, I tried to remain in my bunk, cold, wet, just hoping nothing would break to necessitate another journey up on deck. Several more

145

times we were rolled down beyond 90 degrees, but after the first, the surprise was gone. I had stuffed the openings of the vents into the cabin with rags, so little water came in. Late the following afternoon, conditions had eased enough on deck to gybe and head more east, but the bulletproof remained set as the wind was still extremely strong. With wind of that strength the trailing log was often blown clean out of the water and I spent an exciting half-hour working out beyond the stern perched on my self-steering frame, freeing it from entanglement with the self-steering rudder. The sky was almost clear by sunset and the swells, although still large and sometimes breaking heavily, were regular again. Almost tame. We sauntered off east for a quiet night before sailing again in earnest next morning.

The Southern Ocean, having reminded me of its reality, its potential roughness, now proceeded to show me some of its more pleasant and gentle facets. I rapidly increased our sail area in stages next morning, from bulletproof alone to staysail alone, to Yankee alone, to Yankee plus triple-reefed mainsail. I could have coped with more mainsail area, but didn't want to blanket the Yankee excessively and cause a bout of slatting and chafe problems. It was an absolutely glorious day to be at sea, with strong sunshine, moderate 10–15 knot breeze, and delightfully warm out of the wind. I was near the point in the Pacific where the Antarctic Convergence reaches furthest north, thus the air and water temperatures were cooler than expected: the water was down to only 10.7 degrees again and the breeze chilly to match. Here also I was skirting the edge and trespassing into the region of possible encounters with icebergs, so I tried to maintain a course a dash north of east to keep us clear.

At about longitude 100 degrees west, the line of extreme limits for icebergs dips down again rapidly towards the Horn, so I was aiming to keep at around latitude 45 degrees south until I too set off on my ride down the Big Dipper to 57–58 degrees south to get around Diego Ramirez and Cabo de Hornos. Then up and out. The stars that night were possibly the clearest of the voyage so far, really looking the part of 'the Stars like Dust', dusting the heavens from horizon to horizon when I went up on deck around midnight for the usual course check and general look around. On deck, however, was not a place to linger, unless I changed completely into warmer clothes. The night wind cut through me cold as ice, so after a short but wonder-filled stay I retreated below where, despite being uninsulated, it seemed heated and warm, just by virtue of being protected from the wind.

Boat chores kept me busy on these calm days. Washing, airing, drying, pulling in the log and oiling the mechanism, checking for chafe on the line and adjusting, if necessary. Also, refilling the kerosene feed tank for the stove and the bottles I used for topping up the lamps. Then there was checking and putting more silicone around potential leak spots on deck and around the deck plug electrical connections, tightening and rewhipping self-steering control lines to eliminate stretch, replacing broken slide lashings on my mainsail and replacing anti-chafe protection on headsail sheets. All of these were pleasant chores in moderate weather and sunshine, but most of them became almost impossible in the more normal weather down here. These days of mild weather were welcome, therefore, despite the slower progress. It seemed stable enough weather to set the Drifter again, so I gained some miles back. Although sorely tempted to leave it set all night, I dropped it just before total dark, as a night-time drop of such a large and light sail would almost certainly result in terrible tearing if the wind strengthened.

For the first time since my wintering in Hobart in 1986, condensation reared its ugly head as a nuisance problem. I had noticed a few drops coming down on to me during the bad storm as I lay curled in my bunk, but virtually every opening had been sealed then, so it was not all that surprising. The air must have been very moist here to cause drips even with the aft hatch open its usual few inches. And there were lots of them. I had to wipe little puddles off my chart quite frequently to avoid damage to the paper. Hopefully these conditions were unusual and I would not find the problem a continuous one. Maybe the experts had a point in thinking me crazy not insulating for this voyage! The southernmost part would soon be left astern, though, and I prefer to see any corrosion problems as they occur, early, and not have them hidden behind layers of insulation and fancy woodwork – unnoticed until too late.

If I were choosing to remain in cold climates for any length of time, yes, I would insulate. Living in the cold combined with continual damp would rapidly become unbearable. For this voyage, however, warm clothes would have to do the job of keeping me warm, and hopefully, ventilation would keep excessive condensation at bay.

On the afternoon of 17 January I was overcome for no apparent reason by an overwhelming feeling of sadness. Nothing in my small world, bounded as it was on all sides by a limitless horizon and a clear sky, could have caused this sudden attack. I only hoped that no tragedy had befallen a member of family or friend and that these were the distant vibrations of the event I was receiving. I was really quite upset, and my daily run, instead of bringing its usual bubbling joy, barely lightened my mood. Whatever it was, I would be none the wiser until my return and we had a long way still to go. We sailed on.

The following day was another milestone along the way – our fiftieth day at sea. But there was little reason to celebrate. Conditions outside, with a high barometer and light north-north-easterly wind combined with an overall grey-ness and drizzle, were very similar to those immediately preceding the last big gale. I aimed to get beyond 115 degrees west and off the present chart before it arrived if possible. At least it would then seem as if progress was being made. I wrote in my log that if we made it through the next fifty days in particular, or 100 if I were to include our next major cape, the Cape of Storms, only then would I feel confident of being able to finish the journey.

Not until these two cruxes were behind us did I really feel any certainty as to the outcome. It was still a long, long way to go and so much could happen yet.

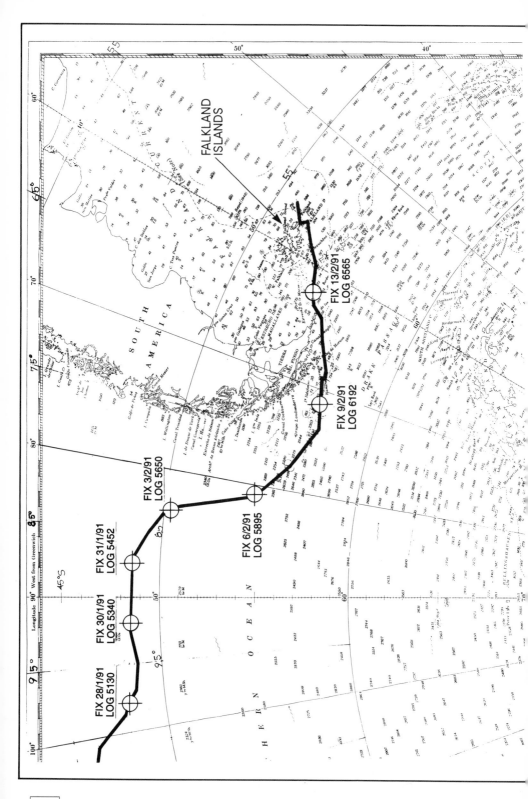

FALKLAND ISLANDS

FIX 13/2/91
LOG 6565

FIX 9/2/91
LOG 6192

FIX 3/2/91
LOG 5650

FIX 6/2/91
LOG 5895

FIX 31/1/91
LOG 5452

FIX 30/1/91
LOG 5340

FIX 28/1/91
LOG 5130

SOUTH AMERICA

Our speed had been very slow so far due to all the becalmed days and very light headwinds, and it was annoying to know how much better our average would have been had I chosen to sail with the Genoa ready to set.

This voyage, however, was not a race and every last little thing aboard had been paid for by my own work efforts, not sponsor's PR dollars. Everything needing repair or replacement would need to be paid for and/or carried out by me also, further reason for care. Besides, until very recently the fashion for destructive, sponsor-financed voyaging would have been considered sheer bad seamanship. I still wanted to complete the journey as quickly as possible, and sailed hard whenever conditions allowed, but not to the point of serious damage. With no radio to call for help, and no life-raft to abandon ship either, my priorities were naturally biased towards seamanship and conservation of resources instead of the throw-away mentality of the age.

I managed to get a time signal from Radio Australia in the afternoon, still not being able to pick up the American stations WWV and WWVH. It was pleasing to see that my el cheapo watch hadn't changed its rate of gain at all in over a year!

Cape Horn and its dangers must have been starting to occupy more of my mind as we approached the point where the descent would begin. Days of greyness and drizzle, but otherwise mild and reasonable for sailing, I now found very depressing, full of foreboding. I consulted Young Mist about most things requiring decisions, and this gave the feeling that we were working out the problems together. It eased the loneliness, which was strong at times, and also helped to clarify my thoughts before action. I made our bunk properly after airing the doonas one day and what luxury it was to sleep again between sheets in a neatly made bunk, Young Mist looking like a princess, tucked in between the pillows and cheering me up through the grey afternoon.

My trusty old wet-weather gear, once the Rolls-Royce of such gear, had now become so porous as to have me wet and cold after even minor excursions on deck. No patching seemed to help, and it didn't seem possible for all the water to come in through my new sewing. I tried the spare new pants for a change. What luxury! What a pleasure! How enjoyable deck work became! My clothing inside remained dry. The jacket of the old gear I continued to wear for its inbuilt safety harness; leaks in the top had trouble getting through jumpers and track-suit tops so were not as noticeable. It was the dry pants for a change that brought joy. Nothing wet with salt water really dried out down here in the cold.

I only wished I had remembered to bring my sea boots. The wet-suit boots I had became very smelly, so I preferred bare feet on deck. Then chilblains attacked my toes to such an extent that I couldn't wear anything. 'Oh well, it won't be this cold all the way,' I tried to reassure my toes!

While lashing the mainsail down securely one day after a hasty drop in a squall, I almost dropped myself. My hand slipped unexpectedly on the wet lashing, sending my fist hurtling into the side of my face, smashing my glasses and nearly knocking me out! Luckily all my glasses from 1966 onward are nearly equal for clarity, so I just switched to a new old pair from 1973. My present and only optical sunglasses are a set of 1966 lenses put in new frames after the plastic of the old ones had just powdered away and disintegrated with the years.

Speaking of disintegration with the years, I felt a little twinge in my shoulder while rehoisting the Yankee during a sail change and ignored it completely since I had never hurt a muscle in years of climbing, where the strain could be very great making some moves. The following morning, however, found me a cripple, and even though it was my left arm, I needed it to steady myself while my right did the work. I couldn't move it enough to put on a sock without being almost stopped by the pain, and all other movements hurt as much or more. I managed to drop all sail except staysail, and went back to bed. Maybe rest would cure it in time for the descent that lay ahead.

For two days we dribbled along sorely undercanvassed while I tried not to move at all, but this was impossible aboard a small boat at sea. When the wind next eased I could resist the temptation no longer, and carefully reset the Yankee, and the mainsail at third reef. If there was anything more depressing than being confined below, convalescing, it was keeping tally of all the miles going to waste and the need for haste in completing as much of the voyage as possible before the long nights of winter made it hell.

Not all cold fronts herald their arrival with dramatics. Some of them crept up on us very subtly indeed, with no change in wind strength initially and such a gradual swing in direction, normally a backing from north-west to south-west, that the first clue to their arrival was the unexpected change in boat motion. With the new wind we would be suddenly pounding into the old waves head on instead of them approaching comfortably from astern, because wind-vane self-steering systems hold the course constant in relation to apparent wind – hence the danger of subtle wind shifts when depending on them near land. It is wise to consult the compass often, especially with land about.

The first time a front arrived in this gradual manner I had been writing up my log in the cabin below. There came seeping into my consciousness a rhythmical bash, crash, bash as we slammed head on into waves not apparent moments before. Crossing the wake of a ship? Self-steering not working? I raced up on deck to find out. Ah ha! A glance at the compass revealed all, reminding me of the barometer that had been dropping steadily as advance warning of a front. Having adjusted our course, I stayed on deck to await developments – in these latitudes I did not trust this mild-mannered change as being all there was.

The first thing to notice before the wind backed further into the south and strengthened, necessitating a reduction in sail, was that we had crossed an invisible line into a new avian territory. Hundreds of a species of petrel new to me were dancing in the new wind of the change, playing with the turbulence created by my sail. Banking and stalling, diving, swooping in and out, then soaring off alone to altitude. A later study of my *Seabirds – an identification guide* showed them to be Stejneger's petrels most probably, from the features I could see. With their dark caps and white underwings, they reminded me of the fairy tern who visits Bernard Moitessier in *The Long Way*.

Unfortunately, I had to interrupt their play. With both hands almost frozen into uselessness I eventually succeeded in dropping and lashing the Yankee securely, then setting the staysail. Under staysail alone, through a frozen grey seascape, we drove our way eastward during the late afternoon and into night.

It was the first time we had been on starboard tack almost since memory began. Every movement around the cabin, every placement of object or reach for security had to be reversed. Hoping I would soon get used to it, after a simple dinner I decided to sleep. Moving around was just so strange!

Chapter Nineteen

Riding the Dipper

Waking to bright sunshine with a brisk westerly blowing, it was like a perfect Blue Mountains morning. I could easily imagine myself brewing a mug of billy tea and warming myself by the campfire prior to setting out on the day's bushwalking or climbing with my friends. How often the memories of those happy weekends together sustained me when the feeling of ultra-aloneness, normally invigorating to me, threatened to become tainted with despair.

This morning though was a joyful one with the conditions almost screaming at me: 'Go for it, kid, now is the time to start your run.' Down came the staysail, back up went the Yankee and our course changed to south-east. We were aimed for 'the Corner' at last, rolling our easting out astern at a comfortable 5–7 knots with mainsail up also at the third reef until dark, when surrounding rain squalls made me decide to drop it for the night. Yankee alone was a more forgiving rig for the self-steering if a squall should happen along. We were close enough to 5000 miles on our way.

The decision having been made, the priority now was miles. Miles put astern of us as quickly as possible, as many as possible until the Corner was safely rounded. A few things decided to hinder this plan. Firstly, the weather once again set out to show the uglier side of its nature, forcing numerous sail changes as rain squall after rain squall overburdened us with wind accompanied by torrential rain. Having shortened sail and adjusted our course for the greater wind strength in the squalls, this would leave us undercanvassed in between and wallowing in chaotic cross seas, requiring the procedure to be reversed.

It could have been worse. Since nights were very short now, most changes could be made in some vestige of daylight. My left arm, however, was now almost immovable again due to insufficient recovery time, making these frequent sail changes very painful. I continued to sail undercanvassed, thus annoyingly slowly, that this problem might be cured. Sail reductions were made in larger jumps than necessary for the same reason – for example, reducing from Yankee straight down to bulletproof in one leap at the onset of a blow instead of trying staysail first to see if it could cope. Losing miles to buy healing time.

Despite these problems, each day had its moments of pure joy. Up on deck delighting in the way we moved through the water, reacted to the wind or danced with the waves as we surged and surfed the never-ending miles, one by one leaving them astern. At these times I would think I was in very heaven and feel lacking in nothing at all. Except when I shifted my attention to the other wings that shared our world. Compared with the locals' grace and perfect adaptation to the Southern Ocean we were obviously just visitors, transients passing through.

From the tiny, seemingly fragile and moth-like storm petrels flitting uncon-cernedly amongst breaking seas that had me at times apprehensive, through the larger but equally fragile-looking Antarctic and fairy prions right on up to the majesty of the great wandering albatross, these local wings fitted their world to perfection. With no more than the feathers that covered them, they not only survived, but thrived in conditions hardly bearable to a human even when protected by the shelter and imported technology of a *Little Wing* and her contents. It was a humbling observation, this demonstration of the inadequacy of unprotected humankind.

And any person incapable of seeking and finding their own non-destructive solutions using their own creativity is no more advanced than unprotected human-kind. Whether this deficiency be due to the pressure and control exerted by the media, religion or society in general, the result will be the same. Creative intelligence is our only protection, our only key to survival. Individual, species or planet.

Ever since the last big one, the gale that repeatedly rolled the cabin-top Dorades underwater for the first time, I had wondered occasionally how much harder we would be hit before getting back to more civilised latitudes. This concern was almost a continuous thread through my thinking now that the descent had begun. My mind reviewed the experiences of those who preceded me and lived to write of their experience and methods to survive. The masters who sailed for the love and not for the fame, in an era when all was experimental and small-boat voyaging new.

Vito Dumas and his sleigh-ride through gale after gale without ever getting down to bare poles. Maintaining speed for manoeuvrability and staying at the helm, unprotected, as required through thick and thin. A true master seaman whose choice of tactics, harmonising with his vessel and her ways, ensured survival.

The great Bernard Moitessier, a next-generation disciple of Dumas and the 'run before at speed' philosophy, was converted to this school of thought only after trying the more conventional 'slow her with warps towed astern' system and along with his wife Françoise, almost meeting their demise. His ideas, as expressed in *Cape Horn, the Logical Route*, had instant appeal to me for a couple of reasons.

Firstly, ever since my days of racing Skates, I have held the belief that for maximum performance each wave has to be taken on its merits and dealt with on its own terms in choosing a course over or around. This proved to be the key to safety in the Moitessiers' survival situation, with performance in their case being equated with safety. One cannot weave a course without some speed.

Secondly, his way of taking waves on the quarter so that large breakers would not thrust *Joshua* straight forward stern over bow in a pitch-pole situation, but rather slew her safely sideways using the fullness of the waterlines and some of the higher diagonals forward in a way equivalent to the turned-up end of a ski, also made sense from my observations. It was akin to the way I would pull off a wave that was closing out ahead of me in my surfboard-riding youth. The necessity being to have waterlines and relevant diagonals sufficiently full forward to have this ski effect, yet not be so full as to be detrimental to windward performance.

This was one of my earliest design considerations when working out my hull lines. The amount of fullness ultimately chosen was derived from years of observation and comparison, combined with a hefty dose of intuition as to what felt right to achieve one without sacrificing the other.

Little Wing was designed to harmonise with the ocean, its waves and weather, not to take advantage of loopholes in totally artificial regulations such as ocean-racing rating rules. These have no relevance to the natural world, and this is why so many ocean-racing yachts or designs derived from these false values come to grief or are useless in true survival conditions. The competitive situation of racing is, I agree, the only way to learn the finer points of boat handling and racing tactics, but after some years of racing and winning, surely there are other things to learn, other goals to strive for, that are equally worthy of study?

I have only raced *Little Wing* once, almost twenty-one years after my last race in the Skate, and how satisfying it was to gobble the competition up again, to windward, as in the blessed days! It was as though I had last raced yesterday, and so satisfying to work the *Wing* through those more racing designs in harbour-racing conditions far more suited to them.

I digress. Another whose experiences in these waters provided much food for thought from the first stages of design through to the present was Jerome Poncet and his experience upside down for a long period in *Damien* during one of their several rollings, near South Georgia. As previously mentioned, this incident was a crucial design influence in aiming for instability when upside down. Although I had read the stories of the others – Smeetons, Lewis, 'Carronade', Robinson, Chichester, Naomi James, Hiscocks, etc – none of these became conscious influences on either the design or sailing of *Little Wing*. Except Robin Knox-Johnston, and the addition of a bowsprit and outer forestay to shift my centre of effort further forward for better self-steering with sheet-to-tiller gear when and if Mr Monitor had a breakdown. I did not manage to read Alec Rose's *My Lively Lady* until after my return, but enjoyed it when I finally found a copy.

Cabo de Hornos was waiting. Would we be struck down by the Ultimate Gale or the Ultimate Sea before we made good our rounding and thence our escape? The intensity of living each day of this final approach was amazing. Every millibar jumped by the barometer, every cloud forming or dissipating in the sky, every swell increasing or decreasing in size, or starting up a cross sea from a new direction, had meaning, was full of inferences to be drawn and tactics to be evolved ahead of time. It was a mix of experiencing, deducing and tactical planning – invigorating, exhausting and exhilarating at times. Each new factor entered the game as a new problem to be dealt with, and our progress depended on assimilating all these factors as they arose and planning ahead to cope with others not yet arisen. We sailed on . . .

One sunlit morning, while I was changing up from the bulletproof for more speed, Señor de Hornos gave me notice, and a warning, that he had woken, was aware of my coming. It was by means of a little tragedy, with a lesson attached, and made it the saddest day of the voyage.

Having downed the bulletproof as the latest gale faded to more manageable proportions, the Yankee was almost hoisted and ready for my dash aft to the cockpit to sheet it home, halyard winch handle in hand – I use the one winch handle for all winches to avoid leaving any around to be lost – but damn! I had caught the Yankee sheets under the bulletproof lashings and it wouldn't sheet in. I raced back forward to free the sheets and drop the Yankee again to sort out the mess if necessary. Crack, crack, crack – the flailing sheets whipped through the air as the Yankee flapped uncontrolled. Ducking and weaving I worked my way forward to sort it all out, ever afraid of another bad knock on my head. They say you don't recover from a second head injury anywhere near as well as the first, and although I chose to believe nothing else of the negatives the medics tried to load me with, this warning deserved caution. Thwack, it had gotted me. Thwap, ouch! That was hard! My precious bini that had been brought back from Chile by my mother and had sailed so many miles, through so many storms, went flying towards the sea. I couldn't let go the end of the Yankee halyard, in my right hand to snatch it out of the air. My left was incapable of speed and finesse. Over it went. I tried running aft to hook it aboard with a foot as we sailed past, but my lifeline brought me up short. Damn! I couldn't go about or gybe until the sheet problem was fixed, so I quickly checked our course for a reciprocal search and went back to the tangle, glancing astern as I worked to keep the bini in sight. Finally, I gybed and aimed back towards the spot. For over an hour I searched back and forth, back and forth, but the wind was strong and so small a thing next to invisible among the 'white horses' everywhere. So, so sad. So sad; but it was a lesson. How easily I could lose myself overboard and be seeing that scene in reverse: *Little Wing* sailing off into the distance as I floundered in freezing water, waiting to die – of cold, long before drowning. I reset our course towards the south, hoping that this would be the only sacrifice demanded for our passage.

The endless procession of white-capped swells around us and their grandeur towering above as they passed by reminded me this morning, along with the chill in the wind, of the Wolgan Valley. Of driving into the valley, adventure in the air. One area was even referred to as 'Cape Horn'!

The days passed. Even with the spurs dug right in to make maximum progress, the intensity of observation and deduction necessary to optimise tactics had a marked time-dilating effect. Contributing also was the sheer length of the days down here. With night proper becoming almost non-existent, the mental effort seemed full on and almost without let-up, lacking anywhere near a normal nightly rest. Spray flew as I pushed us to the limit under Yankee alone, trying not to reduce sail further if at all possible. I was trying to make up for a couple of days of mostly light and variable winds, and now my hull design was in test again, testing to see how she coped with the Moitessier method of running before at speed, taking the waves and breakers on the quarter. A test in tamer conditions than the survival ones of the last gale, just tame enough to observe carefully. I felt the wind and seas were enough, combined with more sail area than was prudent for the conditions, to gauge her reactions in more severe circumstances.

Standing, facing forward, braced against the dodger frame, I watched as we took off and surfed on wave after wave as we hurtled our easting down. This was fun. I watched her carefully when cross seas hit and when she was suddenly rolled and heeled. In complete control she just schussed off regardless, her heeled waterlines forward acting like the turned-up end of a ski. Just as planned. In these conditions it was far more comfortable mentally being up on deck, and I spent most of this day there. In the cabin below you couldn't see what was causing all the different noises and changes in motion, and the explosion of occasional waves over the cabin was dramatic and tension-producing. Way beyond reason when the full situation was observed from on deck.

Some cross-sea explosions would sweep over the cabin completely, from bow to stern, even though we were running before with the main swell direction coming from roughly 20 degrees off dead astern. The combinations of waves down here never ceased to surprise. Literally anything seemed possible once wind and wave were up and running wild.

Our wake shining silver through the moonlit hills, the heavens ablaze with stars, and the flash and sparkle of phosphorescence as we forged our way through the night – all made for wonderful moments in the cockpit at night. But with the water temperature down to 9 degrees and the air about the same, it was not a place to stay long once the spray started flying. Even the warm pink glow from the compass light, reminding me of the warm glow of a friendship forming, could not hold me out there for long when I was spray-drenched and cold. Chilblains were still eating through my left-hand fingers and my toes. I tried to keep them warmer and dryer below. My left shoulder was also still bad, so I avoided most deck work to give it a chance. It could well be needed *in toto* very soon.

Leaving aside for a moment the infernal rolling inherent in running before large and confused seas in strong winds – which you tend not to notice after a while until a super-charged cross sea catches you just as you are engaged in a task needing precision – the sailing itself down here was really quite terrific. Inspiring even, to the point of returning for more.

I had decided, from the fleshy evidence still attached at times, that my log rotor and trail wire got attacked by squid. These were the culprits that so twisted the wire back around the log line in their attacks that the rotor was facing backwards, and not working approximately half the times I pulled it out to check for chafe. I always just straightened the wire and returned it to the water, as it seemed to have prevented the rotor itself from being gobbled now for nearly 20,000 miles of towing. Despite its seduction of squid in Southern Ocean waters, it had proven its worth overall.

It intrigued nearly all of the seabirds that accompanied me. It was amusing to watch them hover and land in our wake, always trying to catch that little trained fishy that followed so precisely astern. Invariably they misjudged our speed. Landing, dipping their heads in for a look, then taking off again in disgust to circle until temptation could be resisted no more. In they would come for another waterski landing, a look-see below, then a flap and run take-off. They never seemed to learn. Greater shearwaters, white-chinned petrels, black-browed, grey-headed and other smaller albatrosses. The only ones to remain aloof from such frivolous fishing were the wanderers and the royals, and those most wonderfully high-aspect ratio of wings, the sooty albatross. All of these maintained their distance and their dignity in the air.

We were almost at 50 degrees south. The wind veered more to the west. I gybed on to starboard heading south-east for our final approach, 50 degrees south on one side to 50 south on the other being the traditional zone of the Horn. How noisy and uncomfortable it was at the start. Everything slightly loose rolling and moving until finding a secure nest for the opposite heel. It was time also to replace my reinforced standard monitor vane with one of my self-designed and constructed specials for the battles ahead. I did not think the other could cope with the ultimate conditions we might hit, and in those conditions it would be impossible to replace a broken vane balancing on the framework beyond the stern.

A night of good progress, but then, yet again, damn, damn. More light wind and drizzle of another interminable warm front. And not enough rain even to catch! Give me real rain and calm, or wind and no rain, but *never* not enough rain along with calm.

Barometer dropping slowly, and already I was in the habit of looking forward to the next gale, as at least we could make some progress, even if carrying minimal sail and running scared. I dropped the Yankee again to minimise chafe, lashed the helm and self-steering and waited for change, all the while rolling like crazy in the left-over swells and cursing having got my rotting hand rain-wet again. But when there was wind, how the petrels loved sweeping and swooping, banking and playing with the eddies and turbulence behind the Yankee. What happy little grey-capped beauties, Stejneger's petrels I think.

Luckily, sometimes, when things were bad and in need of change, conditions never remained the same for very long down here. By late afternoon wind had returned. This time from the south, and *cold*. Having just reset the Yankee, I dropped it again, setting staysail instead. It was interesting to note that in this extreme cold my right hand seemed to become totally incapacitated and incapable of fine movement more rapidly than my already deadened left. Maybe it was just relative, as my left couldn't really tell the difference.

We ploughed on, hard on the wind under staysail and mainsail at third reef, waiting for a shift to the south-west or west which should follow and bring with it a more comfortable motion. Of course it didn't happen that way. I was up at 4.30 a.m. (in daylight) to drop the mainsail completely and press on under staysail alone as the wind freshened and swung. The wrong way. In a strong south-south east to south-easterly we started once more to dance that lovely old lee-shore shuffle, trying desperately to hold a course that would take us clear of Tierra del Fuego. Unsuccessfully initially, but the wind really should swing before long, so I was not overly worried.

With my hands turned to ice blocks just trying to remove the rain catcher, I decided that it definitely was not a high-latitude design. It was something I had bought from a friend forced to sell all his equipment, and I think he made it for more tropical climes. I had had no time to test and adapt it before leaving, but it worked and I resolved to refine it before next time – make it simpler to set up and unrig. The air temperature was 7 degrees without wind chill, the water about the same – cold.

I saw a funny thing while on deck that day, an albatross alighting on the water for the sole purpose of scratching under its armpits/wingpits with its feet instead of its beak, then taking off again to resume its endless search. The cold was now making condensation a real dripping problem down below, despite the aft hatch being open a dash and sunshine appearing outside. Better get around this corner fast, kid! How friendly my lovely petrels were. From a study of tail feathers, there were both Stejneger's and Cook's petrels around. Often flying so close I felt they wanted to talk to me.

Despite the pain in my shoulder now being so bad that I couldn't find a position where the pain didn't keep me awake, I managed to set the Drifter and cross 52 degrees south in the 'Furious Fifties' with it flying defiantly. Hoping to goad the weather gods into sending a lot more wind. We had been becalmed again with no steerage way for most of the previous couple of days and I was utterly fed up. Unfortunately, my virtual inability to move that arm led to a very poor set, the sail being dragged under my bobstay and torn. There was not enough wind to increase the tear, so I merely dropped it a bit early to have daylight handy while I sewed a patch over the damaged area. This was particularly satisfying work, sewing happily and restoring my 'engine' to 'as new' condition while waiting for wind to arrive. A few zephyrs from the northern quadrants kept us moving through most of the night, but they varied considerably in direction, necessitating many compass checks and course adjustments as the slightly different noises of our passage through the water alerted me to change. This at least was motion, so more pleasure than pain.

It was never fully dark down here and as night lightened into day the shade was just a different one of grey. It was a chilled grey, with the water temperature now at 6.8 degrees and the air much the same, but we were moving, so overall it was a happy grey.

It didn't stay that way. Soon I was reefing bit by bit until the mainsail was down completely and the Yankee testing my nerve as to how long I'd hold on. By 1 p.m., with the barometer still dropping, the Yankee was down and lashed and we drove on under staysail alone trying to make maximum miles before dark, by which time it too would come down and be replaced by the bulletproof if conditions remained the same. The positive happy grey that started the day had now become a fringes-of-fear grey as I listened to the whine of wind in the rigging, gauging whether it was strengthening, steady or starting to ease. All the while watching the barometer and barograph for clues. By mid-afternoon I had the bulletproof up early since the barometer had hastened its fall. There was no more to do now as I never reduced sail further than this. Time to curl up and listen and hope nothing broke.

Next day. Oh happy grey! Bulletproof down and Yankee back up as we raced for the Corner through rain and cold grey seas, the wind from north to north-west at 25–30 knots. Aye, it's grand to be down here like this, racing for the Corner, racing time through shades of grey, weighing options, weather signs, chancing sails and gear to stay intact. This was living on the Grand Scale. You forget the cold completely in the grandeur of large seas and breakers to the horizon all around, and us racing through the centre, a little speck of colour and of life. Truly inspiring.

The wind remained steady in strength and direction for a change, all day. At around sunset the cloud layer even showed signs of breaking, so I decided to risk flying the Yankee all night. This progress was too good to waste. Lots of grey-headed albatrosses followed astern, trying to catch my log-fish, and practising their waterski landings. What lovely birds. I was now close enough to be thinking of various possible landfalls, eventually opting for a skirting just south of Diego Ramirez to get some photos if we timed it right for daylight. Then I would try to make VHF contact with Cape Horn lighthouse if I passed within range. Otherwise I would aim for the Falklands to send a telegram. There was still a long, long way to go and it was a lot of time for my parents and friends to be news-less and worrying.

Next morning, Log 6,000 miles, and water temperature down to 6.3 degrees, cabin 7 degrees. After a coffee starter I reset mainsail at third reef and while I was doing this my eyes played tricks. I thought, 'What is that? Am I seeing things?' But no. It was a ship! Passing me slowly to leeward about half a mile away. A teal blue ship with red antifouling, heading on a similar course for the Horn. A factory ship for the squid fleet, or a squid boat herself most probably. What a surprise! The first ship I had seen since Sydney, and where I least expected to see one.

I tried to raise them on my VHF when I remembered, but they were almost hull down ahead by then, and I received no response on any of the usual channels. It was probably Korean or Japanese or South American and probably had no English speakers aboard. Choosing to ignore the foreign 'wog' in his wee little boatie!

By the following morning I was getting into 'Iceberg Alley', Drake Passage, with a latitude of around 57 degrees south. After a careful semi-dismantling while conditions were calm I had ascertained that my starboard primary winch, which had been giving trouble for a while off and on, was really out of action for the duration of the voyage, unless I had conditions as calm as enclosed harbour waters to do a total dismantling and rebuild. The position of my winches prevented my doing this at sea with my dud left and cold-affected right hands. I would almost certainly lose crucial parts and/or tools overboard. I thought of finding sheltered water at the Falklands, since I would probably be sending a telegram from there anyway. Meanwhile I jury-rigged a tandem system, to use in conjunction with the port primary. The two smaller winches weren't powerful enough for real gale conditions down here, so it was important to fix the primary before it led to possibly serious damage of other gear.

It was starting to get tense on board with my intended Diego Ramirez landfall only 160 miles ahead if my latest DR position was correct. After over 6,000 miles of sailing out of sight of land, and with a notoriously unfriendly lee shore lurking over the horizon, I was naturally concerned about the accuracy of my navigation. The sighting of the ship heading in the same general direction and presumably Cape Horn-bound as we were below the entrance to the Straits of Magellan, was a good sign but proved nothing.

I started to take sights several times a day, whenever the sun was visible, if the sea state allowed. I had been slack, I confess, in being satisfied with just one good position line a day across the Pacific (when the sun was visible at all), and as long as it agreed closely with my DR plot from course and distance run, I didn't worry further. There was after all nothing to hit in thousands of miles, I rationalised. Now, however, with land nearby, I was becoming tense. In one of my trips out on deck to grab a quick group of sights (I generally took three sights and averaged them to get the one I'd work through long-hand), the sextant took a slide across the cockpit, bringing up hard against the other side. Hard enough to worry me, but the results worked out OK, just a little optimistic. Maybe we had covered more ground while asleep than expected, thinks I.

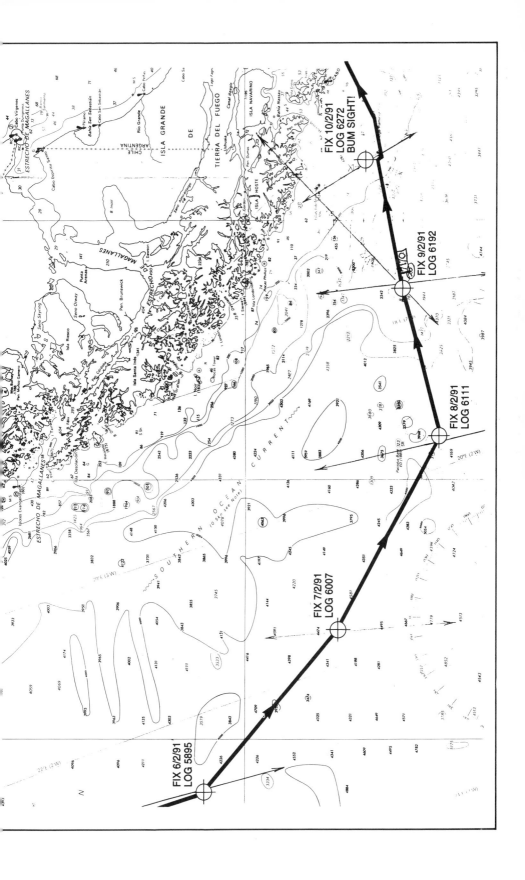

Fool me! Bloody stupid me in fact! I didn't check for index error in the sextant, which I should have done after its knock – it would only have taken seconds more than the checks I did do. Anyway, the wind started up again with some ferocity, so I reduced sail to staysail alone with the hope of arriving near Diego Ramirez two dawns hence for photos. Then, hopefully, passing Cape Horn late that afternoon or early evening in time for photos there. But, as a quote in one of Bill Tilman's books, says, 'Very few plans survive contact with the enemy.'

Chapter Twenty

Ramirez and Around

The following day dawned cold and grey, the water temperature being down to 5.8 degrees and the air to 7 degrees. For the first time I took to wearing the long-sleeved 'warmie' that Marion had made. I had been wearing the sleeveless one almost since day one of the voyage, but in this climate sleeves were a godsend, not a nuisance, as the wind cut like a knife. Three quick sights put me approximately 70 miles from Ramirez, so a dawn landfall the next day was looking good. The sun was very low for these sights and the resultant fix doubtful, but the day proceeded to cloud over heavily soon after, so they were all I was going to get. By noon it was drizzling and I sat becalmed again in typical warm-front conditions. No steerage way, and no visibility. Late in the afternoon a light breeze sprang up from the north once more, simultaneously with the arrival of a group of hourglass dolphins, the first I had seen of this beautiful cold-water species. The delay meant I was quite safe from hitting land unexpectedly in the night, so could maybe sleep a little more soundly.

Golden tendrils of cirrus and pink alto-cumulus lit a beautiful dawn, one of the prettiest of the voyage and suspicious down here. I had been up since pre-dawn darkness hoping to catch a glimpse of Ramirez's light, but to no avail. Haze or distant rain could have kept it hidden at that range, but I was a bit disappointed not to see the islands themselves at dawn. Well, you can't win them all, they say.

Another group of sights later in the morning seemed to confirm our position, so puzzlement started to replace disappointment, but I still didn't relate it to the knock that the sextant had taken a couple of days earlier. I sailed on towards the Horn, thinking we must have missed Diego behind a squall. More hourglass dolphins kept me company during the day, their playful antics distracting me somewhat from a growing concern. If we were where I thought, how come the high land to the north and around Cape Horn itself was not visible? The afternoon was overcast but clear, and the high mountainous coastline should have appeared before dark.

At midnight a strong rain squall caused me to rush up and drop the mainsail completely, continuing under staysail alone. Flash . . . flash . . . While lashing the mainsail securely I thought I saw a five-second flash ahead . . . Diego Ramirez! Which I had thought was well astern! The light then vanished and I thought I must have been imagining it, since no lighthouse turns itself on and off during the night. I raced below to check the chart. An arc of visibility was drawn for the Cape Horn light, but none for Diego Ramirez – visible all around, therefore? What else could I assume? Nevertheless, I hurried back on deck to look again, heavy rain and spray making it rather hard through salt-spattered glasses . . .

Yes, there was a light ahead, or the loom of a light, and it was being occluded by the dark form of land dead ahead! I looked again and saw an island very much like Cape Horn itself in shape, looming to port and I adjusted our course to clear it to the south. I remembered that there were several more unlit islands a mile or two to the north of Diego Ramirez proper, so gybing and heading to the north seemed too much of a risk.

To the south there were some rocks also, but by luffing a bit I thought we would clear these 'minor' hazards easily. But what was that? A band of white flashes skirting a totally black form rising ahead . . . Rocks! A large rock, to windward, with breakers around the base . . . What the . . .! I bore away to go to leeward, between it and the main island, clear of danger, I thought. I had left the cabin light on accidentally after checking the chart just before. I needed all my night vision now, so leaned inside the cabin to switch it off. This was almost our undoing! With a clatter, the head torch was knocked from my head, disintegrating on the cabin floor and making it impossible to sort out the sheet tangle in the cockpit to gybe. I could not feel to sort out the mess. I needed vision, needed light! I saw other rocks rising to leeward, so couldn't leave the helm to search for another torch. We edged closer, I zagged away. I could only see their darker forms against the not quite blackness of the night, and the fringes of foam around their sides. Not enough to gauge either height or distance. Almost blindly we slalomed this course of certain destruction if we hit. At the last moment I noticed a huge black area just to starboard, almost certainly too close to avoid. My thoughts were not on my own end, which seemed inevitable, but sorrow at having let down *Little Wing* so badly. She had proven such a wonderful little sea boat, surmounting all dangers the sea could offer, and now it seemed I was about to betray her trust completely.

Dimly I could pick out a very narrow skirt of foam, hardly any at all – we might just make it. That indicated the rock fell steeply into the sea and as I zigged back to port it seemed we might clear, as long as there were no underwater spires. The

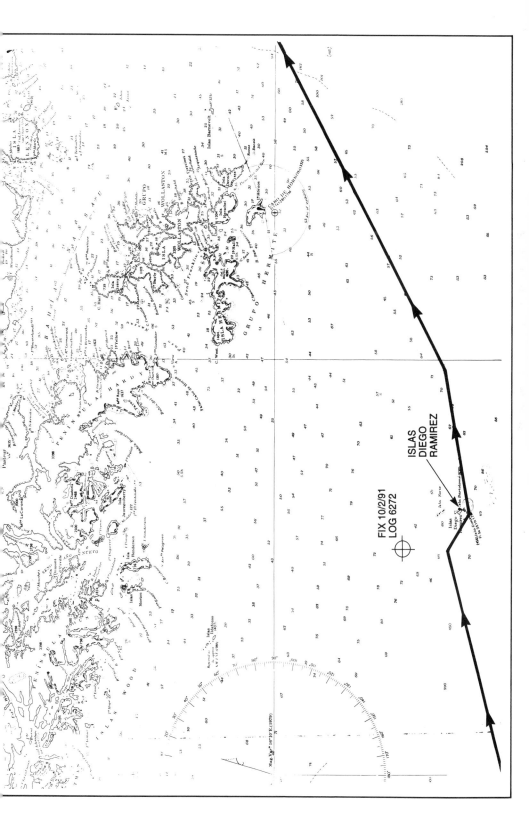

ISLAS
DIEGO
RAMIREZ

FIX 10/2/91
LOG 6272

seconds passed. Less than a boat length clear of doom! Another large lump then appeared ahead and to port. I zagged back to starboard, heading east and hoping we were clear. I stayed at the helm for another couple of hours in order to be absolutely sure. Well, that was one way to get a fix! At least we knew exactly where we were! I set a course towards the south of Cape Horn, approximately 60 miles on, and retreated below to rest awhile, hopefully till dawn.

Huh! The gods were having fun with me. A little before daylight it started to really blow, but since I was so handicapped in the dark I managed to delay a sail change until just on first light. Down came the staysail and up went the bulletproof again. This wind didn't give the impression it was fooling. It quickly settled in at a steady force 9–10 with extended gusts of force 11+. Even with that tiny sail area and only a shade off running before, we were blown almost flat through these gusts – while staying on course, not blown flat due to rounding up or wave action.

In the relatively shallow water between Ramirez and the Horn the waves were like nothing I had ever seen, or hope to see again. Absolutely *huge* surf breakers with plunging tops just like a shallow beach break. But in the order of 60–80 feet high and breaking in 300–400 feet of water with crests well over half a mile apart. The tops tubed over like Hawaiian surf photos for the upper 10–15 feet and below that was varying degrees of steep. Their distance apart enabled me to climb out the hatch several times to fix lashings and halyards threatening to come loose, but timing re-entry to get below and lock the hatch behind me in time for the next onslaught was touch and go. I needed eyes in the back of my head.

On one of these trips out on deck the inevitable happened. A large cross sea combined with the main swell precisely where we were, picked us up ever so easily and tossed us over until the mast was at least 40 degrees below horizontal judging from the trajectory of things in the cabin. The strange places things ended up landing – some I didn't locate until we were back home. I was on deck through it all, luckily near the cabin entry, so I grabbed the dodger frame and stood on the multiple purchases of the mainsheet, normally vertical, as we were rolled over and down. Rolled to leeward, but rolled so far that with the hull above it reminded me of being trapped underneath during some capsizes to windward in the Skate long ago! The solid water of the break was deflected by the hull bottom and dodger to such an extent that I only got a little water down my neck, but down below things weren't so dry. We had been over so far that both Dorade boxes on top of the cabin must have been underwater and were now gushing water on to my bunk, galley and chart table. All were deluged. We sprang back upright almost instantly, so the volume of water that got below was not large, but it doesn't take much to make a bunk sodden. Only someone bent on suicide would have stayed at the helm in that cold and in those seas and I was thankful indeed that Mr M. was doing a job as good as any human. Better, in fact, because a human would be too fearful looking astern to remain at his/her post!

A while later I saw a large ship ahead, visible only with both of us on crests, and I couldn't gauge what it was trying to do. It seemed to be in trouble, with no definite course it was holding, so again I returned on deck to hand-steer us past if necessary. We, at least, were manoeuvrable in these seas.

Barely had I arrived on deck and looked astern than I saw it coming, the daddy of all breaking waves that I had ever imagined. It was breaking like Sunset Beach or Waimea Bay in Hawaii for the upper 15 feet and the rest nigh on vertical to the sides – a real close-out set! In 400 feet of water! It was too late to retreat below and close the hatch, several tons of water would have come in with me. There is a wide cross beam across the middle of my aft submarine hatch/cabin entry. It was the highest point I could get to. I stood up on this, wrapped my arms around the boom and waited . . .

For the second time in twelve hours I just waited, almost a detached observer looking on while time passed very, very slowly. As it reached us it was closing out on both sides, but just peaking to break where we were. Mr M. had the helm and we were in his hands. We tilted forward as the wave picked us up and threw us ahead with it. Down went the bow, down, down until we appeared to be aimed at the centre of the earth, with a trough so deep that I honestly expected it to suck dry until rocks appeared under us. I remember wondering whether the top of the mast would spear the bottom vertically as we free-fell end over end into the trough, or would we be slewed sideways and rolled a few times before reaching it that way. Then I noticed spray peeling up in walls on both sides of me. The spray reached gunwale level just aft of the lower shrouds (about half way back from the bow) and above boom height on both sides by the time it was level with me. Mr M. held us dead in line with the direction of the wave, ideal for a pitch pole. She just lifted her bow and surfed, straight as an arrow, for seemingly an age but probably only 15–30 seconds. I was speechless, the surfing ride of a million lifetimes and almost too much for one day! Before I could recover, the next wave had arrived, but it was a cross swell, and after flirting with the crest we just slewed off and pulled out, as a surfer would do. What a helmsman, Mr M.!

For the rest of the day and night I retreated below and left it to him. We were caught and rolled horizontal several more times and many times I heard that amazing extended hissing of long high-speed surfing runs, but was too exhausted to look. 'La Méthode Moitessienne' to the hilt! I was aiming for deeper water where the waves were more sane but to get there we had to cross these shallows. After that wave of waves and the way we handled it I was full of confidence in our ability to cope at speed. To hell with warps, sea brakes etc., we were out to catch up miles and get clear of the shallows as soon as possible. We averaged over 7 knots for twenty hours under less than 40 square feet of sail. That was sailing . . .

Cold, deep water beneath us and a blue sky above. The morning dawned with us safely in the deep-water escalator of the Antarctic Current, helping us toward Islas de Los Estados, the coccyx of South America. Luckily, no icebergs were sharing the ride. The swells were still very large and some tops just breaking, but after yesterday – a calm! I reset the staysail early, then changed it for Yankee, and by the time Los Estados and its peaks suddenly appeared through the haze, we were back under Yankee plus triple-reefed main and moving comfortably at around 5 knots.

With a landmark now in sight for a bearing, and an accurate DR position, I took sights to try and sort out the mess we had got in at Diego. Aha! The position I got from the sextant was way off. A good 60 miles or more! I checked the sextant throughly now, and found an index error of 1 degree 5 minutes not allowed for since the slide it took days ago. Recalculating the sights of the last few days showed them now all to make sense. I was learning: check for sextant errors often, not just at the start of a voyage! It was almost twenty years since I had done my navigation course and I had forgotten such warnings, never having had that type of accuracy problem before.

During the gale rounding the Horn our course was dictated by the conditions, and we passed too far away either to see it or to communicate via my hand-held VHF. With no message back to my parents and friends from there I now decided to aim for Stanley and send a telegram – via VHF without stopping if that were possible, but I was no longer sure the little radio worked. I had passed another ship rounding Los Estados, aiming for the Horn from this side, and it hadn't responded to a call either. Cape Horn was proving the busiest place for shipping that I had encountered since Sydney! Three ships in five days after none for seventy-five!

My Cape Horn gale had come and gone with absolutely no change in the barometer, and I now wondered if it had been a katabatic wind effect generated by the Patagonian Ice Cap nearby.

Showers of rain, some seemingly stationary and others blown past quite rapidly, veiled most of the peaks of Los Estados as we sailed by. Only silhouettes were visible, but some of these were very impressive and my climbing appetite was thoroughly stimulated. Very steep walls of at least 1000 feet, probably more, were visible amongst peaks reminiscent of Cerro Torre and the Fitzroy group in the Patagonian Andes. Very inspiring, even at a distance of some 15 miles or more.

On rounding Cabo San Juan at the tip of Los Estados, an amazing sight lay before us. An almost dead flat horizon towards the Falklands. No Southern Ocean undulations from the west now South America was blocking their procession. There was still a swell from the south, but it seemed positively calm. What a delightful change – but at the same time it filled me with a little dread. The only sensible way home from here was across two more oceans, neither of which I had even seen, let alone sailed on before. It seemed a long, long way still to go. An almost overwhelmingly long way, but having come so far we should be able to do the rest – with patience, and some care.

It was on the Atlantic side of the Horn that icebergs had proven most dangerous along the clipper-ship route. Between Los Estados and the Falklands were a couple of relatively shallow banks where large bergs often grounded and remained, collecting victims as ships ploughed into them in poor visibility, sometimes remaining a hazard for years before breaking up into smaller pieces and moving on.

The water here was considerably colder than in the shallow waters around the Horn and it was easy to imagine ice not far away. I kept as thorough a look-out as I could at night, but there was little I could see in the dark, at least at a distance, so I tried tactics instead – threading a course between the banks in the hope that they would catch the bergs, leaving the ocean clear of ice in their lee. It was with relief that I greeted each dawn.

The water and air temperatures, having reached an all-time low in the deep water just past the Horn, began to rise slowly after Cabo San Juan. They were still only 6.8 degrees (water) and around 8 degrees (air), but now sunny and dry with ordinary little swells. We sailed happily on towards the Falklands under Yankee and double-reefed main. I was still very wary of sudden changes down here, so kept the mainsail overly reefed to ease my problems in panic reefing situations. I had never succeeded in picking up a time signal from WWV or WWVH anywhere across the Pacific, only getting Radio Australia for a while, then the BBC when nearing Tierra del Fuego. It was time for another check of my watches – maybe there would be new stations in our new ocean. I tuned on to AM to hunt for local South American music first. Instead, loud and clear came the beautiful female voices of the announcers on Falklands Radio at Stanley. What heaven to hear such melodious accents after hearing no speech other than my own for nearly eighty days! I was entranced and listened to several programmes of local news just to hear more of those lovely voices. On one of these, I learned that Jerome Poncet of *Damien* lived there. Well! It would be wonderful to meet him – his experiences with her having been such an influence long ago.

Listening to those siren voices from Stanley had me falling in love with the place and deciding to return for a stopping visit, even without seeing it. On the following morning, while sailing in beautiful sunshine and mild conditions, I decided on one more search in the bilge while the motion was gentle for things still lost or vanished after our Cape Horn rollings. I had nearly dismantled the boat in places in my searches so far, but quite a few things were still unaccounted for. Hardly had I begun burrowing beneath my flooring than I heard a strange sound like an engine droning, but not at all like a ship. I raced up on deck and there was an RAF Hercules circling me! While following his movement I looked astern and on the horizon there was a ship! I looked forward, and there was *land*!! This was altogether too much for the space of a few minutes, after so long seeing nothing but sea. Consulting my charts told me that it was Beauchêne Island I could see ahead – lovely-looking cliffs on all sides from this angle, too. I decided to sail past close if possible, to check it out more thoroughly, but the smell of the guano forced me to keep my distance! After nearly eighty days of seeing no land at all I had now seen three different countries in almost as many days. No wonder I was picking up the Falkland Islands radio station so clearly. I was very eager to send word back to my parents and friends, and at this rate if the VHF were still working I might even get a message off the following afternoon. It had gone flying around the cabin at least once during our Cape Horn antics, though, so I had my doubts.

Chapter Twenty-One
Falklands, Falklanders

I knew the Falklands to be a notorious graveyard of ships, surrounded by strong and unpredictable currents. After my Diego Ramirez experience I had no desire to get anywhere near a strange coast at night, so as darkness fell I tacked away from land, even though this would probably make us too late to send a telegram before the weekend. I had no large-scale chart of the Falklands with me, having forgotten to put it aboard in the rush to leave. Now I regretted it, as they had a very complex coastline with few navigational aids.

Sailing through numerous rain squalls and strong tide races that caused breakers even in the calms between had me regretting having to get close at all. Ramirez had really scared me, and these very variable conditions approaching a strange coast without adequate charts made me long for the open sea. To cap my despair the captive pin shackle at the head of the Yankee chose to let go as I dropped the sail in a squall. The halyard shot up to the masthead, totally irretrievable without an ascent higher than the bosun's chair could take me – only possible in smooth water.

It could have done that during any of my hundreds of droppings and resettings, I suppose, but it was a bloody nuisance now as we would most likely need that sail to power us in confined waters and light winds before escaping from here. I decided to wire the shackle pin permanently shut once it was back on the sail, as the Yankee was all I used that halyard for anyway. Rather like the mainsail halyard shackle that I had wired permanently back near New Zealand. Because I had been transferring the Yankee halyard for use in setting the Drifter I had avoided doing this until now, but I could use the bulletproof halyard instead for that job. Too bad I only thought this right through after the event! Now there were three jobs I really needed smooth water for.

Firstly, dismantling, fixing and reassembling the starboard primary winch – I could see what to do but needed ultra-calm to do it. Secondly, locating and repairing the break in the compass light circuit that had caused it to die rounding the Horn – if it was the plug into the cockpit side, it needed complete dryness and lack of motion to fix. Thirdly, retrieving the lost Yankee halyard. Especially for an engineless vessel, all of these were important to have working, and I decided to ask if there were a spare mooring buoy I could hang off for a few hours in Stanley Harbour to carry out the repairs. My anchor gear was so thoroughly stowed I didn't want to have to tear half the boat apart to get it out, and I had no means of getting ashore. Just to tie up to a buoy for a while was all I needed. I hadn't had sufficiently calm weather at sea for months, and all these things were in constant use under normal circumstances.

Repair sooner rather than later in some unlikely ultra-calm seemed to make more sense the more I thought about it. Two RDF beacons, one at the airport and one at Stanley itself, combined with our course from my last fix gave a reasonable idea as to where we were. But I could not put much faith in a position derived from beacons so closely spaced and decided on remaining well clear of the shore for yet another night. This was turning out to be a very slow and cautious approach, but closing in on a strange and perilous coast without charts demanded caution.

Even though the range was still excessive for VHF, especially for a hand-held set, I decided to try and contact Falklands Radio late that afternoon. It was a Friday, and with everything liable to shut down for the weekend, a successful contact would enable me to clear out, back on my way without delay, chancing that I would hit a good calm sometime soon to fix my problem gear.

Surprise, surprise! I could get through quite clearly on Channel 16, the emergency channel, and discussed things with a most attractive and helpful voice there, but for the telecommunications channels I was still out of range. The friendly female whom I had first spoken to found out the characteristics of Cape Pembroke light at my request, and one on the opposite headland which my oceanic charts didn't show at all. I decided to aim towards these overnight, and close the shore in the morning for another attempt at sending my message. These lights were both of rather low power and short range and she suggested picking up Cape Pembroke lighthouse with radar. This apparently was more reliable, except in conditions of perfect visibility, but not much use for me.

Nevertheless, in poor visibility prior to the arrival of a cold front she had told me of, we continued our collision course with the coast. Continually scanning the darkness for any sign of Cape Pembroke (or any other) light, I hand-steered us in, hoping for the arrival of the front to blow the rain squalls away before we closed land. Around midnight I noticed the possible loom of a lighthouse, through rain, but it was hard to be sure. Shortly thereafter I noticed a loom as from a town, and

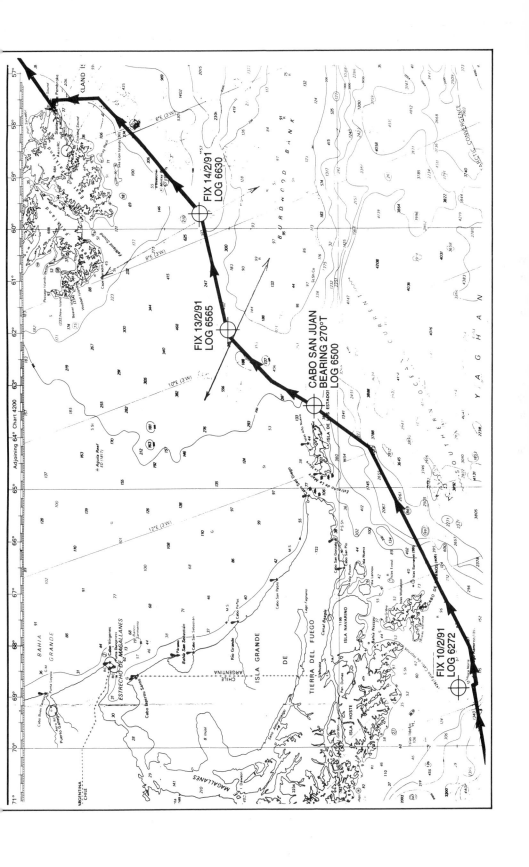

in a quite different direction. With no large-scale charts to work it out, and no local knowledge, I lost my nerve, dropped the staysail and headed slowly back out towards the ocean and safety under triple-reefed main. All but hove-to in a strong south to south-westerly, *Little Wing* looked after us while I dozed lightly until dawn.

I awoke to see land dead astern, and was glad that I had reversed our course in the night, although it looked to be quite a way off. With no details of heights or land formations on my charts, it was impossible to determine our distance off or even exactly where we were. Through large and often breaking seas I just aimed towards the highest point, trusting to spot something recognisable from the *Pilot Book* descriptions once we were close. When closer, and having spotted the lighthouse, I recontacted Falklands Radio for clues as to the correct approach. There were many breakers and kelp patches near us, so I tacked out to sea again. Just at this moment I spotted another yacht approaching from windward, but it being very windy now I couldn't spend much time closely observing its course between the lighthouse and various isolated rocks and islets. I thought he must be a local since he seemed to be cutting it pretty fine around some breakers. I called the harbourmaster again and he suggested keeping 1–2 miles off until he came out to lead us in.

Conical hills like miniature volcanoes with rocky knolls on top led the eye inland to the higher ground of more distant peaks. Scattered clifflines, angular and steep on the lower hills, promised an abundance of crack and corner climbs even if the walls between were disappointing on closer inspection. The wind-blown tussock country seemed to offer wonderful walking. After so long at sea it was an exotic, wondrous scene, truly another world. I was enthralled. Here was a landscape which if the foreshore and sea were included, just begged for an extended visit, a return for proper exploration.

The harbourmaster lent me his large-scale chart of the Port William and Stanley Harbour region to study as I followed them up the Sound towards the Narrows and Stanley Harbour. The tussock country of the foreground lay gold in the sunshine, the high land beyond in the purple of cloudshadow – blue ocean, blue harbour, blue sky. Tufty cumulus sprinkled the sky above with their whiteness, the below world with shadows, and dolphins accompanied us in. Several swirling black and white hourglass ones and large dark bottlenoses arching around us almost in slow motion, particularly after I went below to look for fenders and returned on deck to find us almost immobile in a heavy kelp bed close to shore. A gust from a side bay had self-steered us into danger, and the dolphins, now ahead, seemed to be pointing/correcting/showing the way back towards deep water and our original course.

By this time I had been thoroughly seduced by the landscape I was sailing through and had decided to stop over until Monday (today was Saturday) in order to carry out the repairs, then send the telegram to my parents directly through the local Telecommunications Centre. The harbourmaster suggested tying up alongside the public wharf and offered to tow us through the Narrows since we didn't have an engine. *Little Wing* was designed to sail, so of course I refused.

I dropped the staysail for faster tacking, shook out two reefs in the mainsail for more power, dodged a large Fisheries Patrol vessel coming out, then set us up to head in. The wind chose to die almost completely in the Narrows itself and it was a bit worrying trying to make it through on a single tack, with barely enough speed for steerage way and shallows very close to starboard indicated by flourishing beds of kelp. At last a gust of wind made it as far as us and we snuck through, able to luff a little while the gust lasted. Once through, the wind was steady and I did a few practice circles to reacquaint myself with our turning-circle diameter since I would be coming alongside the French (it turned out) yacht that had arrived just before me, and we had to do it perfectly, at first attempt. This was a public performance now, on behalf of all the 'under sail alone' ghosts and believers.

What a buzz it was to do it so easily, so assuredly. The perfect arrival in an era subservient to engines, motors and mindless use of power. After Customs and Immigration had finished with me we moved *Little Wing* around to the side of the jetty as the Frenchman was moving to another one nearby that had water and electricity available. Having been charged 40 pounds Sterling harbour fees for my minimal visit I was now a 'prisoner' until Monday – then I could change my few American dollars into Sterling when the bank opened.

While moving the *Wing* I got talking to a young local of about my age, Carl Freeman, and his wife Dianne, who had sailed in fourteen years before and stayed. As the weather was unusually perfect for doing all my repair jobs, Carl stayed and helped me during the afternoon. Soon I had the halyard back to the Yankee and 'permanently' wired, then we dismantled and corrected the problem winch. How easy it all was in smooth water. Suitably inspired, we found a break in the wire leading to the compass light deck-plug and, with his two dextrous hands, Carl soon had the plug dismantled, wire soldered back together, crimp connections back on and the whole reassembled, me helping mainly by choosing and finding the various tools and equipment we needed. By sunset all the jobs I required smooth water for were done, but I still had to wait for Monday for the bank/harbour fees, telegram and departure paperwork.

Carl and Dianne invited me to their place for dinner, where I met their lovely young daughters Tracy and Rachael, and we made a return trip to the *Wing* to pick up my Cape Horn bottle of champagne, which I hadn't drunk in celebration yet. Far more wonderful to me than champagne was a wonderfully deep and hot bath, my first really good wash in eighty days. Dianne offered to catch up on my clothes washing for me, but I only had one tracksuit and an extra top dirty at this stage, though everything clean was salty. She offered to rewash these salty clothes in fresh water so they would dry properly and we arranged a visit the next day to show the girls the boat, pick up washing and talk. I returned to the *Wing* to sleep

Grey day – the morning after I arrived in Port Stanley.

as she truly was home now, and I might need to adjust fenders and lines if the wind changed.

For the first morning since before we left Sydney I could in theory sleep a little late. In theory. In practice the forecast wind change back to the west or north-west didn't eventuate, so I continued to be blown against the wharf, necessitating frequent adjustment of fenders and lines as the tide rose and fell. Imprisoned by the wind's direction I could not get away to visit either the Frenchman or a Dutch couple who were already in harbour and who intended wintering over by cruising both the Falkland Islands and their wonderfully convoluted coastlines before a dash south to Antarctica the following summer.

I had met this couple briefly while Carl and I were resurrecting my dead winch, and it would have been interesting to talk to them at some length since their plans seemed so close to my originals for *Little Wing*. Les Halliday and his wife, who had been so helpful to Naomi James when she called in during her circumnavigation some years earlier, also dropped by for a chat while Carl and I were working, this time on the compass light problem. Three fishing-boat captains from Greece, Denmark and Norway who were in Stanley for their holidays completed the afternoon's socialising while we worked, and I hoped I would get a chance to talk with them at greater length before leaving.

My 'imprisonment' was broken late in the morning when the Frenchman came over to visit and compare notes. It turned out that he had rounded the Horn the day after I did, after a non-stop passage from Bluff at the bottom of South Island, New Zealand. He was completing his circumnavigation at Mar del Plata, so was almost home. His worst weather had been in the Indian Ocean, where he had lost his mizzen mast in a roll-down, necessitating a stop at Perth, Western Australia, for repairs and rerigging. He had also called in at Cape Town and spent some time there, after his Atlantic crossing.

*   *   *   *

A colourfully painted mosaic of corrugated-iron roofs led up the house-covered hill behind us. An interesting collection of waterfront buildings spread out on either side. Some of these 'buildings' were the beached hulks of old sailing ships converted to warehouse use by connecting them to the land with linking construction. I could not resist a short exploration ashore. Colourful little houses had their even smaller peat storage sheds, painted brightly also. The flowering shrubs in the gardens, the greenery of grass and trees, the marked lack of vehicles except for a few four-wheel drives all lent the town a child's dream character. Such was its contrast to both the sea I had been alone with for so long and the city I had left behind.

Carl, Dianne, Tracy and Rachael arrived soon after my return, and what fun the children had exploring the confined spaces that I hated so much to work in, the leaking stern region particularly. They reminded me of my own childhood explorations and curiosity and I gave them some little presents I had hunted out as reminders of my visit. Since Carl and Dianne had lived aboard their original yacht at the other end of Pittwater years before, I gave them some photo reminders of their previous 'home' as we talked of places familiar to both of us but somewhat faded in their memories after so long.

I had not been alone for long when further excitement occurred. The British Antarctic Survey vessel *John Biscoe* had arrived in harbour during the afternoon. Now their motorised tender was coming in astern of me to pick up two locals and take them out to the ship – she had just returned from a trip across to South Georgia for zoological survey work. The tender came in fast. A fellow on the wharf jumped down to try and fend its bow away from my self-steering gear and stern. I could not get aft in time myself, expecting a more careful approach. We hit. It seemed a fairly gentle blow and I thought no more of it, there being no obvious damage. I was more interested in the locals being picked up. If my memory of photos from the *Damien* voyages served me well, one of them was Jerome Poncet. What a surprise! I talked to him briefly before the tender moved off, telling him of *Damien's* influence on my design, and ascertaining that the *Biscoe* would be moving to the Fisheries and Harbourmaster's wharf in the morning.

Amongst other town duties, I decided to ask the local architect/designer about job possibilities since an extended return visit was tempting. The friendliness, warmth and multi-instrumentalist nature of the locals was very appealing. Unlike most city folk, these people created their own worlds and amusements and were not dependent on others to do the work for them. This was a refreshing by-product of their isolation, but endangered somewhat by the recent introduction of TV in video form.

As soon as I had the town chores completed, I decided to visit the captain of the *John Biscoe* to enquire what sort of ice-year they had found it to be. If it were a bad year, I would be sailing among icebergs up beyond latitude 40 degrees south (the *Biscoe* was still passing bergs at 35 degrees south a few years earlier), making the entire return journey a tense time, as I planned to be between 40 and 45 degrees south the whole way. This was within the extreme limit line of iceberg sightings and in a bad year would require considerable vigilance by the look-out (me). If it were a good year, with few large bergs on the loose, I should be quite safe skirting the extreme limit of bergs and could be more relaxed when driven well below that line.

The road led on and on, disappearing in the distance beneath a rain squall sweeping in from the sea. Dense tussock grew on all sides, except for the roadway where I walked. Along this windswept ridge and hillside nothing taller could keep hold. Far below lay the wharf and buildings alongside which the *Biscoe* lay. In the shallows beyond, in an adjoining bay, lay a beached three-masted barque, the *Lady Elizabeth*, still with her lower masts and main lower yard standing, and from a distance looking almost intact. She had hit a rock in nearby Berkely Sound in 1913 and had proved too costly to repair, so remains beached, a rusting iron lady.

They had seen no large bergs from the *Biscoe* this year between South Georgia and Stanley, only small ones in the vicinity of South Georgia, calved from glacier snouts there. Some, of course, could have escaped detection, but from their experience it looked a good year. This was comforting news. I would still need to be very wary for the first 1000 or so miles after leaving Stanley on our course approximately north-east up to latitude 40–42 degrees south. Once up there, however, the increasingly long and ever colder nights of winter were unlikely to demand hours and hours frozen in the cockpit each night for unimpaired look-out. We truly were lucky – icebergs were so thick around the Falklands the following year that even the large and fully equipped vessels of the international fishing fleet were severely hampered in their work.

While I was talking to a young lady zoologist after my meeting with the captain, a familiar face suddenly appeared again – Jerome Poncet, who had been with them on their just completed voyage, and who now does zoological work in conjunction with the British Antarctic Survey team. We talked of my voyage a bit, he worrying at the lateness of the season for my return trip alone. I ascertained the titles and publisher of the books he had written about *Damien*, which I had never seen in Australia, and collected his address, an island off West Falkland, to stay in touch by mail. A mini-bus taking crew into town saved me another long walk in the rain, and if the weather didn't worsen dramatically by this time on the morrow we'd be gone.

At the public wharf, sunny Stanley astern.

A few parting beers with Carl and Dianne, dinner with them at home, where Tracy gave me a wonderful drawing (her vision of *Little Wing* in tropical climes) and Rachael showed me her new Brownie uniform – these warm family memories concluded my stay. Next morning the Customs man helped me to move *Little Wing* further away from the landing steps on to the wharf. This involved moving another launch out of the way first, but a tourist ship, the *Polar Circle*, was due at any time, and many tender-loads of tourists would be coming ashore. I would be in danger of damage unless well clear.

This done, and the wind blowing me away from the jetty for once, I made another quick trip into town to post mail, pick up mail – a booklet on the Falklands that a local was sending me – and shop for a few cans of ginger beer. I had developed a great desire for some on the voyage here! By the time I returned, the wind had swung back into the north and was strengthening rapidly, pushing me back into the wharf. I waited as long as I could to show a local man (who had taken some of the tourists fishing for a few hours) over the *Wing*, but it became too windy, too dangerous to stay. The Harbourmaster, though, came to advise me to stay since I had no motor and the wharf region was a lee shore I was hard against.

Although this was true, I reckoned I knew the *Wing* well enough by now to work our way off, but would need help on shore to release the mooring lines in correct sequence. We were bringing up hard against the wharf piles in the increasing chop and every bump made me wince. I had noticed that the wind backed into the north-north-west to north-west for a few gusts every half-hour or so and in such a gust I could get clear. The Dutchman from the other yacht came by at this moment and I explained my plan. Two Customs guys were there, but an experienced sailor helping made me feel more confident. Any confusion and we would be lost.

The younger Customs guy noticed it first. Yes, the wind had gone north-west. I was busy hauling in the wreckage of yet another chafed-through line that had been holding my bow, and getting another rigged. It only had to last while I hoisted sail, but without it we would be driven back on to the sea-wall. There was no room to tack if the first attempt failed. Mainsail up at first reef, we held our own, then gathered way. Bow line off, spring off, stern line off, away! Once out into the centre of the harbour I took in a second reef and reached off towards the Narrows, preparing the staysail as we went. I decided to set it before we arrived at the Narrows as we would need more power if tacking through the confined channel was required. It was not. Close hauled on the port tack we made it through, on past Tussac Point and out into Port William, the long fiord leading to the sea. Startlingly white cumulus, from large masses threatening rain down to isolated tufts of cotton wool, drifted past the receding landscape. The distant peaks, empurpled by shadow, looked tree-covered – only an illusion. The low land of the foreground, with its tussock in the sun, glowed gold. At 3 p.m. I streamed the log – about 11,000 miles to go . . .

Chapter Twenty-Two
South Atlantic

Grey seas with an excess of wind, frequent squalls and biting cold. The South Atlantic was not a pleasant place in the autumn, as we worked our way endlessly on the port tack up toward the 'tropics' around latitude 40–42 degrees south. My previous attempt at this voyage had turned out to be a 'circumnavigation' of the Tasman, virtually all on the port tack, and this circumnavigation of the globe seemed to be shaping up the same. Out of more than eighty days' sailing so far, I could count the number of days of starboard-tack sailing on one hand.

Although the traverse across the Forties was nearly all greyness and bashing to windward, under either staysail alone or staysail plus triple-reefed main, the initial few miles from Stanley at around latitude 52 degrees south, up out of the Fifties, were more pleasant. Brief periods of sunshine and more moderate winds interspersed the squalls, enabling me to set the reconnected Yankee and test the repaired primary winch. What a mood-elevator that sail had become! Every time it was set I could feel us making real progress. On the brink of needing to be pulled down in worsening conditions, though, it was a worry, especially at night.

One good side effect of my brief stop in Stanley had been the formation of more solid scabs on my chilblained fingers and toes, with no need for sail changes in the rain every day. The scabs were still minimal, however, so I avoided long deck outings in the wet until they were more definitely on the mend. Falklands Radio faded out of range astern; and suddenly it felt very lonely without those lovely female voices. Siren voices of the South.

A swing in the wind towards the east-north-east had us heading south of east for a while and further into icebergville and worries, but signs of a change were apparent. I did not think it would be long in coming as it seemed time for a gale. Instead, the wind swung comfortably back into the south-west next morning and gave us champagne sailing. Broad reaching before a moderate 15-knot breeze in sparkling sunshine with flocks of fair-weather cumulus floating overhead. On course for heaven. We were still below 45 degrees south, though, and nearly anything could happen here. Before dark I dropped the Yankee and set the staysail as conditions were worsening, but thought we could hold triple-reefed main through the night in our quest for miles. By 3 a.m. I could no longer bear the noises and discomfort of our 'submarine sailing' beneath breakers at speed, and dropped the mainsail completely. Dawn found us reaching north-east in a force 8–9 north-wester, through and under large, breaking seas.

Although it was rough, the water temperature was up to around 15 degrees, and the cabin nearer 20 degrees, too hot for my 'warmies'. These strong, warmer nor'westers had me puzzled, as they came in with no barometric change at all. This one, a real gale in all senses of the word, reminded me very much of the Cape Horn gale – could it be an effect of the now distant Andes?

Although the nor'westers this side of the Horn were mainly sunny, they were often too rough for good sunsights. With no land around to worry us, though, this was hardly a problem. By nightfall I had upped the mainsail again to the third reef in pursuit of miles. We still needed to get approximately 600 miles north-east to reach the zone of minimal ice worries, and then there was the race with approaching winter. It was going to be more of a sprint, this last 11,000 miles, than the first part of the voyage.

It was still summertime as I passed through latitude 45 degrees south, at least for a day. The water temperature reached 18.9 degrees and the cabin 22.7 degrees during another warm nor'wester. This warm weather unfortunately sent most of my remaining fruit (six lemons and two grapefruit from the start of the voyage) bad, and I had to have a lemon-eating binge to avoid wasting them completely. The two grapefruit I decided to hold off eating until longitude 30 degrees west if possible – a complete semi-circumference. After the regularity and predictability of the weather cycles across the Southern Ocean in the Pacific this South Atlantic region had me beat, barometric changes or lack of them seeming to bear no relation to the gales we were engulfed in.

Yankee down, staysail up, mainsail down, staysail down, Yankee up, mainsail back up at third reef, Yankee down, staysail up, mainsail down, staysail alone, etc. etc., etc. Frequently too rough to risk opening the aft hatch, so too rough to use my bucket toilet. Curse that irreparable pump! The continual bashing, virtually underwater for most of the time, was getting on my nerves. I thought of heading due east for greater comfort, but David Lewis had taken a terrible beating not much further south than my position, so I continued to try and gain northing. One night's midnight gale boost was accompanied by a marked change in the sea and our motion, and I wondered if indeed this was caused by a sea-mount I had aimed to skirt, with only 8 fathoms(!) of water over it according to the chart (continuing my ongoing exploration of sea-mount weather effects).

Atlantic petrels continued to keep me company in large numbers. Some seemed fascinated by my little trained fishy following closely astern, others by the flashes of crystal structure from my solar panel. These latter would hover just above it, their wings in continual fine adjustment to maintain their position before wheeling away, curiosity temporarily satisfied. Despite the frequency of these hovering inspections, they always reserved their closest and most photogenic approaches until my camera was put away, or so it seemed. Their relatively small size also contributed to non-spectacular photos of these pretty birds as I had no telephoto lens.

Nine days out of Stanley the sea developed a peculiar greeny-blue tinge to its dominant grey – plankton? An atttempt to include some colour from a sky trying for blue? In the afternoon, in sunshine, the water changed into a most beautiful blue with hints of turquoise. It was possible for the first time to imagine this ocean lapping tropical shores to the north, the coasts of northern South America and the West Indies in particular. North-west Africa seemed very remote, South America still close at hand. We were at about 41 degrees 30 minutes south, 42 degrees 30 minutes west, so should reach both Forties very soon.

A thousand miles out of Stanley, 10,000 miles from home, and problems, old and new ones, appearing. On the minor side, apart from the last few pieces of fresh fruit going bad rapidly, the tins of fruit and fruit juices in my bilge were corroding through all at once and having to be ditched also. I had made a point of stowing all non-biodegradable rubbish from the start of the voyage, to be put ashore later – all plastics, plasticised cardboard and whatever else would not soon vanish. Tin cans I continued to ditch overboard, as I knew from sailing one just how rapidly biodegradable they were when not maintained constantly. More worrisome was the increase in my hull leak since leaving Stanley. I had no money for repairs or any further harbour fees, and no time to waste with my food stocks now deteriorating, yet I could not push too hard in our quest for miles in case a catastrophic increase put me and *Little Wing* in the biodegradable refuse category also. Going too slow or going too fast both had their dangers. But the miles were falling astern and we were nearly out of the main ice danger zone.

The leak had for fourteen years remained at zero. It went up to around seventy pumps per week after rounding New Zealand, and had remained fairly steady at that until Stanley. In the relatively smooth water of Stanley Harbour it reduced, then returned to ten to twenty per day on leaving. Now, however, it was increasing noticeably after each gale, and was up near fifty pumps per day. A fourfold increase in only 1000 miles, and we were not yet half way around the course.

But it wasn't all bad. Full moon sailing, from evening through night, my Yankee blade driving us to windward over a moonlit but rising sea. Wind nor'east to nor'nor'east and my sights confirmed another milestone passed. Back up to latitude 40 degrees south and across longitude 40 degrees west, across the limit of ice line. All we had to do now was head east, east, east for approximately 7,500 more miles before dipping down again to get south of Tassie, then up to Sydney town. And of course, keep pumping the sea back out as fast as it decided to come in. Simple, but I still didn't trust the weather down here and dropped the Yankee for the night despite almost halving our speed. This continuous South Atlantic gale, and the way the leak was increasing, had me worried.

Checking the bilge regularly for water had its pleasant surprises, though. I was still coming across items lost in our Cape Horn rollings. Items that must have thought themselves billiard balls, judging from their final trajectories. It was very hard to relax enough to write, or even read. I would just lie and listen to the wind in the rigging, the crash of breakers rolling over us and wonder when we were really going to burst a seam and sink like a stone.

Out on deck I could forget these night worries, and each day had its joys. The colours of the turquoise tops, breakers transparent to the sky. Even the greys were warmer here. Working on the foredeck, whipping rope ends again, I spied the first Portuguese men o'war/bluebottles since the Pacific. Do petrels and such peck them to deflate/kill them and then eat them? Heavy rain had me thinking of catching water, but I was nearly back to full capacity, so let this excess cargo pass me by. When not worrying about the leak I was really enjoying the grandeur of it all, particularly on the grey days – for some reason these seemed to prompt more memories and reminiscences. It was a happy grandeur these calmer grey days had. But they were not photographable, they were 'interior' days, their colour and life mainly in the mind.

Not quite half way around the globe, and I watched a little night-time tragedy last night. I was furling the mainsail after dropping it at midnight. While leaning over the boom with furling line in hand I bumped my head torch with an arm, sending it over the side. Landing face upwards it floated away astern, still alight. A lone point of light in a dark night until it vanished a minute or two later. These little tragedies of losing things overboard certainly reminded me of my precarious existence out here and my own fragile mortality.

We continued to make great progress under Yankee alone, possibly over-canvassed, but loath to slow down and a bit scared of changing down in the conditions. Finally I could no longer take the wear on my nerves that this highspeed submarining entailed. Fortified by a morning cup of coffee I success-fully got the Yankee down without damage and the staysail set, but less than an hour later I was thinking of the bulletproof. This damn South Atlantic was proving a wild and windy place, far more so than the Pacific had been. The lateness of the season? I just hoped it got no worse around the Cape of Storms.

How I enjoyed the daily working out of sights, all long-hand. The mental arithmetic of adding, subtracting, dividing, etc., was sheer joy and reminded me of the delights of yacht design. I decided to design a slightly larger version of

Little Wing on my return. The ultimate cruising vessel, more suitable for very long journeys sailed by a crew of two. With all the time to observe and experiment with my own 'baby', and my complete happiness with her, I was sure that no better sea boat could be found than one of these refined versions.

We had to get back first, though, and a new and potentially serious problem first appeared now; suspect self-steering. With hindsight, as the problems increased until I disconnected the system as totally useless and reverted to my old sheet-to-tiller ways, this problem had originated back in Stanley. That knock from the *John Biscoe*'s tender. The blow from astern must have bent the lower casting of the gears, causing them to disengage more and more frequently as time went by. There was mention of this problem in the workshop manual for the system, and instructions on how to fix it, but with the unit positioned so far aft to clear my rudder, and my problems in using one hand, I could not repair it at sea.

It had chosen a most confusing moment to introduce this problem. A cold front had just passed through, with a wind swing of 90 degrees from north-west to south-west, but along with this front had come rain. Rain like solid sky falling, so loud on the deck and cabin overhead that the noise and chaos completely masked the change in motion from our course change. When I reached the deck the blackness was so absolute and the violence of the deluge so overwhelming that for a considerable time I couldn't ascertain either the direction the wind was coming from, or its direction in relation to our course. I eventually gybed and continued until dawn under staysail alone on the starboard tack. I expected a wind squall to follow the rain, so left the mainsail furled, but if it had been daylight it would have gone up. During all this confusion I first noticed us no longer holding course and the gears disengaged.

Morning dawned totally clear with a light westerly pushing us east. I would have preferred more wind as we were back in a real Southern Ocean swell again. Big fellows coming from astern and thereabouts, rolling the wind from our sails. It was cold also, and I was glad my chilblain scabs had finally sloughed off so I could wear wet-suit boots and gloves for warmth. The wind went back into the north-west around noon and I gybed us back on to port. How much more comfortable than that peculiar starboard tack!

What a glorious afternoon . . . sailing as relaxedly pleasant as any in the voyage so far. Just doodling along at a steady 4–5 knots under triple-reefed main plus Yankee. We could have carried more sail, of course, but it was pleasant just to catch up on boat chores, washing, airing and drying while there was a chance. I also tested my spare sextant, an expensive plastic one whose shade colours transformed me to another planet, but the results it gave put us on another planet also – a matter of some concern! I tried every adjustment in the book to make its errors consistent, but was forced to conclude they were neither ascertainable nor remediable by me at sea.

Deck work that night was all done by the light of a bright half moon with no need of a head torch for once. So clear, so peaceful, what a night to be on deck!

The feeling was that we had been almost becalmed for a day, but sights showed us to have held a 3-knot average. These idyllic light wind conditions held into the next day with 5–8 knots of breeze on a broad reach and full mainsail set for the first time since Sydney! I baked two wholemeal fruit loaves, enjoyed the peace while it lasted, and decided that from here to home the voyage was mainly for the enjoyment and evolutionary aspects and taking whatever came in the most pleasant way possible. That is, as fast as was comfortable, with a minimum of worrying night sail changes.

Warned by late afternoon cirrostratus, altostratus coming over from the west and cirrus streaks from the south-west, I put one reef back in before dark, another at 2 a.m. All day I was filled with joy, and by afternoon the 'real' Southern Ocean was back. With a strengthening nor'west to west wind, main back to a triple-reefed state, but Yankee still set in an effort to make up for the calm days of late.

Progress, and the division of the voyage into stages, was measured in two main ways now. Firstly, the gaining of each ten degrees of longitude further east, each ten-degree division being approximately 450 miles at around latitude 40–42 degrees south, where we were. Secondly, when real progress had been made, sailing off one chart and on to the next. It always seemed to take a lot longer to get past the second half of a chart, or the second half of an ocean. Particularly when that ocean was covered by two or more charts. In life until now I had always found the second half of a task to be easier than the first, but out here, racing winter, the reverse seemed true. I am sure it was the lengthening nights and shortening days that created this illusion.

On deck in the strengthening wind, watching the way she reacted, her every move, it was hard to imagine improving on *Little Wing*'s lines in the refined/enlarged version I was intending to design. Her hull form seemed so right out here, dancing on the water, moving sweetly with the swells. By late afternoon I had dropped the mainsail completely, with us averaging over 5 knots under Yankee alone through stormy seas. Scud hurtled by overhead and there was some very theatrical lighting when the sun found a gap in the scud layer. Through the gaps showed a blue sky and strong cirrus wisps far above. With the wind going around towards the south, I gybed us on to starboard for the night.

One hundred days into the voyage, and off the Western Atlantic chart. I ate my second-last grapefruit to celebrate. Absolutely delicious. I was hoping that the last one would keep until we had crossed the Greenwich Meridian, still twenty degrees of longitude away. We would have to get a move on, but again we were beset by a calm. Heading for Tristan da Cunha, but I didn't want to go that far north. I would head south once wind arrived to pass close to the northern (high) side of Gough Island if possible. Islands are particularly satisfying sightings, both aesthetically, with their contrast to the sea, and psychologically. Potential Edens of safe haven? At any rate, a sighting always prompted dreams, ideas, thoughts of possible futures. The sharing of wilderness with another.

We seemed to have cleared the shelter of South America by now, and the long, low swells from the west through to south-west had returned. Like a heart-beat in the rhythm of our life, their presence in our world was always there. Sitting in the cockpit with mug of tea in hand and savouring the warmth of the sunshine, it was hard to imagine a more pleasant place to be. A westerly had cleared the sky. Reading, writing, doing my daily exercises; no need of clothes except in the cool after sunset. The only necessities each day were bilge-pumping, navigating and cooking, with washing of clothes whenever it was fine. Life was so uncomplicated, so simply pleasant. Even the gales were not unpleasant now. Not once I had reduced sail to a stage approaching 'comfort'. Great shearwaters were our most common flying companions, with a few grey-headed albatrosses mainly at sunrise and evening. The shearwaters stayed with me all day, either flying or looking like fluffy bundles of feathers as we sailed past their waterborne forms. From time to time those flitting little maniacs, the Wilson storm petrels, appeared. The flashes of white as they darted crazily about made me think I was hallucinating . . . flashing sparks of light in the falling dark of night.

It was time for the next problem to appear! Dead batteries this time. No navigation or compass lights, no music from my cassette player, no emergency cabin lights or bunklight. Candles and kero. I remember that I had almost decided to start reading again in my bunk at night to use up a little power. The batteries were looking very fully charged. This sudden loss of power had me stumped, so I decided to use no electrical power at all for a while and see if they recovered. I also cleaned the contacts, checked the electrolyte levels and then the batteries themselves with my multi-meter. This confirmed the problem: dead batteries, not dead voltmeter. Remembering that both batteries were linked I then disconnected and tested each separately. One was totally kaput and must have haemorrhaged internally, the other still held a charge. I connected this one back into the circuit, vowing only to use it for navigation and compass lights when needed. This might just keep it 'alive' until home, but both batteries were the same age, so equally likely to die. This series of experiments to ascertain the problem took just over a week – there wasn't much sun around to recharge. In the meantime I used the only kerosene lantern that would stay alight in a breeze. Hung between our backstays over the stern, it was at least a 'psychological' navigation light. I also started convincing myself that the ocean is large, and the ships on it relatively small, and that the chance of collision, even with no lights, remote.

For the last couple of days I had been noticing quite a few 'whale birds', mainly Antarctic prions by the looks, and wondered if we were now crossing a migration route of whales. Just before sunset, one of the leviathans paid me a visit. Alerted by the sound of its breathing, I watched as a whale at least one and a half times, possibly twice the length of the *Wing* cruised slowly past, overtaking us from astern. I didn't see it spout to aid in identification, but from the dorsal fin shape it was most likely a fin whale or a sei, and from its length, most likely a fin.

How's this for automation? I was sitting on my bucket toileting when I heard the hiss of my recently repaired radio starting up. We had just hit a particularly sharp swell. While puzzling over it, I heard time pips, so checked my watch error while I sat. Without even an aerial extended it had fluked just the right angle to get a signal through my cabin windows. Normally I found I couldn't get BBC reception at time-signal times or had a habit of always just missing them. My spare transistor radio, sitting on top of the more powerful one, had just jarred the power switch to *on* with impeccable timing!

I had hoped for a look at Gough Island and had slowed us down by reducing sail so that we would pass in daylight. I also headed us a little further north in case current landed us on top in the night, prematurely. To no avail. By morning the visibility was down to 50 yards or less in mist and fog. I headed a little further north again. By noon it had cleared enough for sights which put us past Gough and 30–40 miles to the north. One more place to check with another visit! I found a little jar of marmalade at last, among the pickles, so could now have toast and marmalade. What heaven. Not only the delicious smells of bread baking when I made it, but now the mouth-watering smells of toasting, as well.

A couple of perfect days of clear Southern Ocean 'tradewind' sailing followed our missing of Gough. Reaching east in a 15–20 knot north to north-north-westerly and glorious sunshine. We could have carried more sail but were averaging 5 knots in absolute comfort, so I got on with boat chores while the comfort lasted. Double-reefed main and Yankee doing the work. At 2 a.m. while I was up for the usual late-night course check/alteration time on deck, the sky was truly ablaze. An infinity of light specks dusted the heavens, the Magellanic Clouds particularly clear. The blackness of the night had now joined us in the day, in the form of white-chinned petrels/Cape hens. These kept their white chins very well hidden, and no matter how closely I looked they appeared to be all black around here.

Like the meteor's trail of light across the sky, our wake blazed through the darkness with its own bright tail. For only the second time in the voyage that I had seen – the first being back south of New Zealand – we left an underwater rocket trail behind us. Our keel, rudder and self-steering rudder were creating a trail of bioluminescence many boat lengths long. An underwater furrow of light complete with large sparks peeling off as larger organisms lit up. There was virtually no phosphorescence in our surface wake, only this milky submarine trail. It silhouetted everything near the stern in its glow. To put in the third reef and slow down would have spoiled the show. I remained on deck watching, around the brink of too much sail.

This was the night before my latest 'revelation' and disconnection experiment with the batteries that had me finding one still alive. Barely. We needed days of strong light to see if it would build up then hold charge.

Mist and drizzle, drizzle and mist, once more mist and drizzle. We had now crossed the Greenwich Meridian and the wind had swung from north-west into south. Our easting was still good, but battery-charging nil. Today, in its greyness, passes slowly. It is sunless, cold and dismal, and my thoughts are of winter coming on . . . I take out a reef, I put back a reef, I am not sure of this weather at all. Our electric, psychedelic wake was with us again last night, but not as strongly as the previous two nights. Could it be related to the moon? The total absence of a moon the other nights?

The numbers of our longitude were increasing, progress easier to gauge. I seemed to have almost sailed out of the territory of the black-capped great shearwaters, with very few around. Yesterday we seemed to have only the black of the petrels in the sky, but some black-capped friends caught up with us again during more days of windlessness and grey. Both they and the petrels were still fascinated by my trailing 'fishy' – mesmerised, it would seem.

My solar panel was now showing no charge despite some weak sun late in the day. I thought there had been enough general illumination in the sky all day for at least half an amp, so this was a worry. I was using no power at all except brief bursts of compass light when course-changing, so chose to ignore this new problem until a really sunny day left no room for doubt.

I didn't get a chance to ignore it for long. On the horizon, almost hull down to the south, and what did I see? A ship passing us. I didn't have enough batteries to run my radar detector all the time; I was saving it for regions where traffic was more probable. I quickly connected it as a test, but there were no blips. Either his radar wasn't working, or it operated on some strange frequency that didn't alert my alarm. Not very reassuring. Particularly with no navigation lights to show. But . . . I guess it missed me, so my small ships, big oceans theory was holding!

We really needed an extended strong sunboost to try and put life into the last battery, and I found the lack of sun particularly depressing. I figured the ship had been on the Rio or Buenos Aires to Cape Town shipping lane. There shouldn't be much more along there. Log reading almost 3,000 miles from Stanley and we had wind again. I took a coffee out into the cockpit to get the feel of the day. I had been avoiding reefing until daylight. I stayed awhile soaking in the signs, and it felt there was more wind to come.

The aerial ballet put on by my flying friends always seemed best at the birth of a blow. This morning's was a beauty. Two large wanderers taking the lead, backed by a considerable number of petrels and shearwaters. The petrels soared high, looked around, then came back down in swooping, banking dives. The shearwaters maintained a more even altitude. I put back in the second reef. It was the first time in the voyage I had done this on starboard tack, so a little reorganising of lines was necessary. Feeling that there was still more wind to come I put in the third reef while I was at it. Not long after, a very threatening-looking rain squall heralded the start of the next round. I returned and dropped the mainsail completely.

The waves were throwing us around quite a bit by now, and when the Yankee accidentally backed (we were running almost square under Yankee alone) it felt and sounded as if it would pull the mast out. It was too nerve-racking. I dropped the Yankee and continued under bare poles white sorting out the staysail for a set. Soon we were heading east again under staysail alone, the wind having swung from west to south-west to south-south-west as it strengthened. So far we were handling it all right and I retreated below. This was the first starboard tack gale since New Zealand.

The waves down here below Africa seem very different from the gale seas of the Pacific. They are far more irregular and unpredictable to the point where you could describe them as vicious. Some are very large, but long and harmless, others short and very, very steep, yet not breaking. Still others rear up out of nowhere, breaking savagely only to vanish moments later into void-like holes. A combination of cross seas and unpredictable currents, I suppose. There were a lot of sea-mounts around here. I was in a 'I don't trust the Atlantic at all, let's get outta here' frame of mind. For so long the gales and seas had seemed so unrelated to the barometer that it was very hard to predict what would happen next.

At 5 a.m. next morning I reset the main at the third reef to make the most of milder conditions. The race was really on to get past this 'corner', past the Agulhas, back into more open spaces. Before the next gale if we could. Soon after, I dropped the staysail and reset the Yankee. I could have taken out a reef as well, but held back, being cautious. Sights put us at 39 degrees 40 minutes south and 7 degrees 0 minutes east, so we had made some progress despite the blow. I had not wanted to sail beam on to the large breaking seas and so had run off more towards the north, figuring it would ease before we had gone too far. It was reassuring that with these sights this was confirmed.

I watched a saddening fragment of life this morning, amongst my feathered friends. A large skua was attacking and bullying a small shearwater, and it was having great trouble in trying to escape. The skua had damaged some of its wing feathers already and was repeatedly attacking the smaller, weaker bird (humankind is more evolved?) The shearwater was trying to stay near the surface, using brains and agility, running and splashing to avoid the attacks. I called to it to come aboard for a rest in safety, but of course I wasn't understood. I hoped it escaped in the end.

The sou'wester has been very cold, my cabin dripping condensation as badly as ever it did in the regions far to the south. 'The winter time is coming, the windows are filled with frost . . . I tried to tell everybody . . . but could not get across.' We must get a move on. My books and everything else in the cabin are getting wet from the drips, the toilet/spare bilge pump unusable. The navigation lights, compass light, emergency cabin light, bunk light, cassette player and radar detector also unusable due to dead or dying batteries. It is no longer as pleasant without these luxuries and bringers of illusory safety. It is cold enough to need socks and Marion's long-sleeved 'warmie' in my bunk again now. According to *Meteorology for Mariners* it shouldn't get much colder than this for the rest of the course, but I expect it to be damned cold below Australia and Tasmania no matter what the temperature charts say.

Dinner these nights consisted of rice + fresh root ginger + honey + black pepper + fresh onions + tinned seasoned green beans, corn kernels or other tinned vegetables + sultanas or raisins, dried apple or variants along these lines. Based on rice, tinned veggies, dried fruit and nuts, honey, pepper, chili, cheese or nutmeat. Alternatively, dishes based on pasta, spinach noodles or macaroni shells along with fresh garlic and onions, tinned tomatoes, tinned ratatouille, basil, black pepper and chili, maybe with some Mexican chili salami occasionally, for a change. I would cook enough on the first night to last for three nights, reheated, with the addition of fresh onion and another tin of vegetables that harmonised with the first. Desserts consisted of tinned pineapple rings or pears, figs, dried fruit and nuts, along with a glass of fruit juice.

In a strengthening wind we hurtled east through afternoon and evening. I spent a considerable amount of time on deck, watching and waiting to drop the main before dark. But . . . We seemed to be coping. On into the night. It was a night of sleeplessness and many visits to the cockpit to observe. Spray flew. A phosphorescent wake streamed far astern. This was moving. I decided in the darkness I might cause more damage dropping the main than risking it up. On we flew, surfing in long runs down irregular seas. Breakers burst astern in explosions of phosphorescent light. I couldn't push us harder. This was some ride . . .

At dawn I discovered that the log hadn't been reading all night. I pulled it in and found the trail wire hopelessly entangled with the log line, stopping it spinning. After fixing, on returning it to the sea, I noticed the eye at the end of the line had worn to less than a hair's breadth of nylon. I replaced the entire line. The world was still all grey except for the birds, our wake, the breakers' turquoise tops. Rain squall, rain squall, rain squall. If it blew any harder I would have to hand-steer . . . or slow down and make it easier to take. This felt like a race between life and death, too finely balanced on a minimality of edge. I started hoping for some sun as this had to be near a '200 miles in a day' day.

The wind eased a bit during the morning, with hints, just possibilities, of sun. The way the swells suddenly build, peak and break heavily is still exceedingly irregular and unnerving. They seem to hold no pattern, these South Atlantic swells. A calm patch, flat and harmless, jumps out of nowhere to a steep and breaking giant. Most odd.

Noon, and sunshine out there now, but only for brief moments – not long enough for me to adjust the micrometer screw for a good sight. Curse that hand. Not a good horizon, though, either. By 3 p.m. it had eased somewhat, with longer periods of sun. *Yippeeee*! 220 miles in 27 hours, and those last three hours 'fairly slow'. *Our first 200-mile day.* It was one of my goals, this trip, to break that barrier. You did it, while overladen too!

No wonder the log needed all those replacement parts this morning. Whenever I went on deck last night the speed and phosphorescence were amazing. Now I knew why. We really had been pushing the limits – the same average speed as the

The calm end of our 200-mile day.

57-foot *Ondine* in setting the Sydney–Hobart race record that stood for so many years. Thank you, *Little Wing*. 22 March, 1991.

'Becalmed' was now a relative word, and next morning we were 'becalmed'. Averaging only four knots. Sewing repairs to my wet-weather gear, clothes washing, rewhipping the self-steering lines to avoid the continual port tack chafe spots and remove stretch. We were back to windlessness and grey by afternoon, heading slowly south-east in a very light easterly. Hardly enough wind to fill the sails. Next morning the lack of wind remained, but it was sunny and I had been joined by a new group of friends. About a dozen black-browed and grey-headed albatrosses stayed with us all morning and into the afternoon. Landing up ahead or close astern, a peck at my log-fish as we went past, then a puzzled look as we left them behind. Off they would run to get up speed for take-off, repeating the process all morning.

I began to think they were doing it just to show off their waterski landings, so often and so close did they land. Sights put me at 40 degrees south/16 degrees east, confirming my DR position and thus also our good day's run. In between conversing with my feathered friends I baked two more wholemeal fruit loaves, then discovered my margarine was going mouldy and tasted very off. Honey or my precious marmalade would be needed to mask the taste. When it got too bad, I would revert to mayonnaise. We kept on the more southern tack, heading south-east, as I wanted to be well south to avoid the Agulhas Current and its tail. Too many ships had vanished or broken up in the seas it threw up with a contrary wind.

Despite two days of calm we had still covered 420 miles in the last three. I was well pleased, sitting in the afternoon sun and watching the aerial ballet of my friends. Wheeling and sweeping, swooping and banking in unison when in groups or pairs, alone at other times. They reminded me of film I had seen of ice skaters dancing. An aerial Torvill and Dean, so co-ordinated were they at times.

A very bright two-thirds moon last night, then watching the stars through the window over my bunk. A great sense of the infinity of space. Memories, memories bubbling until I fell asleep. We were heading happily to windward towards Antarctica. There was a lot of southing in our course, but I preferred this southern tack.

Chapter Twenty-Three
The Cape and The Current

Mild, sunny and warm, to windward under a cloudless sky. A water temperature of 19 degrees C and the appearance of several bluebottles convinced me we were in a tongue of current from the north. Some cirrus appeared at sunset to the south, with altostratus to the north. This slice of summer would not last long. As the wind went further towards the north I eased sheets and headed more towards east. I hoped we would cross longitude 20 degrees east, below Agulhas, with tomorrow's sights. We would be in Agulhas' waters until longitude 50 degrees east. Then, and only then, would I consider this corner behind us.

Since midnight we had moved not a whisker. Windlessness held us in its sway. Rolling in confused seas, not even the Drifter held its shape. Roll, pitch, roll, pitch, roll. These nonsensical seas shook us about dreadfully, and I dropped even the Drifter to save it from tearing. The moon maintained a halo each night, promising wind to come, but each little barometer drop just fizzed. At least the battery was getting its chance, and I was using no power to drain it.

One advantage of the recent calm weather had been to facilitate the discovery of a new heroine, the remarkable Beryl Markham. I devoured her book *West with the Night* in almost one sitting, reading and re-reading large tracts of it, so enchanted was I by her story, her style. It was not enough. I had bought a biography of her at the same time (the year before my first attempts at the voyage), so now I continued to live in her life through its pages. I had deliberately held off reading these until we had arrived below Africa, her spirit home. The wait was well worth it. I felt close in all ways. I had been introduced to the writings of

Isak Dinesen in 1988 by a close friend and had read all that I could get. But Beryl was more African, more real. As I listened to my 1968 tapes of African native music in my bunk these calm evenings I would almost be there in those 'frontier' years.

We seemed to be passing through, or drifting with, a field of plankton, and I expected another whale, but none appeared. I decided, though, that my petrels and shearwaters must eat plankton. This would explain their head-dipping antics whenever they landed – searching out and eating the larger kinds. I had been making friends with one group of about two dozen white-whiskered buddies parked in a group just nearby. One of them became almost tame, eating some tinned tuna from my hand, but seemed more impressed by two large goose-necked barnacles growing on my self-steering rudder. She dived at these time and again. Expecting a heavy dew later, I gave my wind vane a coat of varnish to cover some weathered-looking spots. It should dry in the heat of the day. I then cleaned around our waterline, removing the goose-neck barnacles and green weed that had grown. I also let the tin of tuna drift off for the birds to feed themselves, but none recognised its shape as being food. It was still there as darkness fell, about a boat length away and untouched. Even those few who flew directly over it during the afternoon when restless didn't bother to land or look closer.

An almost forgotten sound, very faint but full of meaning, awoke me at 2 a.m. The whisper of wind ripples against the hull beside my bunk. Rapidly I shot out on deck for a look, catching the moon just as it set. Yes, there was a breeze, a very light west-north-westerly, and just enough to sail in now the swell had flattened.

Drying my work aloft, climbing rack below Africa.

Up went the Yankee again and the lapping of the wind ripples now became the rustle of forward motion. At dawn I dropped the Yankee and reset the Drifter to maximise our miles. We were almost directly below Cape Agulhas, heading east-south-east, and had a sunny and cloudless day. It was a great chance to catch up on treating rust appearing here and there on deck. I spent the day with rust converter and paintbrush in hand, but a really thorough treatment would have to wait until home. I was very tempted after sailing through a marked cloud front from the south-west without change in wind, to leave the Drifter up all night, but lost my nerve. Our 'engine' was too valuable to risk a major tear.

We were getting south into icebergville again according to the charts. It seemed an ice-free year, though, and down here we were well south of shipping lanes, which I considered a more real threat. I hadn't expected such a burst of summer sailing in autumn down here at around 42 degrees south. The breeze held a steady 15–25 knots from the north-west to west for most of the day; we broad-reached in comfort until sunset, when it lightened but for once didn't die completely. I kept to the more southerly course option, aiming to hold it until past the region of the Agulhas Plateau. Even in the moderate and steady wind of morning, the way the waves broke and heaped irregularly at times convinced me that we were in a region of strong current. The water temperature jumped up and down chaotically, more bluebottles appeared and my sights started to differ markedly from DR positions. We were in some tail-end whorls of the Agulhas. An almost full moon lit the night.

Bill Tilman had had strong, strange currents around here also, on his way to Marion and Crozet Islands long ago. I found a flying fish on deck today, already dead unfortunately, but another sign that we were in some tropical stream. As this would probably be our last warm calm, the recently treated rust spots were given more top coat. Only about one mile sailed all night. These calms, this lack of progress were so depressing. Even my birdie friends were all sitting down on the job again today. But . . . I saw the most complete moonbow I have seen, last night, and the water temperature is down by more than 6 degrees centigrade today. Maybe we are re-entering the Southern Ocean again.

At around 8 a.m. all species of my feathered friends put on a show. From wee fairy prions through the shearwaters and petrels to a half-dozen large albatrosski friends. Wheeling in unison with their white underwings flashing simultaneously in the early morning sun, a dark cloudscape behind. But my camera wasn't turned on! Although they continued the aerial dance for some time as they searched for food, never again did they wheel so together, white gold against the darkness beyond.

Evening found us buried again in drizzle, calm and grey. Several times during the night I was up to make course and sail adjustments as the wind strengthened from the north. By dawn I had the Yankee down. By mid-morning we were ploughing east under triple-reefed main and staysail, the reefing having proved quite difficult in irregular seas after so much calm. The water temperature had risen again, we had found another branch or swirl. It held rough and grey all day until at sunset one reddish-pink cloud roll appeared ahead. It looked very like Uluru (Ayers Rock), and on the correct heading too!

The water temperature took a dive to 13 degrees and the wind fell right away. From midnight until dawn we wallowed, stern slapping, log pulled in, helm lashed and Yankee down to ease the chafe. It was drizzling lightly, but not enough to catch. In the past seven days we had been able to sail continuously for twenty-four hours only once. The noises again of halyards slapping, wire rubbing on wire, the transom leak pounding the water every time the counter slapped. A total lack of any sounds suggesting forward motion or its possibility. Very depressing.

Wind! And rain, from that grey old sou'sou'east. Triple-reefed main and Yankee, holding east. For a period last night the waves were truly chaotic and breaking heavily in total windlessness. Another crazy swirl. This morning, once the wind arrived, the waves went 'soft' again, like sailing over hills and dales. We are heading in the same direction as yesterday, with the same angle of heel, but on the opposite tack. No chance of sights today, but tomorrow's should put us on a new chart, a new ocean, and then I can open Fruit Cake No. 2, and Marion's biscuits No. 3.

Sleep is very hard to come by these nights. Once more from 8 p.m. onward we have been rolling and pitching, stern pounding, sail slatting in windlessness. Log pulled in, helm lashed, Yankee down. Waiting, listening, waiting. We were also facing back where we had come from – the South Atlantic high must have come south. What a god-forsaken hole this is. I don't want to be here all winter. A very watery sun, no good for sights. April Fools' Day 1991.

I think *Little Wing* senses that she has escaped that damned Atlantic pond. Sights put us around 41 degrees south, 30 degrees east, and on to the next chart. Sunny and fine, wind 5–8 knots. If only we could get a breeze that would blow all night I would really be in heaven. Three more tins of pineapple and orange juice have eaten through their tins, new ones for this voyage, too. The tin plating must be being skimped on to corrode so fast. All my other tins have remained sound, but these seem to corrode from the inside out. Somewhat like a steel boat! Yes, getting off that last chart and entering a new ocean appears to have done the trick. Broad-reaching east under Yankee and single-reefed main, and all through the night, the first time in over a week.

'But to fly in unbroken darkness without even the cold companionship of ear phones or the knowledge that somewhere ahead are lights and life and a well-marked airport is something more than just lonely. It is at times unreal to the point where the existence of other people seems not even a reasonable probability. The hills, the forests, the rocks, the plains are one with the darkness, and the darkness is infinite. The earth is no more your planet than is a distant star – if a star is visible; the plane is your planet, and you are its sole inhabitant.' Yes, I could relate to Beryl Markham. We both flew alone, and as she said of her own wings; 'To me she is alive, and to me she speaks.'

It was a beautiful evening to be in the cockpit. I watched a satellite passing overhead until it vanished into the Earth's shadow, and a very theatrical moonrise. The moon's rays, just before the moon itself appeared, swept across a region of low cloud like a searchlight. I thought for a while that it must be an aurora until the orange orb appeared. The moving silhouettes of the swells had created the illusion of the moonrise itself darting about. We were entering the tail end of the cyclone alley between Madagascar and southern Africa, and I hoped for more wind to get us across to at least 70 degrees east as quickly as we could.

Another delightful day under Yankee and single-reefed main in a moderate 8–12 knot breeze. Not enough for the rapid progress I would prefer, but I was enjoying the peace, and couldn't be bothered with setting the Drifter or Genoa, or full main with its rushed reefing in emergencies. But the sounds of sail hanks wearing on the forestay, wire halyards rasping on wire, mainsail slatting back and forth as we rolled, gooseneck straining, stern slapping, rudder jarring and galley storage rattling, returned that night. When wind rose again, a nor'wester, grey and with drizzle, I continued a little south of east. I just couldn't get the rhythm of this ocean yet. It was rather similar to the Atlantic for a considerable while after leaving the Falklands. Maybe due to the proximity of a large landmass in both cases. South America and southern Africa. The most truly predictable weather had been during the long Pacific haul where there was no land near at all.

My Cape hen friends (white-whiskered petrels) had become quite reliable short-term weather forecasters. When they sat around in small groups on the water while there was still plenty of wind for flying without needing to flap their wings, it was a sure sign that a marked wind increase was imminent. Time to prepare mentally for the next sail reduction. Meanwhile, it was time for more of our nocturnal rocketship impressions. Our underwater wake stretched several boat lengths astern, with bright sparks of phosphorescence igniting in the overall milky glow. The wind was from the north-west, getting stronger. I put a second reef in the main and went below. A deluge of rain, a wind shift of 180 degrees, and I was back on deck to put in a third. I gybed and headed east-south-east.

Morning found us close reaching east in another heaping grey confusion. Swells were coming from three different directions at once. Two directly opposed to each other, the third at right angles to these. The water temperature was up almost 7 degrees centigrade also, indicating another current swirl. I repaired our only usable candlestick and did further sewing repairs to my disintegrating wet-weather gear. Homeward-bound stitches, they used to be called. Rough and ready, only meant to last for the return journey. I dropped the Yankee and re-set the staysail to slow our headlong rush through the irregular seas. We were crashing through solid water to pulpit height. The Yankee was nearly torn from its lashings. The barometer continued to fall. I dropped the mainsail completely, and continued under staysail alone. When the real blow arrived I preferred to have only one sail to control. Was it a monster low approaching from below, or a cyclone coming down on us from above? Let's get outta here!

Beryl's solo east-west flight across the Atlantic, the first by a woman, in 1936, was a flight I could relate to closely. Flying an overloaded plane without radio or any means of escape other than successfully completing the task at hand, she was criticised before the flight as irresponsible and her journey devoid of purpose. Much the same as the so-called 'well adjusted' thought when I set out. We can laugh together Beryl, when I die! In comparison with hers, modern so-called adventure flights (except for the likes of the *Voyager* flight) seem tame indeed, making use as they do of thoroughly proven equipment riddled with safety gear.

We appeared to be coping as darkness fell, so I lit the kero lantern for getting into my wet-weather gear in a rush and lay down in my bunk to wait. The barometer continued its fall. I couldn't sleep, but I attempted to doze, knowing that something big was about to happen and the signs were now stronger hour by hour. Lightning put on quite a display nearby, rain came and the wind fell away, losing direction as it died. The self-steering disengaged once more – it did this now whenever our speed fell and/or the seas were strange – it was not a night for rest. At 5 a.m., in the dark, real wind arrived and I hastily donned my gear and went on deck. A strong south-south-west to southerly had arrived. I tried to head east, but soon there was too much wind to risk the staysail any longer and at first light down it came, with the bulletproof in its stead. By 6 a.m. it was blowing a steady force 11 and I had my worries about even this being too much sail. I ran us off further to the north and retreated below.

It was totally impossible to see anything out of the cabin. Flying spray, flying rain and breakers covering us continually. It went on and on and on. Not the slightest sign of a let up. Nothing gave way on deck, thank heavens, and Young Mist and I remained in our bunk, flippers and fingers crossed that it would ease. Over two days we were rolled to horizontal or beyond at least half a dozen times, and the wind-driven spray hit us with the force and sound of a sand-blasting with pebbles. The waves here were ugly, brutish, heaping, irregular. Breaking in vertical collapses and avalanches and awesome in their violent formlessness. Literally mountainous in size, this scale lent a peculiar slow-motion appearance to their movements. The water temperature had dropped 7 degrees C in one day and I thought that at last we might have escaped the Agulhas/tropical/Southern Ocean mix that I suspect brewed up this gale.

A funny thing happened as the gale began to ease. I could hold on no longer and simply had to use the toilet bucket. It had been too rough until now to consider opening the aft hatch for me to get out and empty it. I went about my business and then, horror of horrors, the hatch wouldn't open. The violence of the gale and quantity of water breaking over us had untied a lashing keeping a hold-down bolt out of the way, and it had fallen into its slot, locking me down below. I propped the bucket as securely as possible (we were still being thrown around a lot), praying it wouldn't spill. For the first and only time in the voyage I then opened the forward hatch and got out, luckily while no breakers swept the foredeck, raced aft and fixed the problem, then returned forward and below, fastening the hatch closed again behind me. Finally, myself plus loaded bucket exited via the aft hatch for emptying. What relief!

The log showed us having averaged around 5 knots for the duration of the blow, but in which direction only sights could confirm. The large westerly variation here was rendering both my inside compasses unreliable, and it had been far too rough to open the hatch and check the real compass. Somewhere north of east was about all I could be sure of. The temperature was real winter again, with the air at 11 degrees C. With the boat having been so sealed up, condensation was now horrendous. What had not been drenched by the immersions of the Dorades during rollings was rapidly becoming sodden from the dripping of condensation. It was necessary to wear wet-weather gear at all times, even below. Otherwise, my sodden bunk would wet me from below while the drips showered me from above. Now that conditions were mild enough for me to notice it, I discovered the solar panel to be dead again, but it was too cold and wet to locate the cause.

On deck at sunset, just soaking in the scene, it had very much the wintry, solitary feeling of arriving at Lockleys Pylon in the evening with bad weather coming in. Very stark and lovely as a place, windswept and with little shelter, but invigorating in its isolation, its exposure. Bushwalking alone, Southern Ocean alone, just different facets of wilderness, and I loved them both. We were now making just over 6 knots under staysail alone, and it really was quite pleasant. I had decided by now that up to around force 8 it was very pleasant sailing down here, and better still with sun out to alleviate the cold and damp.

A new form of lightshow had brightened the last few nights. The waves washing over the top of the cabin sent shooting stars of phosphorescence across the cabin window above my bunk and down the window opposite. I was still unable to sort out the new solar panel death and my remaining battery was losing charge steadily. Without a calm spell for repairs the battery would be beyond saving. My day thoughts and night dreams were becoming more involved with people and life after my return, so I must have been thinking I'd make the distance. It was now the sixth successive day with wind never below the 30–40 knot level, and the barometer was falling again! I must confess I was getting sick of the sight of large, grey, breaking waves looming over us every time I looked outside. It was still too rough to open a hatch even a smidgen for ventilation/drying, and the cockpit was now growing green weed even on the seats, having been underwater so constantly. The stove burners were also worrying me, having been drenched with salt water so often, and I had no more spares. Despite these anxieties I spent a wonderful couple of hours in the cockpit during late afternoon. Alone with the vastness of the greys.

A more familiar lightshow appeared in the distance astern after I'd put out the candle for the night. Lightning. It resembled the distant electrics that preceded the last big blow. I sat up and waited, but I must have dozed off. All hell suddenly broke loose outside as a furious electrical squall hit. Lit by almost continuous discharges from the big flashbulbs in the sky, I dropped and lashed down the staysail, sure there was more to come. It was impossible to distinguish rain from spray from wave tops blown to smithereens by the squall. All the while lightning exploded around us, light simultaneous with sound. Up went the bulletproof to take us wherever until dawn, but after the squall, nothing. At first light back up went the Yankee, followed soon after by the main at third reef. It was sunshine early, and a relative calm (only 20–25 knots of wind), so time to get my solar panel alive. I quickly located a shorted wire where the external lead joined the through-deck lead. I recrimped and insulated them, sealing them better than before. I knew full well, however, that this was only patching over the problem. I would have to replace the entire wiring from solar panel to electrical board with one continuous lead, sans joints, that I had brought along for the purpose, but the job was too big for me yet.

I had decided by now to take us up to latitude 39 degrees south, to follow along this to sight Amsterdam and/or St Paul Islands, and thread the gap between them. A reasonable navigational exercise, especially if visibility were poor. By then we would have covered about 6,500 miles since leaving the Falklands, and the west face of Amsterdam was supposedly sheer or unclimbable for 3,000 feet. Irresistible. I must have a look, then maybe return for a climb. The aft hatch was open nearly all day, my bedding draped everywhere to dry. It being impossible to move down below, I remained out on deck where I saw a most wondrous sight. An entire rainbow arc down in the trough between two swells. We were so high on one swell that the top of the arch didn't even make it up to horizon level. What a novel reminder of the size of these seas! To make the sight even more memorable a huge wanderer came in for a landing under the arch as I watched. There were four to six wanderers with us all day, two with juvenile plumage. Maybe a family group? Also many Cape hens, and I noticed that these tended to give way to the wanderers aloft, when collisions seemed likely. We passed the 5,000-miles (from Stanley) mark overnight.

Some days of perfect weather followed. Not rushing from sail change to sail change in the blind pursuit of miles. It is such a privilege to be out here in these conditions that it seems almost a crime to spend all one's energy racing to get out of them, racing to return to land. An early autumn heaven. Replete with evenings of peace and nights of reasonable sleep. The early mornings in the cockpit, still chilly while drinking a morning coffee, do make me restless, though, to get off this chart and on to the next. I am restless for climbing, for bushwalking again with my friends. Not at all desirous of the city where one is more solitary amongst the defensive masses than ever one is alone in wilderness. Mankind, caged in the city, so lacking in openness, so afraid. So unhappy with themselves apparently that they have no room for others less brainwashed, less narrow in their dreams.

I think one of the young wanderers keeping us company today could well have been a very rare Amsterdam Island albatross instead, but the proof eluded me. To be sure I needed to ascertain the colour of its lower mandible, and binoculars were not always handy. The results of my sights over the last few days when I had been able to get any had shown an increasing error in my DR position, in the form of a substantial time difference between assumed and actual time of meridian passage (of the sun). Since we would need pinpoint accuracy to thread the needle between Amsterdam Island and St Paul safely in conditions of poor visibility, this was a worry. Over the next few days I had a navigational frenzy, eventually putting our progress back a couple of hundred miles. Those weird-shaped swells and wild fluctuations of water temperature over the past couple of weeks had been current-created, as I thought, but the backward component was way beyond expectation. Reminded of the sextant-induced error back near the Horn, I had checked this out first. No change. From here on to home my sights and DR remained in close agreement all the way. Bill Tilman had been set up to 60 miles in a day near here. It had been the Cape and the Current.

Chapter Twenty-Four

Amsterdam, Aye

We had a target now, relatively close, and with it returned all the fears of landfall. The double-checked sights, the more often checked compass, renewed worries each time the self-steering disengaged. With sheet-to-tiller systems my stable course options in light and heavy conditions were limited and it was likely I would need to do a lot of hand-steering. Or aim to bypass the islands well to the south. Too far north and we risked getting caught in the Indian Ocean High, and I had had enough of windlessness for one voyage! While waiting in the cockpit for the next cold front to arrive I watched a lone Arctic tern fly past. At first I had thought it was a rare Kerguelen tern but further reading suggested an Arctic tern, bleached from the Antarctic summer, on its long, lone journey back north. It flew with a very erratic flight as if hunting insects in mid-air, repeatedly dropping close to the water to inspect things it had spotted on the surface. A very delicate bird, more fragile-looking even than a storm petrel, with its pale colouring and very high-aspect ratio wings. We were getting into warmer waters up here at latitude 39 degrees south. I found a flying fish dead in the cockpit at morning, and a squid in the scuppers to boot. We were inadvertently catching local fauna as we all flew through the night. I returned them to the sea for recycling.

Although the water was warm, at 17 degrees, the wind definitely was not. It was too cold to remain comfortably on deck without sea boots, and these were forgotten, at home. I expected new outbreaks of chilblains on hands and feet at any time. Meanwhile, we were rattling off the miles very nicely, covering 90 miles overnight when there was wind. At present, 25–30 knots from the south to

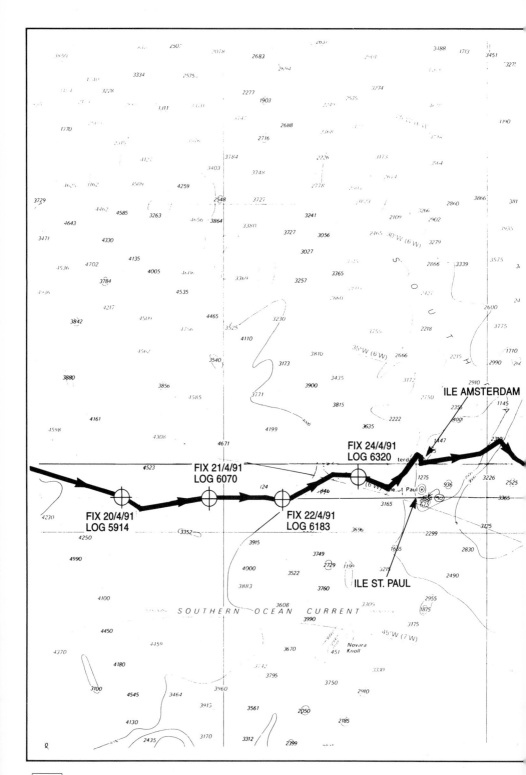

ILE AMSTERDAM

FIX 24/4/91
LOG 6320

FIX 21/4/91
LOG 6070

FIX 20/4/91
LOG 5914

FIX 22/4/91
LOG 6183

ILE ST. PAUL

SOUTHERN OCEAN CURRENT

Novara Knoll

sou'sou'west, ideal for Mr Monitor, Yankee plus triple-reefed main. I could have handled more mainsail, but with the self-steering damaged and disengaging when strained, I sailed undercanvassed to avoid further damage.

My solar panel was now dead as a dodo. This time the panel itself, not a break in the circuit. I had noticed its latest death the day before, but in the overcast and rough I could rationalise it away. Today, however, was calm. Calm enough to act, at any rate. I removed the junction box cover at the back of the panel. What had begun life as shiny connecting wires and pristine terminal blocks were now a corroded mush. Sealing with silicone as recommended had not been enough. Theory had not been capable of coping with the force of repeated assaults by wind-driven seawater during gale after gale.

If I were to save my last battery, it was time now for a complete replacement. I would need to remove the present panel and its timber frame totally from the stern, along with all its support fastenings and leads. This done I would remove the panel from the frame, replace it with my spare and rewire completely, with one continuous lead to the electrical panel below. It sounds so simple. It involved much work below decks in my unlit, unventilated, now leaking stern. It involved, also, the removal then successful realigning of some fifty perimeter fastenings with their pre-threaded holes. No latitude for error. I had thought this task too difficult to attempt even on the mooring at home. I worked until darkness without breakfast or break, but compensation came with morning. Everything worked, the gauges read power, the battery might live.

The electrical work day had cost us miles, my concentration having been elsewhere. Now I was pushing to make them up, holding on to the last before reefing. We had wind enough, so I set my sights on another 200-mile day. It was a sleepless night, holding double-reefed main plus Yankee. At first light, able to see again, I put in the third, then shortly after, when the wind strengthened, dropped the mainsail completely, before the self-steering lost control. All day we surfed eastward in 30–40 knots of wind from the west-north-west. We were at the limit all day, even under Yankee alone, but I held my nerve and by evening it had eased to 20–30 knots from the west. Not enough wind for a 200-mile day now, but it was like heaven out on deck as evening came. Standing facing forward, holding the dodger frame for support, I stayed out watching us surf wave after wave until I was lit by moonlight alone. We in turn watched by the stars overhead. What a marvellous little boat, how beautifully she moved!

It was about the only time since Stanley that we had had comfortably strong sailing winds for more than a few hours at a stretch without radical change. We were doing over 170 miles per day in comfort, and this could have been more had Mr M. been intact. We needed some mainsail area if we were to nudge 200 or more. Maybe I was getting a bit worn down and tired, not wanting to push quite so hard. These westerlies were cold, not just cool; they were telling me it was winter, not autumn, down south. We were also entering a new avian territory. Gone were most of my white-chinned petrels, their place having been taken by large numbers of soft-plumaged petrels. Putting in an appearance also were a few sooty albatrosses. How light and elegant these looked with their ultra high-aspect ratio wings. They almost appear too fragile for the weather down here, too prone to damage if accidentally dipping a wing. So highly refined that the black-brows and others were made to look heavy, almost clumsy in comparison.

I lost a dear friend today. I was down below writing up my log as we sailed comfortably, almost slowly along. Glancing out of the cabin window above me for some reason, I noticed the Yankee luffing. What?! Off-course in these mild conditions? I looked aft and noticed the wind vane missing. Puzzling though this was, it didn't yet worry me, as the vane was attached to the rest of the mechanism with a safety line. But on reaching the deck and looking over the side to retrieve it, it was not there. Nothing. The line chafed through by wind. That vane had taken us through everything, gales and calms, from latitude 50 degrees south on the western side of South America. From the start of our dip down to get below the Horn until now. Faultlessly through every gale.

The chances were about the same as finding a needle in a thousand haystacks, but I turned us around on the reciprocal course and began to search. I didn't know for how long it had been missing, as in these mild conditions we had probably held our course without it for quite a while. I was trying to sail us always so well balanced now as to need Mr M. for fine corrections only, because of the disengagement problem. And now we were being penalised for holding course so well! I sailed back for 20–30 minutes along our track, my eyes peeled for a glimpse of the floating vane. I then gybed and returned the distance, continuing a search pattern for over an hour until a gigantic line squall approaching us was too close to ignore. It was time to get sail down and prepare for the blow.

What a fraud. The huge roll of cloud stretched straight as an arrow towards the horizon until it was swallowed by perspective and the atmosphere. But no wind reached out from under. Just a blanket of darkness to bring a premature end to the day. We wallowed in confusing dark and windlessness while brief little squalls came and went, started and stopped, from all points of the compass. Mr M. was disengaged repeatedly. Savagely his castings had their teeth gnashed and ground together as the confused swells slammed the watervane from side to side. There was no forward motion to cushion the blows. I lashed everything I could to limit the damage/put a halt to the slamming, but the darkness and my lack of dexterity foiled all attempts. Pouring rain further obscured vision. I tried hand-steering in an attempt to get forward motion to solve the problem, but not even I could find a course to steer. How could I expect it of Mr M.?

Approximately 5,000 miles to Sydney and 300–400 to Amsterdam Island. Although I succeeded in improvising sheet-to-tiller/Mr M. combinations that kept him working intermittently for another 3,000 miles, Mr M. was dead from this night as a reliable form of steering. I would die of cold if I had to hand-steer long gales, so every trick in the manual I tried. The whole unit being mounted so far aft to clear my transom-hung rudder rendered repairs at sea impossible. My

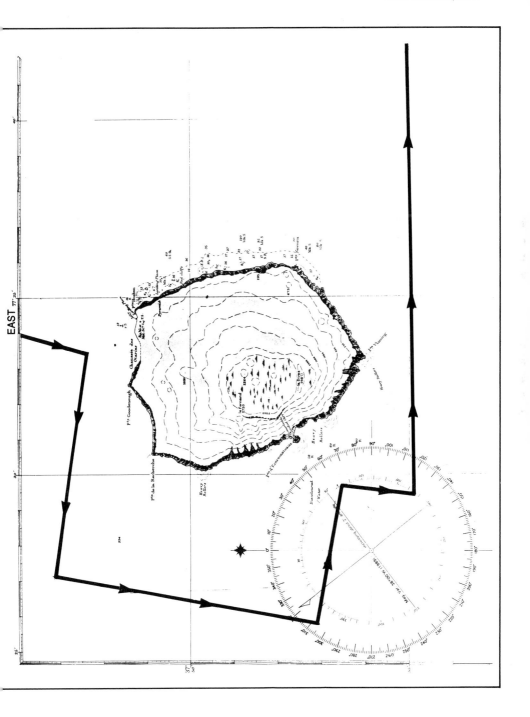

tactics now would have to be aimed mainly towards getting back in one piece and repairing everything then. The quest for speed becoming secondary. I still wanted to investigate the west coast of Amsterdam Island, so was ready to hand-steer as necessary until we were clear. It was about the same distance away as a Sydney to Lord Howe dash and I could almost keep awake for that if desperate enough.

As the self-steering became less and less reliable, less and less reading was possible. I had bought many books in the two years preceding setting out and had left these unread especially for the voyage. Most now remained unread as time to read rapidly approached zero.

Every day now until I disconnected Mr M. completely below Australia I would work perched out beyond the stern trying to re-engage his gears. Up to ten or twelve times a day, day and night, trying to find settings that would keep engaged for more than one narrow wind and sea combination. The colder it became, the more I realised how the success of this trip so far had depended on him. I tried everything to keep him alive. To keep an accurate DR position in my head I checked our course hourly between noon latitudes and longitudes. Light to moderate breezes and clear skies for sights aided our approach, and Mr M. allowed brief bursts of rest. We were only 90 miles off. If my navigation were correct we should be there tomorrow, and be gone.

Sunrise, 27 April, and up early to reset the Yankee. I had slowed us down by sailing with staysail overnight so as not to hit land prematurely. An island that wrecked so many fully crewed ships that a provision depot and cattle were kept there deserved respect. I was unlashing the Yankee and had hardly begun, when . . . I looked again. Yes, Amsterdam Island, visible off the starboard bow between rain squalls. Just a dash further to the south than I had expected. Nevertheless, safely in sight, and within range of studying and passing at close range if the wind held, but of course it didn't. It swung until we were approaching hard on the wind, with current and leeway taking us past. I held course until within a mile or so of the meteorological station visible ahead, then tacked clear to keep us away from land effects on the breeze. It was no time to risk getting caught in a 'hole' and swept into the cliffs by current.

Cloud was formed continuously near the tip of the sheer western wall, keeping the highest peak completely wreathed and hidden for all but brief moments. We worked our way from the north down around the western side, to clear the island to the south. Streamers of cloud peeled off the long knife-edge ridge that formed the tip of the western wall and led up to the summit itself. Late afternoon light lit the precipitous faces, the ridges and gullies, all sans vegetation except for tussock or grasses glowing gold. Darker eroded areas of bare earth or rock swept sheer to the sea. A band of dark cliffs protected the island from easy landings wherever the full height wall let up. It was an impressive sight. What splendid isolation. What magnificence of nature. What a heaven to share with a loved one, just the two of us with the wildlife and the weather, the refuge and the storm.

Approaching Amsterdam Island
– cloud forming continuously on the Western face and peeling away to leeward.

The West Wall Amsterdam Island – the reason for our detour north.

Fur seals came out to leap and play, some ultra delicate little black-capped terns, and I am sure I saw one of the rare Amsterdam Island albatrosses, seated, as we sailed by. I had to tack out to sea again at sunset, to clear the long, gently sloping ridge heading to the southern headland, but tacked back before dark to see if we were going to get past. It was a tense bit of windward sailing, in gathering gloom and a fading breeze, but we made it past in intermittent moonlight, sailing along the moonpath heading east.

Amsterdam Island had an amazingly powerful effect on me. I felt as lonely leaving its perfection of isolation behind, or more so, than I had on leaving the Falklands and their human warmth. Something about creative challenge, and the sharing, the melding of dreams. Imagining the climbing, the exploring, studying the natural world there with a loved one by my side as keen as I. At sunset on that high and knife-edged ridge perched amongst the clouds. Ocean to the horizon on all sides except maybe a glimpse of St Paul Island to the south on a clear day. The wind-blown tussock, the ocean's pound and roar, the winds from calm to screaming. Through the night we sailed away – so quietly, calmly – dreaming. Self-steering sans any self-steering at all. Balanced sailing, full moon rising, in a very light south-easter until becalmed. The deck and cockpit so white by moonlight, enveloped in a world of silver-grey. The swells smooth and barely rippled, whatever ripples caused by their motion through still air. Almost two days spent sailing away yet there it was, clearly visible still at 60 miles.

Several seals paid us a visit one of these tranquil afternoons. Popping their heads up about 18 inches above water level and swivelling slowly for a good 360-degree look around. Diving under the boat, swimming alongside, then rolling on their backs to sunbake, flippers pointing towards the sky.

By the third evening after clearing that southern headland our Amsterdam Island 'holiday' was over. Finally out of sight astern with the next land to be seen either southern Tasmania or the coast of New South Wales near Sydney. Western Australia and Cape Leeuwin just snuck in there on the edge of our present chart (Indian Ocean, Eastern Portion), but we would pass several hundred miles to the south of them if all went well. Meanwhile, our all but non-existent south-easterly backed further towards the east, sending us creeping ever so slowly toward the tropics. It was the less losing tack, however, despite not wanting to be driven north and trapped in the Indian Ocean High. Signs of approaching change had been in the sky for some time, but nothing came. My sights put us at nearly 38 degrees south, the water temperature had become a tropical 17 degrees C; it was time to tack towards the south and the mythical westerlies – they certainly weren't reaching up to here.

With our dreadfully slow progress over the past week came fears of spending the entire winter at sea, battling darkness, more breakages and gathering despair. I had never been able to get us to self-steer adequately under sheet-to-tiller systems in hard going downwind, but unless we got some of these conditions soon, our progress would remain abysmal. The progress would make the hand-steering worthwhile, despite the cold. While I had working self-steering nothing seemed too big a problem to solve. Now I was losing all confidence, we were getting nowhere, just wearing things out one by one . . . And our last battery died today. We had had no navigation lights except for emergencies. Now we had none at all. No compass light either, no emergency cabin light, not enough small batteries for the radar detector or frequent use of torches, no music to listen to and dream. With the leak still doubling every gale, this was becoming a voyage to hell – at least in my more depressed moments. But with the arrival of wind I rejoiced, and we set happily about covering those last mere 4,500 miles.

Chapter Twenty-Five

Things Almost Always Pick up at Dawn

Things almost always pick up at dawn. If you can hold out until dawn, you will probably hold out until the end.

Bernard Moitessier, *The Long Way*

Darkness descending simultaneously on more fronts than one. For over a week we have averaged less than 50 miles per day in calms never ending. Days noticeably shorter, the nights lasting an age. In miles this was now our longest voyage, exceeding Sydney to Stanley on 2 May. A short force 9–10 of only twenty hours' duration livened things up and had us running before at the limit under staysail alone. Again with no barometric change, and this time out of a clear sky. The preponderance of calms had me always driving to the limit when there was usable wind in large doses. To the limit that my weld-tearing, leak-increasing fears of sinking would allow. We were surfing frequently in strangely breaking seas – a sensible limit probably – keeping intact. The sunlight brought no life back to my dodo batteries, despite charge going in. We would remain an unlit ship, unseen through the darkness of the night.

Large left-over swells made progress very hard once wind was gone. Our apparent wind angle changed radically as they charged on through beneath us. Cross swells, not enough wind to steady us, no Mr M. The weather of the world seems to be dying down here. Humanity, their noxious fumes and cancerous growth would appear to have destroyed the balance of life on our water planet. Slatting about in windlessness, almost ready to take a leap into the deep for a little peace and quiet. Moonrise. Again the searchlight fanning the sky effect just before the rise. Sky clearing, stars except for in the south, and wind again. Keeping company in the cockpit with Mr M., enjoying the novelty of motion in a 15–20 knot westerly which held all through the night.

There was a lesson here for my moments of despair. As I had learnt so long ago to accept that all storms must pass and not to worry as they blew, so I came to learn the same of calms, that even they pass, too. Despite the endless slatting, rattling, pitching, slamming, rolling-on-the-same-spot blues. Oh, for more than a few hours of good sailing breeze at a time. My prayers were answered by the goddesses that be and on we ploughed in Yankee-only seas. Wind and wave too much for Mr M. with mainsail set. Then came the dawn . . .

Firstly the cirrus wisps catching the early pinks, pre-sunrise, in an otherwise featureless sky. The shades of neither night nor daylight hid the structure lower down. Sipping coffee, idly thinking, suddenly aware. The air around us colour-flooded, immersed in light. Pinks. Golden pinks, orange pinks, rusting pinks like blood – little scales of pink against the grey now turning blue. The entire eastern sky ablaze with flame pink fire as the altocumulus lit up sky-wide. Higher still the cirrus tendrils glowed gold in direct sun. Around us and ahead the sea reflected back the sky, but rippled, flecked with shadow remnants of the night.

This dawn dealt out a warning of less pleasant things to come and soon after came the line squall, came the change. Mainsail down, Yankee down, staysail up, mainsail up at third reef, self-steering disengaging, disengaged. New tack, try sheet-to-tiller gear but all in vain. So wet below from deck trips in one day that you would think the wet had been here for a week. The next morning, coffee cheered me once again, and I promised Young Mist we *would* make it, despite our troubles. The nights were now near fourteen hours of total dark. Fourteen hours a day reduced to a cripple. Trying to work over the stern these nights for hours, hypothermic, on Mr M. – hands frozen, screaming out their pain. Hurrying to round Tassie and head north to longer days.

Mr M. now needed absolutely steady state conditions to keep his gears engaged. Conditions too rare to be useful often. I hardly dared change sails any more unless I could keep our motion constant during the change. This was almost impossible unless very carefully thought out and rather complex sequences were followed. Long hours over the stern in all weathers, day and night, were no longer the exception, were the rule. If we had had only a few hundred miles to go, these reaching conditions, hand-steered, would have been almost ideal. Reaching, however, in breaking cross seas stressed the skeg welds ferociously, and the daily increase in bilge-pumping told of increasing weld tears somewhere underwater, out of reach. With our only working bilge pump possibly near worn-out, I felt a growing urgency. Would we get there before sinking? I was still hanging on to sail as long as possible, hand-steering worried miles. It was our longest voyage in terms of days.

With winter now fully ensconced it was satisfying to notice that, despite being cold and wet for most of each day, I was never even slightly ill from coughs, colds or flu. No doubt thanks to the lack of humanity and the illnesses they carry. As well as my morning cup of coffee and afternoon cup of tea, I was now in the habit of having a cup of instant soup around the middle of the day. With some fresh onion, sultanas, raisins, basil or pepper added, these were quite acceptable and easy to prepare, sometimes with instant mashed potato also to make a thicker soup. The tins of concentrated soups I saved for evening meals, again with additives to suit each type.

A radical change in seabird populations took place while I was in the cockpit, steering. We had been sailing all day through a marine desert, devoid of birds. Suddenly we were surrounded, engulfed in a flock of hundreds of whalebirds/ prions on all sides. Maybe we were crossing another whale path/migratory route, but I saw no sign of whales. Again the wind left us becalmed for the night. A night of drifting backwards, Mr M. broken down and not enough wind for sheet-to-tiller gear. Continually trying to forestall the next trouble through unexpected breakdowns combined with darkness, cold and my bloody useless hand. It was easy to despair.

I broke my right wrist, I think, this morning, in a final burst to try fix Mr M. The cripples creep on without even one intact hand on the ship. I managed to take in a reef using teeth in lieu of hands, but broke off a large filling in the process. I hope it is the only one that breaks, as without using teeth now I couldn't sail at all. I can't even bandage the wrist due to the other hand. Since the triumph and joy of Amsterdam Island I have been steadily losing confidence in completing this journey. The leak, the breakdowns, being reduced to a cripple for most of each day by long nights, and now my only useful hand put out, with every bump or movement shooting pain. I feel more fragile out here now than at any other time in the voyage. Every passing wave hurts, but I can't sail no-handed or we would get nowhere at all. I have a bad case of the 'it takes just so damned long to get off the last half of the chart' blues.

Managed to furl mainsail completely using left hand and teeth, barometer heading down. God only knows how I'll manage Yankee if that needs dropping too. I eased us off further south than desirable to try and keep it up. I just have to go where she'll sail herself for the time being. After a good porridge breakfast, lack of progress started hurting more than my wrist, so I reset the main at third reef. In the afternoon I shook this out and went back to the second, thus giving myself a night of no sleep as I lay listening for trouble. By daylight we were back to third reef; soon after no mainsail at all. By late morning the Yankee was down and we continued under staysail alone, sans Mr M., steering herself between reach and close reach. Waves were again breaking clean over the cabin so often that it was reminiscent of the miserable grey gales south of New Zealand.

Despite all woes, however, parts of every day were joyful and wonder-filled. Subtleties of colour and movement in the sea and sky and our motion through

Indian Ocean, molten.

them; sudden avalanches of happy memories, strings of past and future dreams, ideas and plans triggered from nowhere seemingly, just surfacing and flowing through my mind.

Cape Leeuwin is not wanting to be outdone in the 'Great Capes producing Great Gales' department. Last night was almost as rough as any we have had. Probably only due, though, to trying to hold staysail and make miles. I couldn't face a night change yet, in seas like these, sans hands. The very confused swells around here are reminiscent of the Good Hope/Agulhas region; there must be current swirls. My bilge pumps have nearly doubled in the last three days. This Aussie gale seems the most enduring of the lot, or is it just that the winter makes it seem so long? It has been over a week since any sights were possible, so I remain trapped on the old chart until I get a positive fix. A sliver of moon appeared through a gap in the clouds at dusk. A new moon for a new continent, Venus near the moon. Mainsail back up at third reef and pumping several hundred per day.

Totally becalmed last night, helm lashed, log in, Yankee down – twice. A brief reset between. A light easterly came with the dawn, so back to single-reefed main plus Yankee, port tacking to windward once again. The skeg welds tearing beyond pump capacity was now my greatest worry, with Mr M. almost forgotten. Despite the nuisance of having had to sail the last 7,000 miles or so always at half throttle to try and maintain some spark of usefulness in him. Sights put us directly below Leeuwin at around latitude 39 degrees south and aimed for 40 or below. Australia continued to throw up the most sustained piece of variable, unpleasant weather. Not a star seen at night now for weeks, only that sliver of moon. Reefing, unreefing, headsail changes, no chance for the wrist to get some rest. Rain, rain, rain, confused seas and little wind jumping suddenly to gale and then back. So much for Australian sunshine. This is the most extended period of sunless, sightless, unpleasant weather I can remember. The irregular tossing about makes even reading next to impossible.

Beneath the Bight, at latitude 41 degrees south, and at last a clearing sky. Cleared slowly from the north and west during the night. In the cockpit, moon astern, stars above, my own Antares blazing brightly red directly overhead. Morning crept in cloudless, all my washing out to dry. I finally drank Marion's Cape Leeuwin miniature of rum. She had wrapped little miniatures of different spirits and liqueurs for each Cape among her bag of presents for the voyage. The name of the Cape was written on the wrapping, and now only one remained. I would not, however, open the Tassie one until well into Bass Strait, several hundred miles past. I made a habit of doing this so as not to risk annoying the Capes by premature celebration. So far this had worked and we had not been driven back.

> Radiant as burnt Antares
> blazing in a midnight sky
> that warm red glow of friendship growing
> Stirs me,
> I'm alive.
>
> You burst into my life, my dreamscape
> stretched to give you room to move . . .
> One blue-suede hero died,
> it moved me
> Deeply,
> so do you.
>
> Raud (written the day after Elvis's death, 1977)

Our Drifter has been set since early morning – trying to pass 9,000 logged miles before dark. We almost found a new way to rip the Drifter this morning by having an albatross fly straight through it, confusing it for sky. A large wanderer mistook its pale blue for part of heaven's dome and only radical evasive action at the last moment took it clear by inches. It looked quite funny from on deck as it even paddled with its feet in mid-air to help make the turn. A whopper line squall appeared early afternoon, so in the space of about an hour, I dropped the Drifter, reset the Yankee, put second reef in the main, put third reef in the main, dropped main completely, reset main at third reef, settling finally on the second reef. What a fizzer! The wind died completely in the night, but I managed to get us to sail on a dead square run, very slowly under Yankee and single-reefed main. Just with the helm lashed central, and we sailed this way for hours, for 10 miles without change or adjustment required. I was waiting for the cold front to arrive, and it came about an hour before midnight. Took second reef back in, freed Mr M. to steer, have been making 6 knots ever since.

Fifteen to twenty degrees north of east our course, in 20–25 knots from sou'sou'west. I will head more east when it eases a bit for Mr M. After a morning coffee I put back the third reef, just for him. A splendid winter wind, this one, fresh, clear and biting. Albatrosskis in the air – sootys and black-brows, sunshine in the sky and happiness at progress in the heart. A day of perfect light wind sailing followed, keeping spirits high. My deliquescent doona drying in the sun, or trying to. I had to wear wet-weather gear when under it or drown, it had become so wet. Up around eight times in the night for minor adjustments, but nonetheless a restful night. Drifter up again at dawn and once again my 'fish-net' in the sky almost caught game. This time a sooty barely avoided its sky-blue trap. Foot flapping, side slipping, air braking to get clear.

The sea a leaden grey in the late afternoon light with not a trace of sunsparkle on its heaving surface to lighten its message from the south. The sky was an even darker grey, in places hinting at storm. A thin band of pink-tinged cloud brightened the horizon at sunset for a while, some albatrosskis silhouetted in its glow. Two black-brows, a young wanderer and *Little Wing* came together for the dance, the light fast fading, the wind picking up. In separate worlds we travelled into night. By dawn both black-brows were gone and only the young wanderer remained. Wheeling and soaring down the endless searching path, alone . . .

Racing to round the corner before the next blow from the south. Already large swells were marching in long strides from the south-west. I suspect our peaceful easting may be coming to an end. Heading a dash south of east, at latitude 42 degrees south, longitude 135 degrees east or thereabouts, under single-reefed main and Yankee. Playing dodgems with cumulonimbus all around, picking a course to take us through them in the dark, avoiding being blasted in their path. A few sootys and a grey-head my only companions until a solitary pintado, the first I've seen since only a few days after leaving Sydney, joined us at dusk. On the edge of reefing, holding on, ears open all the night.

Dodged the storms OK, the *Wing* threading her own survival line through lightning and cloud monsters on all sides. The onset of misty rain had me put in the second reef at 10 p.m. for caution, but at 2 a.m. I took it out again after a few hours' sleep, there being no increase in wind. Still aiming to get around this corner in comfort of sorts. The air temperature in the cabin staying around 10 degrees C, cooler on deck. I am wearing my long-sleeved 'warmie' again down below. Low cloud, mist in patches, an increasing swell. Our 100th day at sea. Still moseying along a little south of east under single-reefed main and Yankee, hard on the wind. Sailing over rippled swells, moonpath off the starboard bow, full moon.

Morning found the wind around to north-west, cool and crisp, wintry, but with blue sky early. Sights put us at latitude 43 degrees south, longitude 141

217

degrees east, so have taken out the second reef, square running in pursuit of miles. I can estimate distance covered each day accurately now purely by counting the number of pumps to clear the bilge. Next morning, 31 May, found us going for the corner in earnest in a freshening nor'wester. Heading 20 degrees south of east to clear safely Pedra Branca, Eddystone and the other hazards of the corner if the wind switched hard from the south. Sights put us at approximately latitude 44 degrees 30 minutes south, longitude 143 degrees 30 minutes east, just over 100 miles east of South-West Cape. Another day of this would see us around.

Ran out of wind at 3 a.m., back into rain and drizzle, warm front stuff. Hard on the wind again under single-reefed main and Yankee, but not enough wind to keep the sails filled. Cape Horn is the only cape we will have rounded not hard on the wind. My only working kero lantern seems to have broken down, and is leaking kero badly. As our only available navigation light of sorts, we would need it when near shipping. I set to work. Very cold and wet out on deck. So miserable in fact that when we passed a pair of seated albatrosses out there in the rain I almost called to them to shelter under the nearest bus-stop before remembering where we were. Wind came on dark, so back to second reef and staysail for the night as there could be more. Very confused seas again indicated current swirls and I headed further east. I didn't fancy hitting the unlit rocks hereabouts in the dark. Log at 10,000 miles since Stanley, back to third reef and below to sleep.

Staysail down, Yankee up and out with a reef at dawn. This windward crossing beneath Australia has not been bad, really, enabling the *Wing* to steer herself, without Mr M. for over 90 per cent of the time. For the last 3,000 miles, in fact for the last month, Mr M. has only been of use for a few hours here, a few hours there. Most of the steering has been done by choosing correct sail combinations alone. At sunset, a wanderer in young plumage, mainly brown, was circling around. As I watched, it opened its beak and yawned deeply in mid-flight, presumably before going back to sleep. An instinctive flyer!

Wind arrived gradually from the north during the night, so on we go, port tacking, hard on the wind forever. Morning saw it strengthen as it backed more to the west, settling at around nor'west. Back to staysail, down to second reef. If it swings more west I will reset Yankee for more drive, more miles. The barometer remains low, but the weather is sunny and the feminine voice of Hobart's 'Country Hour' lady such a treat. Thoughts of settling down in Hobart. How those siren voices call. First the Falkland Radio ladies, now my Hobart town. It was hard to sail past.

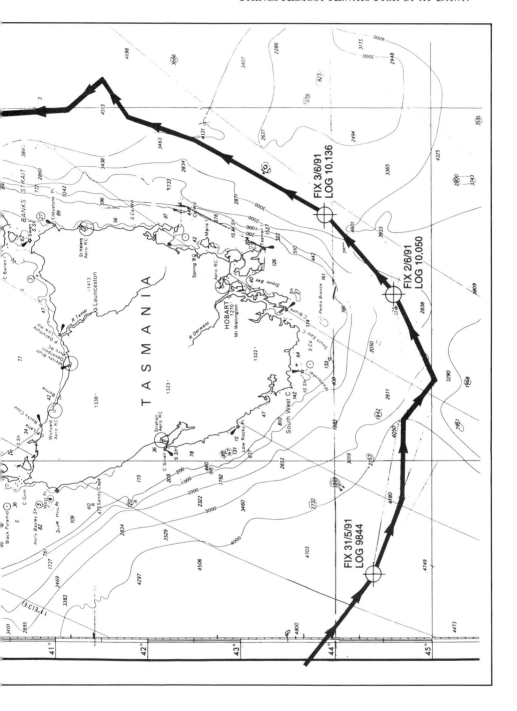

Chapter Twenty-Six
The Bubble Bursts

It started innocently enough, a ship's lights seen to leeward, about a mile away on a nearly parallel course. I was under second reef main and staysail, working slowly north. It would soon be past and gone, I thought. As it became darker another light appeared, this one dead astern and closing on us fast. I watched its bow rise up, then fall, crushing swells (or anything else) that lay in its path. Brute force. I bore away to try and get clear. I switched on my radar detector, but it didn't respond despite the point-blank range. Since it worked with other ships (later), these must have been driving blind or using radar of very different type. I would get no warnings of their approach except by sight. My batteries were dead, my navigation lights dead, my kero lamp too dim. I decided to stay up until we had them out of sight.

But more appeared, and more. From horizon to horizon, rank after rank, and all night long. A whole armada, a Japanese fleet methodically raping the ocean, my home and that of my friends. I had been sharing existence for so long with only those who harmonised with, were part of, the natural world: storms, seabirds, sky, clouds, sea mammals and waves. It was with the utmost horror and revulsion that I was forced to watch this attack on the world I had come to love so much. For a lifetime of sorts I had been living a life complete, but with very few comforts, very few stimuli from beyond the natural world or from within. Yet how fulfilling it had been, in harmony within and without. How superfluous the addictions, the entertainments, the so-called 'needs' of supposedly civilised men and women; and how destructive of our planet, our only home. I remained awake all night, avoiding collisions with these planetary vandals, these criminals against nature worldwide – greed their only god.

Surely the most revolutionary pictures shown to humankind were those first photos of our planet seen as a whole against the night-black backdrop of space. At least for those with imagination, clarity of mind, vision. Sadly, history has shown since just how blind, how incapable of comprehension most remain. Science gave us all the chance to see how finite, what a fragile beauty was our only home. Yet wars go on. Man against nature, man against man, brainwashed fool against brainwashed fool. And the imprisoning of minds goes on, fatal for all.

The use of land for the purpose to which it is inherently best suited (intelligent land use) has been of deep interest to me since I discovered Ian McHarg's book *Design with Nature* in 1970. In the following year I evolved my own computer-based variant on his work for my final-year design and architectural science theses. In much of Tasmania and the south-eastern corner of New South Wales I was sailing past *insane* use of natural resources, and it hurt. The wanton destruction of entire habitats and natural forest ecosystems for

The Japanese Fleet

short-term gain to prop up dinosaur technologies overdue for extinction beggars belief for anyone capable of thinking more than a couple of years ahead. Likewise the destruction of landscape and resources not even for local gain but for the benefit of foreign masters.

Rough seas, rain squalls, staysail stay suddenly gone slack with a twang. I investigated thoroughly, but could find nothing broken or missing. I tightened it again at the segment between deck and keel. The wind vane clamp on Mr M. disintegrated, falling in the sea, so no more wasted efforts there. I was now returning from below Tassie the same way that I first sailed down in '86. Sheet to tiller and sail balance self-steering alone. A great load was off my mind. For the first time in months I slept without having to keep one ear always open for sounds of Mr M. about to fail. Creeping tiredness from this was affecting my decision-making again, and I was too easily upset. When I lost the fleet, what a wonderful sleep, but all the hand-steering to avoid them had not helped my wrist. It was too painful now to even write.

Bash, bash, bash, bash, to windward now in a howling nor'east. Of all the unlikely winds, midwinter, and still below 40 south. If this keeps up, Gabo will turn into another Great Cape, needing rounding from the west. And another to round to windward. Nearly all of my southern ocean birds have now deserted me. Just a few prions, some storm petrels, and now mutton birds remain. It makes me feel like nothing else that I am leaving the south behind. Saddening, despite our troubles, our discomforts there.

Force 8+, unwavering in strength or direction for four days now. It is hard to remember when there was last any pleasure in this voyage. A lee shore all the way to Sydney if we last that long, if nothing breaks. So close and yet in many ways so far. I feel as if I'm going down like Jacques de Roux, in the waters off Gabo. I was near terminally tired, despair was easy. It was time to finish this voyage. Even New Zealand wasn't as consistently bad as this and I was fresh then, at the start of it all. The East Coast Current took us nearly 80 miles backward yesterday, it seems. A rising barometer means nothing here, a falling one, likewise. No wind had blown this way, at this strength and from the same direction for so long, anywhere. *Little Wing* is being tortured to the limit bashing out of this mess. Everything aboard is sodden from rain, spray or condensation from not being able to open the hatch for days. A jarring, noisy, dripping hell. Eating not possible due to hand-steering.

But joy! Two young wanderers rejoined me today, two different juvenile plumages, two different ages. Lows above me, a low forming beside me and no sunsights since the middle of Bass Strait. Uncertainty always, all ways.

Safely astern at last, Gabo, and the south-east corner. Like Jacques, astern, but not forgotten. Just as the vandals were attacking the food and life-chains out at sea, so they were destroying the remaining indigenous forests of the south-east corner for the same masters. Destroying the futures of others through lack of ideals, of imagination, of the ability and desire to evolve. Like so-called 'adventurers' selling out for sponsors' dollars, here was a society at large prostituting itself for foreign trinkets. Living on borrowed resources, borrowed time – destroying their own life-support.

11 June, and I really tried hard to get to Sydney that day. The wind having swung towards the south-east I hand-steered in the cockpit for sixteen hours straight through every conceivable kind of rain squall. Square running before them, my wrist beyond pain but semi-numbed by the cold. Drenched to the bone and frozen, I could no longer steer a course after 9 p.m. so, for the first time in the voyage, hove-to. We had been surrounded by so much lightning and phosphorescence that I could no longer steer a course towards Sydney's loom. Every breaking wave with its burst of phosphorescence was a 'loom' to my tired eyes, and I often gybed unintentionally. With the pain and visual distractions ruining my steering, I gave up. A compass light would have helped.

3.30 a.m. put the staysail back up in the darkness to get us moving again, with the mainsail at the third reef. Took the third reef out. Then staysail down and Yankee up, third reef back in. Third reef out, third reef back in. Working in towards Sydney in a gusty west to north-westerly all day. By evening we had the distant smoke plumes of Kurnell refinery abeam to port, backlit by the setting sun. Considerable aircraft activity in that direction confirmed our position off Botany Bay. We had now crossed our outward track off Sydney, 190 sailing days out. But for the problems with Mr M. after the knock in Stanley, my original goal of under 180 days would have been possible. Well done, *Little Wing* . . .

With the strength of the set further south and the days of strong headwinds since, I thought the East Coast Current would be running ferociously up here too. Since we were a long way offshore, with not even the loom of a lighthouse visible, I decided to delay the inshore losing tack until the wind swung again . . . A knock on this tack, a lift on the other. No luck. We found a lighthouse at dawn, but not Sydney which should have been the next strong light to appear. Norah Head! I had been hand-steering in the cockpit almost the entire night, yet had not seen even the loom of Sydney's light. There must have been no set running at all when we tacked inshore, so we overshot. I have always found Sydney a dreadful place to get to!

Back south we headed, again to windward, as the wind had swung south-west. It was a very pleasant, sunny day coastal sail, but with enough high cloud coming over to warn me to hurry. In gathering darkness we approached the Heads, with barely enough wind for steerage. I managed to get a kero lamp working for a navigation light of sorts, and switched on the masthead light despite the voltmeter reading dead. It worked, but for how long? A game-fishing boat came past into the harbour with deck and cockpit lights so bright that no navigation lights could be seen against them, and 'music' blaring forth from outside speakers. What a terrible change. From the peace and contentment and inner quiet of the Southern Ocean we were back in the world of mechanised madness, engine-addicted moronity. I had only seen either a kerosene lantern flame, candle or soft compass light for nearly four months, and the lights of Sydney and its harbour traffic were almost too much to take.

I was studying a particular piece of streetscape ahead, trying to decide which streets were which. Scanning it closely when I saw . . . a red light . . . a green light . . . and a bow light! A ship heading straight at me out of the Heads. No streetscape this. The scale of things had me beaten, as did the windlessness, almost. I managed to alter course enough to let it past, but only just. Altogether too close for comfort. In very light wind conditions we worked our way up harbour, avoiding two more huge ships on their way out by the time we reached Bradley's Head. How ever did I sleep at sea with those massive walls of steel passing by? Unseen by us – us definitely unseen by them. I suppose I just couldn't worry about everything, only the problems most real.

It was a most magical sail. Dodging ferries, dodging ships and unlit buoys, but all the while the lights, the colours. It could only be compared with sailing for hours through the heart of a black opal, with colours and light all around. The wind was such that the Customs wharf could not be reached sans engine. Exhausted as I was I repeatedly headed us back into the narrow slit of a bay, trying through momentum alone to reach a mooring pile. Again and again, while dodging ferries at full speed servicing four wharves in the vicinity. I gave up before an error of judgement caused our demise, having failed on two occasions by a boat length or less. I was too tired and my wrist too painful to use the sculling oar. About seven hours after we entered the Heads I found a vacant mooring 100 yards from Customs, caught it and slept.

Sydney. Back where it began.

Chapter Twenty-Seven
Landings

I had let Sydney Radio know of our impending arrival via VHF when off Sydney Heads. This was to make arrangements with Customs for re-entry. The wind having suddenly died, however, we reached the vicinity of Customs far too late. I had also requested that they not let my parents or others know of our return. I wanted just to sail back on to my mooring and see how long it took for anyone to notice we were back. It didn't quite work out that way. My father, estimating that I should be nearly back by then, phoned Customs to enquire if they had heard from me. Just after I had finished re-entry formalities and headed back out to sea towards 'home'!

Damn!

In a fresh southerly I retraced my path of yesterday back north, arriving at my mooring late in the afternoon. Bells, horns, clapping from the few who knew, then some friends arrived. Jenö, Marion, Frank and Cassie, and Penny, who all helped my preparations in one way or another. We opened and shared some of the undrunk celebratory bottles of champagne that I had taken for each Cape. How pleasant it was to talk with friends, to share their news and moments of the voyage. Rain had set in in earnest by now, so after a rather rough and ready furling of sails we adjourned ashore where I proceeded almost to make them sick with my swaying allowances for the next movement of the ship.

Life is a voyage, not a destination. One little voyage was over now, but the main one was still happening, was almost just beginning. I was now 'free' for the first time – in my head. I no longer needed to prove anything to anyone, being happy with myself and my creations. Having achieved the most genuinely single-handed circumnavigation south of all five Great Capes by anyone, from anywhere, ever, I was free at last for sharing life's voyages and adventures.

It took several months of emptying different portions of the boat completely, then watching out for signs of water, finally to locate the source of the leak. It appeared for a while that there might be more than one. If the source had been only those found initially at sea the leak should have stopped back on my mooring. It didn't. So I didn't dare remove the silicone I had spread so lavishly at sea. Not until we were out of the water, where we couldn't sink. We would if the problem was as I had feared. I slipped her as soon as I was convinced the problem lay only at the stern. Once out, I removed the silicone, and there . . .

I found approximately 2½ lineal feet of splits on both sides of the skeg, completely through the steel hull plating. I could see bands of light through them. At each wriggle of the skeg, for over 18,000 miles, these splits would have opened and closed anything up to ¼ inch, the tears lengthening all the time as this happened. It had been as my worst fears thought, but which I had denied to myself as best I could, since the leak was basically kept at bay. Only my liberal use of silicone in trying to stop the two tiny initial leaks had kept us afloat for 18,000 miles!

I thought I had found all the crook welds done by the Dutchmen in their final rush, but some I had missed. The frames taking most of the skeg loads had broken at two of these. This allowed excessive flexing of the bottom near the skeg attachment, thus metal fatigue and splitting. My friend Jenö, who had helped me

Rainbow arch over Sydney Harbour Bridge (on the skyline at right) – about 4 hours after my arrival off Customs.

fix all the other suspect work, helped me weld in extra stiffening frames and other remedial work. *Little Wing* is now up to design strength at last.

My birthday came around in due course, and as a special present, the chance to share old friends, new rock. I had never climbed on the granite outcrop of Evan's Crown, Tarana, despite granite being my favourite stone to climb on and quite a few attempts having been made to get there. Not having my own car, I was dependent on friends for a lift out, and unplanned events or changes in weather had always led to trips being cancelled. We were on our way at last. Chris and Heather, Ron and Helen, Russell, myself and a few others. Aaah, Granite! That lovely bite of crystal friction sticking feet to rock – on almost nothingness. Fingernails and bitter ends of fingertips doing all the work of hands. Real thinking climbing this. The epitome of climbing as I first fell in love with it. Thought behind every move and nearly every move an experiment. Tentative at first, confidence and joy soon taking over despite not a single hold large enough for using my left. 'Single handing' doesn't stop just because I'm back from sea!

Most landsfolk looking out to sea see a vast expanse covered by a monotony of waves, all similar. To a sailor, each wave is different, with its own unique shape and complex of movements. Information to be observed, deciphered and made use of in choosing the path of least resistance across the water. Similarly with the sky. To a sailor without the outside assistance provided by weatherfax, long-distance radio communication and satellite information, each cloud, its shape and movement, its growth and decay, is packed with information. Clues to help in making correct tactical decisions. To most city dwellers, the sky is not only substantially occluded by the built environment, but virtually meaningless. About their only 'tactical' decision that is influenced by weather is what to wear.

Arriving at the slabs that day, then having climbed some routes, the same discrepancy was apparent. To a non-climber, observing from near the base, how dull, how uninteresting these slab routes must look. To a climber ascending, however, what an incredible amount of information is packed in the surface. The faintest rugosities, any larger than average individual crystals, micro flakes and breaks only large enough to take one fingernail behind them, all provide clues for ascent. These details prompt the creative act of gaining height successfully on a route. Clues often invisible even from an arm length away. These climbs were delicate, and one fingernail could save you from a fall.

*　　*　　*　　*

That familiar buzz, exposure, brought a smile to my face. I reached for the slit that would take a finger and steady me as I moved up to the start of the flake proper. Booroomba. Having just led Counterbalance, I was now leading Ivory Coast, two favourites and my first visit since the sea. Booroomba, first granite met, first love. It was good to climb here after Tarana, to compare. It seemed less steep, fewer fingertip ripping edges, fewer flakes. Sort of 'softer' on the hands . . .

fewer holds? Less need? I found them both quite easy, almost too easy now. Still pleasant, but no longer the challenge they once were.

* * * *

A climbing acquaintance from a few years back, Carol, had returned from overseas. Finding some redirected mail from me, she rang to say hello. By the end of the week, Tarana seemed a good idea and Saturday morning found us headed west. Rain and drizzle set in persistently as we crossed the mountains but it could be clearer to the west; we drove on. Pale blue skies behind hill crests golden dry. A few tufty white cumulus the only reminders of the cloud cover back east. Clumps of dark exotic pines where homesteads used to be. The pastureland dry, but surprisingly green here and there. What a joy to climb in this rural setting. The granite outcrops hove in sight, some wire-brushed streaks of routes becoming visible as we drove . . . So glad it was dry.

* * * *

Climbing that day, happy to be sharing with another, happy to be on the rock on such a fine day in such an idyllic setting, reminded me of thoughts I had had at sea, namely that I would prefer to share future life and adventures with one I loved. The battle to preserve any semblance of intelligent life on our planet is too big, too complex to fight alone, but shared example can be a powerful tool for change.

Everyone still wants 'to have their kayak and heat it' (to quote from Frank Muir or Denis Norden of 'My Word'), and I find it hard since returning to live in a world almost devoid of ideals: ideals as timeless as the oceans or the hills, that transcend the brainwashing by the media and other social pressures that paralyse most people's ability to think. It has been hard to return from the purity and timelessness of the ocean's wilderness to a society so obsessed with comfort and material ease, and achieving these only by stealing from the future their chances of even basic subsistence/survival.

As I would tell Young Mist during the more despairing, bleaker periods of the voyage: 'It's a longi way, Young Mist, a longi, longi way . . . but we'll get there. It's just a longi, longi way.'

A long way for us, as we made our way around her surface, but not for Spaceship Earth herself. The distance we had sailed during the past six months she had been covering more than three times in an hour, every hour for billions of years. And this considering only her motion around the sun, ignoring the Grand Tour of the Solar System as a whole . . . Simultaneously nurturing the only forms of life detected so far. Single-handing the only known life through Space . . . No possibility of rescue from outside, no lifeboats. Only ourselves to solve the catastrophes of our making.

Chapter Twenty-Eight
The Wing Dreams (Remain)

Through time and space we set the pace
we wore white lace, we left the race
vanished, without a trace . . .
to isles bathed in contemplation
a life of no more condemnation
Content, we remained, the seasons drifting by.

We lived and loved amongst those isles
promised, planned, enjoyed the land
before it broke asunder –
set adrift by separate forces
moved apart on different courses
each towards an unknown goal.

Raud 1968

Where were we going?
was it to Vila,
Noumea,
Ouvéa?
the sun veined the ocean in patterns of purple
by day
then the moon gave us shot-silken nights . . .

and driving hard, south of Diego Ramirez
that crazy long slalom through turrets of ice
our love kept us strong
it was warm, and sustaining,
and gave us new dreams to share,
kept us alive . . .
Out of space, out of time.

Raud 1975

Voyage

In the land of mauve
the evening's glow
above deep purple sea . . .
a darking sky
a restless mind
thoughts, elusive
She.

Dominant Astronomy
dark hours sliding by
bodies heavenly, suspended,
starlit, alone,
I.

The endless quest
Love's safe harbour
sharing, caring there . . .
melding with the moon
enpinked
exquisitely
triumphantly
We.

Raud, 1986 (this was written entirely in my head sans pen or paper during the final fifty-two-hour stint at the helm single-handing to Hobart on our maiden voyage).

Appendix: Reflections on *Little Wing* and her equipment

(i) Hull form and construction. I could not have been happier with *Little Wing* as regards hull form. She is fine enough in her forward sections not to hinder windward progress in virtually any sea conditions, and yet contained enough buoyancy in those forward sections to prevent pitch-poling or any sign of touchiness when running before at speed. Even in survival conditions. In all but the lightest winds, where skin friction is the dominant factor impeding progress, wave making resistance is the main form of drag. Our consistently high average speeds whenever conditions held steady, along with our negligible wake at speed, both indicate a hull form with minimal resistance to motion. Even when heavily laden, as we were. Our 200-mile day was achieved with a displacement for this voyage of around 8½ tons – almost 2 tons over her design displacement.

(ii) Hull construction. Steel would still be my first choice for construction medium if I were building again. However, I would do all the welding myself next time around to be sure adequate care was taken. The increasing leak I dragged around the world with me for at least 18,000 miles of worry would not have occurred if the welding had initially been as thorough as my friend Jenö's repairs after completion of the voyage. These new welds were thoroughly tested by being beached sometime later in heavy surf for two days. Forty-two original welds were cracked or broken in this beaching, although she still didn't leak a drop when I sailed her back home. These cracked and broken welds were all of the type that led to the skeg leak/tearing problem. Now she is stronger than ever, with all dud welds having been tested to destruction and redone more carefully and strongly. I added six new structural floors at this time to spread the keel loadings better. All set for another southern circuit! The main thing I would do differently next time would be to pre-sandblast and prime all interior steel and build up an adequate high-build epoxy primer substrate to allow for trouble-free insulating of the interior.

(iii) Spars, rig, rigging, bowsprit. As mentioned earlier, I decided to seal the mast and boom at both ends and step the mast on deck instead of through to the keel. This was so that if they were lost during a rolling they would hopefully remain intact, and would float until stowed aboard for restepping later – once land had been reached under jury rig. Deck-stepping, however, gave less structural support to the lower mast and unless the rigging were kept very tight there was a risk of the mast jumping out of its step in extreme conditions. The righting moment provided by the mast and boom as sealed columns of air during our numerous roll-downs (when the mast was driven below horizontal) almost certainly prevented some of these becoming full roll-overs. This was an intended side effect of my sealing them at the ends and appeared to work.

I had no trouble with the rig at sea nor during the beaching, which was a far more violent test than any during the voyage, with the *Wing* being hurled bodily from mast facing up the beach to mast facing down towards the sea as we were repeatedly flipped over on to solid ground. Mast and rigging both remained intact. All my shrouds and twin backstays are of 10 mm galvanised wire rope (7 × 7), with all three of my forestays being of 9 mm stainless steel (1 × 19) to minimise wear on the bronze headsail hanks.

The third forestay crept in when I added the bowsprit to the original cutter rig so as to be able to shift the centre of effort of the Yankee (and storm jib if necessary) further forward to aid in self-steering if Mr M. broke down. I kept the Yankee set on this outer forestay for the entire voyage, and it definitely enabled me to utilise more mainsail area on all points of sail while maintaining good balance. And when the wind was too strong for any mainsail at all, we could still drive harder for longer under Yankee alone using this forestay.

(iv) Sails. There was no serious damage to any sail, only minor wear and tear. All headsails were set hanked to their forestays, with no roller furling used. I wanted no 'unfixables' at sea.

(a) Mainsail: Only a few slide lashings on the luff needed replacing during the voyage. No battens were lost (it has four short battens) and no seams gave way. I had every seam above the third reef reinforced, including along the leech, with extra rows of stitching since I used triple-reefed main instead of trisail (to avoid disconnecting and maybe losing the mainsail halyard in setting it). The trisail had its own separate track on the mast but needed a separate trisail halyard to avoid such problems. A new trisail half to three quarters the area of my triple-reefed main would be ideal, but I had neither time nor materials to make it. And triple-reefed main had survived days on end of continuous force 10–11 south of New Zealand on my first attempt without damage.

(b) Yankee: Set for virtually the entire voyage except when becalmed. Minor restitching required at some chafe spots, otherwise no damage; not even a single

hank needed replacing during the voyage – much to my amazement, since many were well worn before I set out.

(c) Staysail: again, only some minor restitching needed en route to catch chafe damage from rolling and slatting. No hanks needed replacing.

(d) Drifter/MPS: only minor tears, easily repaired at sea, from getting caught under the bow/bobstay during a few problem sets and drops.

(e) Bulletproof jib: my ultimate storm weapon. No damage whatever. A very heavy (12 oz) little sail (approx. 30–40 square feet in area).

(f) Genoa: not used at all. I was afraid of irreparable damage if caught with it up in a sudden violent squall, such as those experienced during my second attempt. I couldn't afford any major breakages. This said, I could have set it for much of the voyage for probably a 20 mile a day better average and with very little risk as it turned out. C'est la vie.

TABLE OF SAIL AREAS
Mainsail: 260 square feet, 9¼ ounce cloth (US)
Yankee: 235 square feet, 8 ounce cloth (US)
Staysail: 125 square feet, 9¼ ounce cloth (US)
Drifter/MPS: 400 square feet, 1¾ ounce (US)
Genoa: 315 square feet, 6½ ounce cloth (US)
Storm Jib: 30–40 square feet, 12 ounce cloth (US)

All shrouds below the lower spreaders were covered with plastic hose to minimise chafe from the 7×7 wire, and this seemed to work well. I rigged anti-chafe hose on the sheets where they rubbed against shrouds also. No sheets gave out during the voyage.

(v) Deck equipment. The problems I had with my primary and halyard winches were due to mistakes during rushed reassembly when I serviced them before leaving. After servicing again on my return neither problem has reappeared. All winches were oversize according to the sales brochures, but proved just right for Southern Ocean conditions. By choice, no winches were self-tailing (for better feel and less rope wear). All winches were Barlow's – 27s for primaries, 25s for secondaries, 23s on the mast for halyards (all two-speed), and smaller single-speed 16s on the boom for reefing winches.

(vi) Self-steering. The Monitor proved a better helmsman than myself in extremely cold and rough conditions, working tirelessly through the worst gales. After diagnosis by careful observation back in smooth water, I corrected the problems I had for the last 8,000 miles without any rebending of gear sets necessary. A Teflon bearing broke during the later voyage that ultimately led to our beaching in heavy surf. Apart from the original wind vanes broken on the second attempt, this has been the only breakage in nearly two Southern Ocean circumnavigations. A half-hour's work in smooth water fixed this problem also, using parts from my spare parts kit. In hindsight I could have carried out both these repairs at sea in calm conditions, and saved myself much worry!

Little Wing will sail herself to windward with tiller free and no self-steering at all if the correct sails are chosen for the conditions. She will also self-steer very well with sheet-to-tiller rigs with the wind anywhere forward of the beam, but with the wind from astern in rough conditions these proved inadequate. Only Mr M. or a helmsperson could keep her driving hard and on course in these. I still intend trying a trim-tab on the rudder combined with a wind vane utilising some of the Monitor gear. I think I can work out a system to change easily from one to the other, even at sea, but haven't located suitable friction-free trim-tab bearings yet. When I remove my rudder again would be a good time to install a tab. Meanwhile, Mr M. works fine so there is no rush.

(vii) Dodger and cockpit/drains. My low windage dodger (a continuation of the curve of the cabin) and dodger frame were godsends at sea. The dodger itself for shelter from the wind and spray (even keeping me all but dry during the rolling to 40 degrees below horizontal while out on deck near Cape Horn), the framework both as a foothold beyond the end of the cabin while reefing and as a secure handhold and support to lean against while in the cockpit taking sunsights or just observing.

Two 3-inch diameter tubes drain the cockpit to cockpit seat level by direct lines aft through the transom. Two more square section drains, of around 2½ inches square, drain whatever remains in the shallow cockpit well. Although breakers regularly flooded the stern to an extent such that green weed even grew on the cockpit seats, these drains proved very efficient at getting the ocean back overboard, thus keeping the stern buoyant for the next assault.

(viii) Solar panel/s. If the junction boxes had been thoroughly packed with Vaseline and sealed before I left, no problems would have occurred. Especially if I had had time to rewire without joints in the wiring before setting out. For getting more satisfactory output, though, in low-angled sun and dim light, two panels should be carried, angled up towards the centre such that one is always working efficiently on either tack. With the winter sun to the north I received very little charge when sailing east on port tack. Solarex panels were taken for both 'in-use' and spare panels – the 40 Watt model.

BELOW DECKS
(i) Stove. The kerosene stove was never a problem, with never a hint of unwanted fire or flare-ups. The key to this might be using Tilleywick starters to prime the

burners, saturated in metho. Only 3–4 litres of methylated spirits were used for priming over the entire voyage, and only 5–10 litres of kerosene, even though I used the oven for bread-baking during the last half of the voyage. I took far more kero, nearly 50 litres, but this will last me for years!

(ii) Lighting. While the batteries and solar panel were working I used an inside fluoro with orange cellophane wrapped around it as an emergency interior light, and a small halogen bunklight for reading at night. After the electrics konked I used kerosene hurricane lamps for interior and navigation lights, or candles in the cabin when calm enough. For deckwork and searching for things in the dark I used a variety of cheap head torches using AA cells. Of six head torches taken, two or three are still working.

(iii) Inside steering. Despite setting up a whipstaff for emergency inside steering, using part of my original tiller extension as a vertical tiller, it was hardly ever used. Visibility out of my large cabin windows was fine, without needing the dome, but Mr M. steered so much better than I when using the stretchy yacht-braid tiller lines.

(iv) Cabin Windows. My oversize cabin windows, dependent on strength through curvature and their lack of resistance to water flow from any direction in order to survive, have withstood everything the Southern Ocean and two days of beach pounding in heavy surf could throw at them. Not the slightest trace of a leak or stress cracking. They make a far lighter, airier boat to live aboard, but a bit too like being in an open boat when waves were breaking clean over.

(v) Hatches and ventilators. Neither of my self-designed submarine hatches leaked a single drop when dogged shut, no matter what the conditions outside. My modifications after the failed attempts proved totally adequate. I removed the ventilators and put sealing caps over three of my five Dorade boxes for this trip (the forward and both aft vents). I kept the two cabin-top vents functional, as only in the most extreme of conditions did these ever leak (when rolled down to horizontal or beyond) and we needed ventilation to help ease condensation problems. I also tried to keep the aft hatch a little open most of the time to aid through ventilation.

(vi) Toilet and pumps. Both Whale Tip-Toe pumps (fresh and salt) to the sink worked faultlessly for the duration of the voyage, as did my spare bilge pump. The toilet pump/other bilge pump almost certainly died because of a hole already in the replacement diaphragm/s that I took with me. I will change the diaphragm again and use it as a spare pump. Otherwise the toilet worked faultlessly, and still does now that I have replaced the pump. The toilet is a standard Lavac operating through a standard Henderson Mk 5 pump. The 'spare' bilge pump used for nearly the entire voyage was a standard RM69.

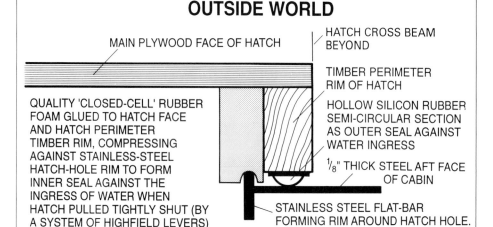

Cross-section through aft hatch waterseal system

A LIST OF MOST OF THE MODIFICATIONS TO BE CARRIED OUT BETWEEN VOYAGES (TO MAKE LIFE A BIT EASIER ON MY SUCCESSFUL ATTEMPT)

(i) Waterproofed the aft hatch by gluing a wooden rim around the perimeter with hollow silicone rubber sealing strip around bottom of the rim. This acted as the outer seal (see drawing).

(ii) Glued softer, springier closed cell rubber sections around the inside of this new wooden rim to seal against the existing stainless steel hatch opening rim. This acted as the inner seal (see drawing).

(iii) Replaced closed cell rubber sealing strip around forward hatch with new, springier material.

(iv) Removed running backstays.

(v) Replaced the fore and aft cabin lifelines to eliminate the chafing of headsail sheets against them. Used softer rope, and deck level lines forward of mast.

(vi) Designed and built new light but ultra-strong wind vanes for Southern Ocean conditions. Six of them. As it turned out I didn't break any, but lost one overboard.

(vii) Removed polypropylene Drifter halyard to eliminate chafe on Yankee luff region.

(viii) Designed and made a new larger storm jib, but had neither time nor money to make a new trisail.

(ix) Made and set up a permanent pouch for storing my glasses near the head of my bunk.

(x) Made and set up a permanent pouch for a head torch near the head of my bunk since I need both glasses and light in order to use my left hand effectively.

(xi) Change solar panel lead to electrical panel to eradicate suspect deck plug and cable connectors (no time, I eventually did this at sea as described).

(xii) Replaced all stove burners.

(xiii) Add harness like galley harness to use at chart table (no time to do this).

(xiv) Pre-cut spare headsail sheet lengths and headsail tack pendants.

(xv) Fitted anti-chafe rollers on the wire life-lines around deck, as well as on all rigging below lower spreaders, to minimise chafe.

(xvi) Added timber lining over and beside my bunk to lessen the condensation and heat loss problems when lying against cold steel.

(xvii) Rig up some form of reel storage for sea-squid towing lines (no time, and anyway these drogues were never thought necessary to use).

(xviii) Replaced the original 9 mm lower shrouds with heavier wire (10 mm) to match the rest.

(xix) Bought spare ring spanners for easier one-handed 'blind' operation.

(xx) Bought spare kero lamps/wicks, and mantles for pressure lamp.

(xxi) Made a fixed cloth bag to store all rope tails of halyards and reefing lines neatly at the base of the mast.

(xxii) Hinge electrical panel for easier access (no time to do this).

(xxiii) Buy a spare new battery as a replacement (not enough money).

(xxiv) Check and correct all self-steering alignments and meshing of gears as per manual. (I ran out of time. This would have ensured Mr M. worked fully for the entire voyage in hindsight!)

FOODS

By inclination I have been predominantly vegetarian for about sixteen years and this made sense for my voyage since I had neither the power nor space to waste on refrigeration of food and drink. In the Southern Ocean this would seem superfluous, anyway.

Ever since taking up scuba diving about fifteen years ago and learning to relate to marine life in its own environment, I have given up fishing also. It would seem like torturing and murdering friends. Especially when I was alone at sea, when all living things in the world around us were as welcome as friends. To talk to, to amuse by their antics, and to stimulate thoughts and ideas.

On a more general ethical level, if the human race and any of the natural world are to survive, the extravagant and wasteful practice of grain-feeding livestock must cease. Without a more equitable use of food resources, world conflicts will ensure insufficient stability to solve *any* global problems.

Vegetarian cooking requires more imaginative use of ingredients to produce interesting meals, but this is part of the fun, surely. Improvising is far more interesting than following recipes or rules.

From Sydney to the region of the International Date line I lived almost entirely on fresh fruit and vegetables so that as few as possible would be wasted. Onions lasted the whole voyage, as did root ginger, which I eat a lot of. My fresh garlic had shrivelled by below South Africa, so I finished the voyage with bottled flakes. My grapefruit lasted half way around the world, lemons almost as far, but my oranges were eaten early to save moulding and waste.

Once my fresh vegetables were gone, I improvised with various tinned vegetables, rice, pasta, instant mashed potato, and a variety of spices, sauces, home-made pickles and chutney. Processed cheese lasted the whole voyage, the more interesting ones were eaten by the Falklands before they went off. I made my own muesli mix, using powdered soy compound instead of milk, and in cooler times ate porridge as my first meal of the day. Apart from porridge for breakfast, I cooked a different hot meal virtually every evening before dark. During the day I ate dried fruit and nuts, or fresh bread if I'd baked it. I liked to bake wholemeal fruit loaves when the weather was calm enough, but had plenty of savoury biscuits if it were too rough to bake. Neither butter nor margarine lasted the distance, either eaten or gone off, but mayonnaise was a reasonable substitute. I took some lamb dripping also, which lasted the distance perfectly – because I forgot about it until I found it after our return! I had a cup of coffee to start each day and often a cup of tea in the afternoons – other than this I drank water or fruit juice.

My water was stored in various sizes of cheap plastic jerry cans (25l, 15l and 12l), and empty 2l fruit juice containers (none of which broke en route). Altogether about 240 litres of water. On top of this I carried about 60 litres of various fruit juices in 2 litre plastic bottles. By making use of my rain catcher, I arrived at Stanley with almost as much water as when I left Sydney. I carried a bottle of champagne to celebrate each Cape, but drank only the Cape Horn one, when dining with my friends in Stanley, and the New Zealand/Dateline/Christmas one. The other Capes were no real cause for celebration, so I saved them until home. A bottle of Grants whisky given to me by John Grant, my previous employer, was finished at the Falklands. I developed a desire for ginger beer approaching the Falklands, so bought half a dozen cans for the return journey. A desire for something non-alcoholic but fizzy. My consumption of water for the voyage as a whole worked out at no more than a litre per day with cooking included, plus up to half a litre of fruit juice each day.

NAVIGATION
Navigation was all by sextant in conjunction with the *Nautical Almanac* and HO 229, of which two volumes were carried: Those for latitudes 30 to 45 degrees, and 45 to 60 degrees. A GPS or sat-nav unit would have made life easier rounding the bottom of New Zealand and Cape Horn due to the lack of sun and rough seas preventing sight-taking for much of the time. But this would also have been cheating the spirit of single-handing in my opinion (see Chapter 12). These devices also greatly reduce the skill level and judgement required in making

difficult landfalls, and this would have vastly diminished my satisfaction in completing the voyage successfully. Star sights were never used, due to lack of clear horizons at dusk and dawn, and no desperate worries about position when good conditions did exist. My timepieces consisted of a $39 wrist watch whose rate of gain was very consistent, with another $49 one as a spare, whose rate was almost as steady. Both could be checked every month or two by a cheap short-wave transistor radio, of which I also carried a spare. Both watches were cheap Casio's.

COMPASS

The main compass was a Sestrel Major mounted in the cockpit and so sited, partly through luck, partly through design, as to need neither compensator balls nor correction magnets – and modified by the addition of a self-designed transparent cover to protect the vulnerable light circuitry from immersion.

Sixteen charts were used during the voyage (see list following). These covered all but a small region of the southern Pacific Ocean between charts, due to the next of a series being unavailable at the time of purchase. I used a plotting sheet and South Polar chart to cover this area. I forgot to take a chart of the Falklands in my last-minute rush. This would have saved me a couple of days and considerable worry. The lack of an arc of visibility for Diego Ramirez light (on the South-Eastern Tierra del Fuego chart) almost lost me *Little Wing*, but this would not have been a problem had my index error been as believed. As luck would have it my line of approach happened to be in line with the only few degrees that the light was occluded by higher ground.

List of Charts
    (i) INT 601: Tasman Sea – New Zealand to South-East Australia
    (ii) 4612: South Pacific Ocean – Chatham Islands to Pacific Antarctic Rise
    (iii) 4611: South-West Pacific Basin to Pacific Antarctic Rise
    (iiia) a plotting sheet which I set up to cover me to 102 degrees west and 48 degrees south
    (iv) 1240: South Polar Chart
    (v) Ice chart for the Southern Hemisphere
    (vi) 4212: Drake Passage
    (vii) 1373: South-Eastern part of Tierra del Fuego (Diego Ramirez light problem)
    (viii) 2127: Atlantic Ocean
    (ix) 2444: South Atlantic Ocean – Western Portion
    (x) 4021: South Atlantic Ocean – Eastern Portion
    (xi) 4072: Indian Ocean – Western Part
    (xii) 4073: Indian Ocean – Eastern Part
    (xiii) 748a: Indian Ocean – Southern Portion
    (xiv) INT 709: Australia – South Coast
    (xv) AUS 422: Cape Otway to Gabo Island, including Tasmania
    (xvi) INT 601: Tasman Sea – New Zealand to South-East Australia (second copy)

BOOKS AND MUSIC

I sailed with my entire boat library of some 500 books, Ranging from expensive large hardbacks to ordinary paperbacks, although I found very little time for relaxed reading. These covered many topics that interest me: Literature, poetry, art, natural history/biology/science, astronomy, meteorology, science fiction, biographies, yacht design and sailing, architecture and design. I told myself that all these books lining the cabin acted as insulation, and I dare say they did to some extent. Less than half a dozen were water-damaged to any degree. One book that I carried was very experienced in high latitude sailing: my great-grandfather's Bible, which had lived through many Cape Horn roundings, but none since his clipper ship days. It was overdue for another, a re-acquaintance with the real world of its youth, and it seemed appropriate that I take it. NB:- Psalm 139 verses 9–10: 'If I take the wings of the morning, and dwell in the uttermost parts of the sea; Even there shall thy hand lead me, and thy right hand hold me,' – underlined in his copy! A girl I met pointed out this passage to me at about the time of my first attempts . . . '*Little Wings* of the morning'!

I took a music selection consisting of 150 cassettes from classical through jazz, blues and native musics, although I preferred listening to silence, and the sounds of our motion through the outside world. Every little boat noise meant something – these natural sounds – so I didn't want to mask the messages. I made an exception of listening to a cassette while lying in my bunk on calm-ish nights or when conditions were steady. Also, when doing my daily running on the spot exercise to help pass the time for thirty minutes or so.

I also took along a trumpet to learn while at sea (since I had played bugle back when school cadets were compulsory), and my blues harmonicas (which I have played since 1965, jamming with many bands over the years).

I wrote up to a thousand words of ship's log and thoughts each day and completed the first 90,000 words of the first draft of this book while at sea. There was a lot to keep me mentally active apart from boat maintenance, navigation, sail maintenance, and helming. I was never for a moment bored.

VHF: the same hand-held VHF that I bought for my maiden voyage in 1986 is still in use (an ICOM M5).

CLOTHES

My friend Marion made me a sleeveless and a long sleeved 'warmie' out of fibrepile material that I had had picked up for me in the US by Jane years before. I basically lived in these, several new and second-hand tracksuits, and some polo-neck hand-knitted woollen jumpers. Socks also, of course, when down below. For deck work I put on my chest-high wet-weather gear pants and top with built-in harness over. Also a bini and wetsuit boots (having forgotten my full sea-boots). I never got around to wearing my thermal underwear, although I took two sets. It was too hard to get in and out of with my bad hand, especially in a hurry.

On my bunk I had an artificial fibre-filled doona, and sea-rug, with cotton sheets whenever I bothered to make up my bunk properly.

Glossary of Climbing Terms

Belay to hold the rope to protect the leader or the second. Also the act of tying oneself to the rock.

Bridging climbing with hands or feet or both, wide apart on opposite walls of a corner or chimney.

Chimney a crack large enough to contain the entire body.

Corner a feature rather like the inside corner of a building or open book.

Crux the most difficult move or moves on a climb.

Edging using the feet on very small holds such that the stiff edge of the boot (the inside or outside edge) is brought to bear on the hold, usually with the foot turned sideways a bit to use the front inside edge.

Flake a piece of rock that has peeled away or detached from the main face. A flake may vary in size from something the size of a fingernail to something as large as the side of a large building.

Friends a form of protection consisting of four independently operated and sprung cams, which when load is applied bite deeper into the placement. Their versatility, ease of placement and ability to provide protection in previously impossible situations have made them and their variants popular across the whole spectrum of performance levels.

Hold anything to put your hands or feet on while climbing, varying from large jugs for the hands, and ledges, down to fingernails on individual crystals and feet on minute edges or smearing using friction alone.

Jamming climbing by jamming or wedging hands, fingers or arms, legs or feet, into a crack.

Karabiners/Krab also referred to as snaplinks. These come in two styles, locking and ordinary. The gate of a locking krab can be secured by a closed-screw sleeve or spring-loaded sleeve. Ordinary krabs just have spring-loaded gates. Nearly all krabs are approximately D-shaped or pear-shaped, the latter used more for locking krabs.

Leader/Lead a Climb the leader is the climber who ascends the climb first, belayed by the second. Since the leader is not protected by rope protection from above, this is the most dangerous position, but also the most rewarding, and the leader can protect him or herself to a certain extent by judicious placement of runners/running belays along the way.

Move an individual step or movement on a climb.

Nuts also called chocks and wedges. Shaped pieces, usually of aluminium, threaded with a wire or rope loop used for anchors on main running belays. Placed in cracks and natural pockets along the route. Common types are hexes, stoppers, rocks, and RPs (smaller, brass wedges).

Pitch a long climb is split into sections between places where a climber can stop and bring up a second climber. These sections are called pitches.

Pro/Protection the runners or places where runners are able to be placed along a pitch. Runners usually consist of: nuts; placed in cracks along the pitch; friends, similarly placed; slings placed around natural features; or bolts pre-placed in holes drilled for them where no natural means of protection is available. These are then clipped by means of placing a bolt bracket over, then two karabiners in the form of a quick draw to bridge between the bolt and the rope. The karabiners (krabs) are joined by a short tape sling to provide a very flexible but strong connection.

Rack a climber's bundle of nuts, friends and slings, for runners and main belays.

Rope Length a pitch this long is around 150 feet between stances.

Runner a running belay, one between stances on the pitch itself, used by the leader for protection.

Run Out the distance between places where it is possible to place pro. Long run-outs mean long distances climbed between few runners.

Second/second a climb the second puts the leader's rope through a belay plate to hold the leader should he/she fall, after first anchoring him/herself to counter the forces transmitted by such a fall. The second then follows the leader up the pitch, removing and collecting all runners placed along the way. He/she is protected by being brought up by the leader with the rope itself acting as protection from above.

Slab a relatively lower angled (up to around 80 degrees) area of rock climbable on friction alone.

Smearing climbing on footholds so sloping that the foot only stays in place by friction; making use of even the slightest scoops and depressions to help this; faith in friction: climbing typical of steep slabs.

Stance the place or ledge at the end of a pitch where the leader anchors him or herself before bringing up the second.

Thin a section on a climb with small, almost non-existent holds. Delicate moves required.

Wall a steeper area of rock, usually less than vertical or vertical, but often feeling as if overhanging.

Glossary of Sailing Terms

Abeam on a line at right angles to the vessel/abreast of the vessel.

Apparent Wind the wind that flows over a moving boat. The sum of the true wind and the wind created by the vessel's motion.

Astern behind the vessel.

Below/Down Below below decks, inside the vessel.

Block the nautical term for a pulley.

Boom-Brake a frictional device to limit the boom's motion and slow it down, preventing damage in accidental gybes.

Bosun's Chair either a canvas bucket seat or hard seat on which a person can sit and be hoisted up the mast to carry out repairs aloft.

Bulletproof Jib a very strongly made storm jib I designed never to need taking down, even in the most ferocious weather.

Chine the junction between two flat segments of the sides or between side and bottom segments of a hull.

Cutter a single-masted yacht with inner and outer forestays to set a greater variety of headsails, thus increasing available options.

Dodger a canvas continuation of the cabin to give protection from wind and spray out in the cockpit.

Dorade/Dorade Vent a type of ventilator allowing air to get in, but keeping water out in all but the most extreme situations. Named after *Dorade*, the first yacht to use them – an invention of Olin Stephens, her designer.

DR-Dead Reckoning (from deduced reckoning): the art of calculating the boat's position from records (either plotted or kept purely in the mind) of past movements. It can only be regarded as an approximate position.

Drifter/MPS the largest and lightest headsail. Used downwind in lieu of a spinnaker, and generally in very light breezes. My 'engine'.

Easting/Running the Easting Down sailing eastward around the world along the old clipper ship routes through the 'roaring forties' and 'screaming Fifties' (latitudes 40–60 degrees south), using the so-called westerlies for motive power.

Foot the bottom edge of a sail.

Genoa a large headsail which extends aft of the mast. Too large for ease of handling alone in strong winds.

Halyard the rope and/or wire by which a sail is hoisted.

Handy-Billy a block and tackle arrangement of two double blocks useful for everything from hoisting oneself up the mast in the bosun's chair, to holding the boom down hard as a vang, and a myriad of other uses.

Hard-on-the-Wind sailing to windward with the wind from dead ahead, pointing as high as possible for best performance.

Heave-to to stop or slow the boat, usually in strong winds, for greater comfort until the weather eases and progress is possible again.

Index Error an error of adjustment in the sextant, causing a wrong angle to be read off whenever it is used. It can easily be ascertained in normal conditions, and allowances made.

Leech the aftermost edge of a fore and aft sail.

Leeward away from the direction of the wind.

Log in my case a 'Walker' – a distance-measuring device consisting of a small rotor towed over the stern that transmits its spin via the towing line for conversion into distance at the dial.

Luff the leading edge of the sail.

Main the mainsail. Set either as the full mainsail or at the first, second or third reef to reduce its area, depending on course and weather.

MPS/Drifter the largest and lightest headsail. Used downwind in lieu of a spinnaker, and generally in very light breezes. My 'engine'.

Pinch to sail too close to the wind. When sailing to windward particularly, the sails could be sheeted in further on other points of sailing.

Pitch-Pole to be rolled through 360 degrees longitudinally, stern over bow, but most likely finishing as a transverse roll in the process of coming upright.

RDF/Radio Direction Finder an instrument used in navigation which allows bearings to be taken from navigational radio beacons. Only of use within the range of the beacons, usually less than 100 miles.

Reef to reduce the sail area by folding or rolling a portion of the sail's area out of action.

Roller Furling a modern means of reefing by rolling the sail around its forestay to reduce area. If the swivels that allow this motion, break, reefing is not possible.

Running backstays temporary backstays set up to augment the permanent backstays. From the same height as where the inner forestay and intermediate shrouds meet the mast.

Sat-nav/GPS satellite navigation systems making navigation easy for the incompetent, if you have blind faith in solid-state circuitry that can't be repaired at sea. The sun and stars have proven far more reliable over time.

Sea squid a form of drogue/sea anchor which if towed astern slows the vessel in a controlled way. I carried two but never used them, preferring the Moitessier method of running at speed in survival situations. My hull design allowed this method to work every time, without undue worry.

Sextant instrument for measuring angles, used in navigation.

Sheet a rope attached to the clew of the sail (usually with a bowline knot) in the case of headsail, or to the boom itself in the case of the mainsail, allowing the sail to be trimmed.

Shrouds the transverse rigging that supports the mast. Divided into lowers, intermediates and cap shrouds.

Skate high-performance planing centreboard class, 14 feet long. Mainsail jib and spinnaker with twin leaning planks for stability. Too inherently unstable and unforgiving of error to become really popular, but cheap and extremely fast. Planing to windward was the norm as soon as the wind reached 8–10 knots, and several times we overtook a B class racing catamaran from behind while broad reaching in 20–25 knots of wind.

Stays the rigging that supports the mast fore and aft. Forestays and Backstays.

Staysail the heavy small Genoa set on the inner forestay of my cutter rig. When the wind became too strong for the Yankee, I would drop it and set the staysail. When too strong for the staysail I would drop it and set the bulletproof. I never reduced sail beyond the bulletproof once I had it properly set up.

Tiller the attachment to the top of the rudder by which the rudder is controlled/ vessel is steered.

Topping lift a wire or rope used to support the outer end of the boom.

Trisail a triangular, loose-footed sail fitted aft of the mast and used instead of the mainsail in rough weather.

VJ a one design class of planing centreboarder approximately 12 feet long, with mainsail, jib and spinnaker, and twin leaning planks for stability. The most popular Australian racing class for teenagers for decades, but now less popular after the influx of international classes.

Whipping method of binding the ends of a rope to prevent fraying.

Windward towards the wind.

Yankee a smaller headsail than the Genoa, with the same length along the luff, but a high-angled foot to keep it well clear of the water.

Index